After 2015: International Development Policy at a
Crossroads

Rethinking International Development Series

Series Editors:

Andy Sumner, Fellow of the Vulnerability and Poverty Research Team, Institute of Development Studies, UK.

Ray Kiely, Professor of International Politics, Queen Mary University of London, UK.

Palgrave Macmillan is delighted to announce a new series dedicated to publishing cutting-edge titles that focus on the broad area of 'development'.

The core aims of the series are to present critical work that:

– is cross disciplinary;
– challenges orthodoxies;
– reconciles theoretical depth with empirical research;
– explores the frontiers of development studies in terms of 'development' in both North and South and global inter-connectedness;
– reflects on claims to knowledge and intervening in other people's lives.

Titles include:

Simon Feeny and Matthew Clarke
THE MILLENNIUM DEVELOPMENT GOALS AND BEYOND
International Assistance to the Asia-Pacific

Andy Sumner and Meera Tiwari
AFTER 2015: INTERNATIONAL DEVELOPMENT POLICY AT A CROSSROADS

Rethinking International Development Series
Series Standing Order ISBN 978–0230–53751–4 (hardback)
(outside North America only)

You can receive future titles in this series as they are published by placing a standing order. Please contact your bookseller or, in case of difficulty, write to us at the address below with your name and address, the title of the series and the ISBN quoted above.

Customer Services Department, Macmillan Distribution Ltd, Houndmills, Basingstoke, Hampshire RG21 6XS, England

After 2015: International Development Policy at a Crossroads

Andy Sumner
Research Fellow, Institute of Development Studies
University of Sussex, UK

and

Meera Tiwari
Head of International Development Studies
University of East London, UK

First published 2009 by
PALGRAVE MACMILLAN

Palgrave Macmillan in the UK is an imprint of Macmillan Publishers Limited, registered in England, company number 785998, of Houndmills, Basingstoke, Hampshire RG21 6XS.

Palgrave Macmillan in the US is a division of St Martin's Press LLC, 175 Fifth Avenue, New York, NY 10010.

Palgrave Macmillan is the global academic imprint of the above companies and has companies and representatives throughout the world.

Palgrave® and Macmillan® are registered trademarks in the United States, the United Kingdom, Europe and other countries.

ISBN-13: 978–1–4039–8772–3   hardback
ISBN-10: 1–4039–8772–6   hardback

This book is printed on paper suitable for recycling and made from fully managed and sustained forest sources. Logging, pulping and manufacturing processes are expected to conform to the environmental regulations of the country of origin.

A catalogue record for this book is available from the British Library.

Library of Congress Cataloging-in-Publication Data

Sumner, Andrew, 1973–
    After 2015 : international development policy at a crossroads / Andy Sumner, Tiwari, Meera.
        p. cm. – (Rethinking international development)
    Includes bibliographical references and index.
    ISBN 978–1–4039–8772–3
        1. Economic development–Forecasting. 2. Globalization–Economic aspects. 3. Globalization–Social aspects. 4. International organization. I. Tiwari, Meera, 1960– II. Title.
    HD82.S85176 2009
    338.91–dc22   2008053019

10   9   8   7   6   5   4   3   2   1
18 17 16 15 14 13 12 11 10 09

Printed and bound in Great Britain by
CPI Antony Rowe, Chippenham and Eastbourne

Contents

Acknowledgements

I would like to thank family, friends and colleagues past and present for their support.

Andy Sumner
Fellow, Institute of Development Studies,
University of Sussex, UK.

I would like to thank all who have inspired me and continue to inspire.

Meera Tiwari
Senior Lecturer, Department of Anthropology and International Development,
University of East London, UK.

List of Boxes, Figures and Tables

Boxes

Figures

Tables

List of Abbreviations

AENP	Approximate Environmentally Adjusted Net National Product
AGOA	African Growth and Opportunity Act
AGRA	Alliance for a Green Revolution in Africa
AIDS	Acquired Immune Deficiency Syndrome
ANNP	Annual Adjusted Net National Product
AREAR	Annual Report on Exchange Arrangement and Exchange Restrictions
ASEAN	Association of South East Asian Nations
BRICETs	Brazil, Russia, India, China, Eastern Europe, Turkey
BRICs	Brazil, Russia, India, China
CAADP	Comprehensive Africa Agriculture Development Programme
CAS	Country Assistance Strategy
CBP	Citizen-based policy
CFA	Commission for Africa
CGIAR	Consultative Group on International Agricultural Development
CIDA	Canadian International Development Agency
CPIA	Country Policy and Institutional Assessment
CSO	Civil society organisation
DAC	Development Assistance Committee (OECD)
DANIDA	Danish International Development Agency
DFID	Department for International Development (UK)
DHF	Domestic Hidden Flows
DPO	Domestic Processed Output
DS	Development Studies
DSA	Development Studies Association (UK and Ireland)
EA	East Asia
EADI	European Association of Development Research and Training Institutes
EAP	East Asia Pacific
EBP	Evidence-based policy
EC	European Commission
EF	Ecological Footprint
EPAs	Economic Partnership Agreements (EU)

EPI	Expanded Programme on Immunization
EPICs	Emerging Processes and Issue Clusters
EU	European Union
FAO	Food and Agriculture Organization
FDI	Foreign Direct Investment
G77	Group of 77
GATT	General Agreement on Trade and Tariffs
GDI	Gender Development Index
GDP	Gross Domestic Product
GEM	Gender Empowerment Measure
GPI	Genuine Progress Indicator
GTZ	German Technical Assistance (Deutsche Gesellschaft für
HDI	Human Development Index
HDR	Human Development Report
HIPC	Highly Indebted Poor Country
HPI	Human Poverty Index
ICT	Information communication technologies
IDRC	International Development Research Centre, Canada
IDT	International Development Targets (see MDGs)
IFAD	International Fund for Agricultural Development
IFAP	International Federation of Agricultural Producers
IFI	International Financial Institution
IGT	Inter-generational transmission of poverty
ILO	International Labour Office
IMF	International Monetary Fund
INGO	International NGO
ISEW	Index of Sustainable Economic Welfare
ISO	International Organization for Standardization
LAC	Latin America and the Caribbean
LDC	Least Developed Countries
LIC	Low Income Country
LICUS	Low Income Country Under Stress
LLDC	Land-Locked Developing Country
LMC	Lower Middle Income Country
MAI	Multilateral Agreement on Investment
MCA	Millennium Challenge Account
MDGs	Millennium Development Goals
MIC	Middle Income Country
N11	Goldman Sachs 'Next 11'
NAS	Net Additions to Stock
NEPAD	New Economic Partnership for African Development

NGO	Non-governmental organisation
NIC	Newly Industrialising Country
NNP	Net National Product
NORAD	Norwegian Agency for Development Cooperation
NPE	Net Primary Enrolment
NPM	New Public Management
NPPRC	Net Primary Product Relative to Consumption
ODA	Official Development Assistance
ODI	Overseas Development Institute (London)
OECD	Organisation for Economic Co-operation and Development
PEG	Poverty Elasticity of Growth
PPA	Participatory Poverty Assessments
PPP	Public Private Partnerships
PPP	Purchasing Power Parity
PQLI	Physical Quality of Life Index
PRA	Participatory Rural Appraisal
PRGF	Poverty Reduction Growth Facility
PRS	Poverty Reduction Strategy
PRSP	Poverty Reduction Strategy Paper
RAPID	Research & Policy in Development (ODI)
RBM	Results Based Management
RF	Resource Flow
RRA	Rapid Rural Appraisal
SADC	Southern African Development Community
SAPs	Structural Adjustment Programmes
SD	Sustainable Development
SDI	Sustainable Development Indicator
SL	Sustainable Livelihoods
SSA	Sub-Saharan Africa
SWAP	Sector Wide Approach
TDO	Total Domestic Output
TMR	Total Material Required
TNCs	Transnational Corporations
TRIPS	Trade-Related Aspects of Intellectual Property Rights
UMC	Upper Middle Income Country
UNCRC	United Nations Convention on the Rights of the Child
UNCTAD	United Nations Conference on Trade and Development
UNDP	United Nations Development Programme
UNEP	United Nations Environment Programme
UNICEF	United Nations Children's Fund
UNIFEM	United Nations Development Fund for Women

UNMP	United Nations Millennium Project
UNRISD	United Nations Research Institute for Social Development
US	United States
USAID	United States Agency for International Development
WA	Western Asia
WC	Washington Consensus
WCA	Western and Central Africa
WCED	World Commission on Environment & Development
WDR	World Development Report
WDM	World Development Movement
WeD	The Well-being and Development Research Group (Bath University)
WHO	World Health Organization
WIDER	World Institute of Development Economics Research
WIID	World Income Inequality Database
WRI	World Resource Institute
WTO	World Trade Organization
WWF	Worldwide Fund for Nature

Introduction

1.   What is this book about?

It is 2015. George Clooney is US President. Bob Geldof and Bono, respectively, Irish President and Prime Minister. Politics is still an unpredictable business. What about economics? China has just overtaken the US as the world's largest economy. India is not so far behind. Some of the UN poverty targets – the Millennium Development Goals (MDGs) were met. Some were not. Progress in Africa accelerated following large aid flows from new donors (such as China) but repayments are now looming. The other MDGs were missed, though not as badly as expected. Climate change – or chaos – has intensified with many of the impacts felt in the South. Urbanisation is accelerating. What next?

This book is triggered by the closeness to the 2015 'line in the sand' or the target year for the MDGs which were agreed at the UN Millennium Assembly in 2000. Income poverty is to be halved on its 1990 rate. Hunger is to be halved too. All children are to complete primary education. Infant and child mortality are to be reduced drastically and the spread of HIV, malaria and other diseases is to be reversed. The MDGs have played a major role in focusing policy since their original incarnation in the 1990s and some development agencies have gone as far as to judge the value of *all* their activities on the contribution to achieving the MDGs. What happens when we no longer have the MDGs – what will guide policy after 2015?

2.   How is the world changing?

Development and development policy have changed radically in the last 50 years. However, the current pace of change is accelerating and

1

creating both challenges and opportunities. The world in 2015 and beyond is difficult to predict. There have been various discussions of possible global futures. The most notable are the US National Intelligence Council's *2020 Project* and related *Global Trends 2010, and 2015*. There are also the EU European Development Co-operation to 2010 and 2020 projects.[1] For those who like a long-term view, the University of Denver's Pardee Center for International Futures may be of interest.[2] Available via their website is a long-term integrated modelling system covering demographic, economic, energy, agricultural, socio-political, and environmental subsystems for 182 countries interacting in the global system. One can download the software and explore alternative future scenarios oneself. The centre conducts work for the US NIC, EC and UNEP. It is currently estimating development in the mid-21st century and beyond.

Computer simulations aside, we need a pause for thought, noting Taleb's (2007) *Black Swans* thesis regarding the unpredictable. Thinking back, who would have imagined the spread of the Internet, the collapse of the Soviet bloc or the post-9/11 world? What can we say at this stage? There are some major global and regional transformative processes and emerging issues. The character of these processes and issues is marked by increased inter-dependence between the North and South (or East and West) above all else. Commentators have also noted the tendency of such processes to destabilise existing livelihoods, unravel social fabrics, create conflict and exclusion as well as disrupt international markets (see epilogue on global financial crisis).

These processes are also reinforcing the diversity in what was once the 'Third World'. There are, on the one hand, a group of accelerated developers in the BRICs (Brazil, Russia, India and China), the BRICETS (add Eastern Europe and Turkey), and the Goldman Sachs N11 emerging economies (the 'next 11' countries expected to experience fast growth in economic indicators). At the other end of the spectrum there are the LICUS (Low Income Country Under Stress) or 50–60 countries that might be classified as 'fragile states'. Global changes are likely to increase the inequality between and within these groups and reshape livelihoods and lifestyles of everyone. So, the question is how can we promote pro-poor development policy after the MDGs and amid complex changes, some of which mediate in favour of the poor, and many do not?

3.   Where are we now?

In spite of five decades since Truman's 1949 Declaration to spread the benefits of industrial progress to the 'underdeveloped areas', or four decades since independence for many developing countries, or three decades since Seer's 1969 The *Meaning of Development,* or two decades since the end of the Cold War, many questions remain controversial. Should countries focus more on growth? or less? Should we talk of well-being and what people can do and be, rather than of poverty and deprivation? Should the focus be on poor people or poor countries? What is the policy narrative? What works? Who or what are the drivers of policy change? These are just a handful of the questions this book seeks to discuss. Not surprisingly many others are also seeking to address such questions. Indeed, one might be forgiven for exclaiming, 'what a lot of books there are about poverty and development and what to do about it!'.

Over the last few years there has been a re-emergence of attempts at a big idea or a grand- or meta-narrative, notably from Paul Collier, William Easterly, and Jeffrey Sachs but also Alice Amsden, Ha-Joon Chang, Dani Rodrik, Wolfgang Sachs, and Joseph Stiglitz to name but a handful (see Chapter 1 in particular and throughout for discussion). Each author presents some kind of diagnosis of the 'problem' of (mal) 'development' and entry points with most leverage for (good) change.

However, at the same time as meta-narratives or universal ideas have re-emerged in development policy so has a deeper interest in context specificity, path dependency and 'messy realities' in a set of ideas known as Complexity Science (see for example, Ramalingam *et al.*, 2008; Rihani, 2005). In Complexity Science, systems are made of multiple elements and processes which are not only connected but inter-dependent through feedback loops, non-linear processes, and sensitivity to initial conditions. Within these systems agents are co-evolving and adaptive (see for discussion in Chapter 1). Our book aims to critically engage with these diverse debates.

4.   Who is this book for and who are the authors?

This book is for researchers, students, policy formers, influencers and practitioners of international development policy, practice and studies. The aim of this book is to provide a middle-ground book between a topical research contribution and a book that will have broader appeal, especially so to postgraduate students of development studies and related fields.

One issue for development researchers and practitioners to consider individually and collectively is that of 'positionality' or 'situationality' (see for further discussion Sumner and Tribe, 2008). By this we mean individual and group backgrounds or 'identities' (our race, gender, age, nationality, social and economic status, and other characteristics) which directly and indirectly influence our experiences, values, preconceptions, ideology, interpretations and research. The 'positionality' or 'situationality' of the authors of this book is affected by their backgrounds in economics but both have a strong interest in cross-disciplinary research. It is widely argued that DS is, or should be, cross-disciplinary, and this book takes this position. Additionally, both of the authors work within UK institutions and are influenced, as much of DS is, by the context of a post-colonial world. In sum, our backgrounds and experiences inevitably shape our writing but we can be open, with recognition of our limitations.

5.   How is the book structured?

The book consists of two parts. The first emphasises the MDGs and the world up to and beyond 2015. Where are we now? How did we get there? Where will we be in 2015? How is the world and the context for 'development' changing? How does policy change happen? The second part of the book relates in particular to what we have called the 3Gs or three policy arenas – governance, growth and globalisation. We argued that the 3Gs provide a 'centre of gravity' in the sense that they almost undeniably play a role in shaping contemporary development and need to be debated not just here but around the world. However, although there may be consensus that these areas matter, the nature of each and what to do is still hotly contested. We discuss 'good' governance and the role of participation in policy-making and implementation processes. We discuss the linkages between growth, inequality, poverty and sustainability. We discuss the nature of globalisation and its relationship with growth and poverty reduction via private capital (trade and private investment) and public capital (aid).

In Chapter 1 we set the scene. We consider how the world is changing and ask what is the state of global development now? We then turn to review the resurgence of big ideas in the Sachs, Collier, Easterly and others attempt to define the 'problem' and the 'solutions'. In Chapter 2 we consider the MDGs and how they fit in a brief history of 'development'. We ask should we concern ourselves with poverty or something else? In Chapter 3 we ask how does policy change happen? We consider the shifting nature of policy processes towards greater 'fuzziness'. We consider theories of policy change and trends in the contemporary policy process architecture. We propose a model of change that focuses on drivers and impediments to change via actors and networks, context and institutions and policy narratives and evidence. Chapters 4, 5 and 6 then turn attention to the 3Gs. Chapter 4 is concerned with governance. Chapter 5 with growth. Chapter 6 is concerned with globalisation. In each chapter we discuss a brief history of debates, the interaction of governance, growth and globalisation with the MDGs and poverty reduction, and consider future directions. Finally, Chapter 7 concludes and we provide an epilogue in light of the global financial crisis. Our objective is – explicitly – not to establish *absolute* 'closure' on any issue, rather to propose some pathways. We hope that the book will stimulate debate as a basis for a positive future for international development policy. Comments are welcomed.

January 2009
Andy Sumner
a.sumner@ids.ac.uk
Meera Tiwari
m.tiwari@uel.ac.uk

Notes

1 See respectively www.dni.gov/nic/NIC_2020_project.html and www.edc2020.eu
2 See http://www.ifs.du.edu/

Part I
The MDGs

1
Development Policy at a Crossroads

> The contest of ideas in... policy making can evolve independently of their intellectual merit and empirical credibility (Beeson and Islam, 2005:197).

1. Introduction

In this chapter we set the scene. We consider the changing context for international development in terms of climate change, the rise of China *et al.*, migration, urbanisation and so on and ask what is the current state of global development? We then review the resurgence of big ideas in the Sachs, Collier, Easterly and others' attempts to define the 'problem' and the 'solutions'.[1] The chapter is structured as follows. Section 2 addresses how the context – the world – is changing. Section 3 focuses on the baseline – the state of global development. Section 4 discusses the resurgence of big ideas or meta-narratives after the Washington Consensus. Section 5 concludes with discussion of the 'centre of gravity' in the 3Gs or governance, growth and globalisation.

2. How is the world changing?

The current pace of global change is accelerating and creating both challenges and opportunities. There are some major global and regional transformative processes and emerging issues. The character of these processes and issues is marked by increased inter-dependence between the North and South (or East and West) above all else. Commentators have also noted the tendency of such processes to destabilise existing livelihoods, unravel social fabrics, create conflict and exclusion as well as disrupt international markets. We can identify five global and regional emerging

9

processes and issues clusters (EPICs) as they are evolving now (see Table 1.1). These EPICs are:

- Market EPICs – i.e. economics and markets
- People EPICs – i.e. demography and employment
- Natural EPICs – i.e. the environment and natural resources
- Techno EPICs – i.e. technology and technological innovation
- Political EPICs – i.e. changes in policy actors, contexts and policy narratives

In terms of shifts in economics or markets there is the rise of a number of 'emerging' economies, notably China and India, which is in part fuelling a commodity price boom and having various other impacts on other developing countries not only via markets and Southern TNCs but also via geo-politics. There are major moves to regional economic integration and there is the emergence of public–private partnerships as a fashionable modality of (public) service delivery. Further intra- and inter-country remittances as a result of migration patterns are increasingly influential. Estimates put international remittances at around US$300bn and intra-country remittances (usually urban to rural) at an equivalent level. There is also a large increase in aid promised, a changing aid architecture, new donors (such as China) and the emergence of huge private foundations in development with multi-billion dollar spending power such as the Gates Foundation. Additionally, the global financial crisis has increased uncertainty.

In terms of demographics there are the labour market consequences of population growth, particularly so in Africa, and higher dependency ratios as population growth creates a higher proportion of younger people at the same time as aged populations are growing too (and the working age population may actually even be contracting in size due to HIV/AIDS). There is also the issue of migration and its impacts – both nationally in terms of urbanisation (past the 50% tipping point), and cross-borders in terms of the effects of international migration. In terms of environmental changes there will be major shifts in agriculture patterns, livelihoods and prices as a result of climate change, and likewise with the expansion of bio-fuels and the spread of bio-technology globally. ICTs and mobile technologies in particular are likely to play a significant role in future development (take for example mobiles acting as banking systems in developing countries via credit transfers).

Table. 1.1 Emerging Processes and Issues Clusters (EPICs) for 2015 and Beyond

EPIC	Meta-changes	Details	Implications
Market/ economic	International markets – trade and capital flows, global value chains	Volatility in global markets – food, fuel and finance. Credit crunch. Investment flows likely to fall. Aid under threat and likely to come from more diverse sources/less conditionality/new conditionality (see below). Global value chains with fewer links, more contracting in advance, and more impersonal dealings. Supermarket chains prominent in creating new arrangements in agricultural supply chains.	Growth threatened by volatile prices and recessions in western markets. Countries may lack expertise to manage trade and investment flows.
	National dynamics – economic growth, urbanisation, resource scarcity	High growth in many countries including Africa in recent years vulnerable now as led by natural resource prices, more rapid urbanisation, driven in large part by migration from rural to urban areas (see below).	Volatile oil prices, food and transport prices threaten to disrupt economic growth. Growth of populations and economies are likely to increase pressure on natural resources of all kinds. A scramble for resources by large economies that lack reserves of natural resources within their own frontiers is evident: those of the USA, EU, Japan, India, China, for example and played out in many parts of the developing world.

Table. 1.1 Emerging Processes and Issues Clusters (EPICs) for 2015 and Beyond – *continued*

EPIC	Meta-changes	Details	Implications
People/ demographic	Population growth and differentiated demographic transitions	South-central Asia will have to accommodate 759 million more people by 2050. However, the most striking evolution remains Sub-Saharan Africa (SSA) with a 100% increase of the population by 2050: nearly 1.8 billion people in 2050, more than double the 2010 population. In 2050, the population of SSA could exceed that of China, and hence will be one-fifth of the world's population.	More people may lead to greater conflict over resources.
	Evolution of age structures and labour markets	South-central Asia and Sub-Saharan Africa will have dramatic increases in labour supply. In contrast, East Asia (EA) will have a sharp decrease labour supply. SSA will carry on bearing the burden of a large inactive population for at least another decade. EA will soon have to deal with an age structure much less supportive of economic growth.	Faster rates of economic growth will be necessary to meet labour market expansions.

Table. 1.1 Emerging Processes and Issues Clusters (EPICs) for 2015 and Beyond – *continued*

EPIC	Meta-changes	Details	Implications
Natural/ environmental	Climate change	Changes in rainfall and rises in sea levels, with major consequences for natural life on the planet and increased variation in climate (cyclones, droughts, etc.). Of the changes predicted, those with the most widespread effects arise with rainfall. Patterns will alter, with different areas becoming wetter or drier. Some relatively well-populated areas already with semi-arid climates are likely to become drier. Water scarcity in such cases will be exacerbated (see below). The seasonality of rainfall may become more pronounced, with greater potential for flooding in the wet season and for droughts in the dry. Rising sea levels threaten coastal areas with higher tides, storm surges, flooding of low-lying coastal areas. Some low-lying coastal areas, most notably river deltas, may become uninhabitable. Changed climates are in turn likely to affect ecosystems. In some cases this may mean that insects as disease vectors spread to previously unaffected areas (e.g. malaria).	Increased variations in agricultural production in response to more variable weather. More frequent storms and tidal surges will probably harm the poor more than others, since the poor often live in places with least protection and limited resilience to extreme weather – such as low-lying areas or unstable slopes liable to collapse when soaked by storms. More people living on even fewer resources or mass migration. Migration from one rural area to another may lead to conflicts over land access with existing residents, especially where the latter have been using the resources extensively and claim rights over large areas. Migration out of areas with declining resources may also be to urban areas, throwing up the large encampments of environmental refugees living in extreme poverty on the margins of urban life.

Table. 1.1 Emerging Processes and Issues Clusters (EPICs) for 2015 and Beyond – *continued*

EPIC	Meta-changes	Details	Implications
	Water scarcity	Water scarcity will get worse due to economic and population growth will increase the demand for water, increasing the likelihood of additional areas facing acute scarcity of water. And climate change as described above will change rainfall patterns, make them more erratic, and reduce storage in glaciers. While overall water supplies may not fall, uneven distribution through space and time will make for more scarcity.	For health, both quality and quantity of water are essential issues. Contaminated water increases the likelihood of enteric disease and parasites, with young children most at risk. Lack of water means that washing is likely to be minimal with consequent potential for the spread of enteric diseases. In more humid areas, the rural poor may be affected by water scarcity in irrigation systems.
Techno/ technological	The spread of existing technologies – biotechnology and transgenics, and vaccine technology	Expansion and pirating of biotech. Large investments and 'rolling out' of vaccines.	Biotechnology optimists advocate that it is rural farmers and poor who will benefit the most from higher yields, lower risks, and larger outputs which will control the growth of food prices. Sceptics argue that it is the poor who suffer the most because biotechnology exacerbates trends towards industrialisation of agriculture, erosion of the diversity of agro-eco systems and undermining farmers' rights.

Table. 1.1   Emerging Processes and Issues Clusters (EPICs) for 2015 and Beyond – *continued*

EPIC	Meta-changes	Details	Implications
	New(er) technologies – industrial biofuel technologies, and	Increase in industrial production of biofuels for large-scale usage.	Debates on biofuel technology and its impact on the rural poor are fraught.
	information communication technologies (ICTs)	Increase in range and spread of ICTs.	ICTs have a range of impacts on the poor in terms of access to information, impacts on livelihoods and so on but cost is something of a barrier.
Political/ Governance	Aid	New policy discourses and narratives: the evolution of the aid effectiveness and ownership discourses.	More aid and more diverse aid. There may be large increases in aid from various sources and a greater diversity and new types of aid.
		New actors and roles: new donors such as China and the philanthropic foundations, new roles for the EU following enlargement and NEPAD.	More voice for national governments internationally. Potentially more voice for the poor but this depends on national governance structures.
		New contexts and institutions: the Paris Declaration on Aid Effectiveness and reforms in IMF voting rights.	

Table. 1.1   Emerging Processes and Issues Clusters (EPICs) for 2015 and Beyond – *continued*

EPIC	Meta-changes	Details	Implications
	The public sector/ services	New discourses and narratives: the New Public Management (NPM) and Public-Private Partnership (PPP) discourses.	Conflict between greater claims for citizen voices and decentralisation whilst voice and freedoms are retreating in many countries.
		New actors and roles: the changing roles of states due to changes in state financing, the expansion of state decentralisation, the increased role of private actors in service delivery in modalities of PPP and via the emergence of new agencies under the New Public Management paradigm.	More finance available for public services from natural resource revenues, aid and (contentiously) the private sector.
		New contexts and institutions: tension between greater calls for citizen voice in public services at a time when there are changes in democratic space and the NPM.	

Source: Sumner *et al.* (2008b).

The net outcome of all the above is a lot of change – of lifestyles and livelihoods. Larger migratory movements nationally as well as internationally are likely as is an increased potential for conflict over resources as a result of people on the move. One might then be forgiven for feeling overwhelmed in thinking about policy planning amid so many changes. Even development policy itself is reconfiguring. We have:

- new actors – China and other new donors, and the new large private foundations such as the Gates Foundation;
- new contexts and institutions – a new aid architecture, decentralisation, and terrorism legislation, and
- newly emerging policy narratives – the resurgence of the idea that economic growth is key to development, and the more nuanced agendas of citizenship, participation and empowerment.

Such changes may reshape policy processes in favour or not of the poor and marginalised. So, the question is how can we promote pro-poor policy after the MDGs and amid all these complex changes, some of which mediate in favour of the poor, many do not?

What is certain is that international development policy-making already does and will continue to take place in the context of significant and likely rising uncertainty. However, the extent of uncertainty in different contexts can vary considerably. There has been a recognition that policy-making in Southern contexts is qualitatively different from policy-making solely in Northern contexts because of greater levels of uncertainty in the policy-making process. These levels of uncertainty can be due to such factors as noted above, for example:

- shifting contexts (sometimes rapidly so) due to processes such as decentralisation and democratisation;
- the changing roles of actors such as civil society and donors;
- trends in policy discourses (notably donors' changing frameworks, for example);
- low demand for, and supply of, evidence (and access to it) and limited technical capacity to factor for uncertainty;
- changes in technology may have unpredictable impacts in shifting and diverse contexts;
- weaker structures for aggregating/arbitrating interests of society may lead to exclusion/conflict.

There is a further complexity peculiar to development policy: it is a product of the interaction of Northern and Southern contexts.

Development policy involves donors – i.e. Northern contexts – as well as actors in developing countries – i.e. Southern contexts. There is the aid effectiveness agenda and the alignment of countries' and donors' frameworks and harmonisation of donors' approaches (see Chapter 3 discussion).

How can we make sense of such uncertainty? The dynamics, impacts, consequences and arising opportunities and adaptive capacity of people to respond are uncertain and determined by a myriad of factors, not least their context, type of household and intra-household dynamics. As Leach *et al.* (2007:1) sum up,

> today's world is experiencing social, technological and environmental change at an unprecedented pace, across a variety of scales... processes are not only dynamic in themselves, but also interact in complex ways. The result is a variety of possible patterns – or pathways – of change... In many cases, different people and groups – in different settings, at different scales, with different perspectives and priorities – will experience and value actual and possible pathways of change in very different ways.

We thus need attention to the major changes themselves, to their inter-connectedness and interaction, to their scales and to their existence as a system where the whole is more than the sum of the parts and where agents are adaptive, reactive to other agents and co-evolve over time.

Until recently, understanding has been driven by a static, linear and equilibrium analysis. An emerging understanding of development is one of development as complex, dynamic, diverse, 'messy' and uncertain. What do we even mean by complex, dynamic, diverse, uncertain systems? Scoones *et al.* (2007:1) note:

> by dynamic systems we mean ones characterised by complexity, non-linearity and often non-equilibrium patterns exhibiting high levels of incertitude in system properties. 'Dynamics' refers to the patterns of complexity, interaction (and associated pathways) observed in the behaviour over time of social, technological and environmental systems.

For example, Chambers (1997) cited Waldrop's (1994) 'edge of chaos' (structure among uncertainty) theory as a possible explanation of why community groups in rural areas are able to exist in, and adapt to, a permanence of development pressures and social change. Warner

(2001:11) too notes rural organisations' adaptive capacity to respond to changes:

> in India, farmers have successfully made the transition from rain-fed to irrigated crops; in Nepal, forest 'user groups' have formed to exploit new community-friendly forestry policies; and in East Africa, government wildlife departments and local communities have developed joint management arrangements for exploiting and sustaining safari hunting and tourism. By voluntarily venturing a small distance away from the order and familiarity of their traditional practices, these organisations have been able to restructure, learn new skills, develop synergistic partnerships and adapt to their changing environment.

How can we seek to understand the system and the capacity of agents such as the rural poor to adapt? A body of ideas that has emerged in development research since Chambers' citation of Waldrop on rural adaptation could be loosely called Complexity Science or Complex Adaptive Thinking (see for discussion with regard to development, Ramalingam *et al.*, 2008; Rihani, 2005; Warner, 2001 for example). This focuses on *inter-relationships* rather than linear cause and impact and pays attention to *processes of change* rather than snapshots (Senge, 1990). Eyben *et al.* (2006:203–4) outline Complexity Science as follows:

> Complexity theory posits that it is not possible to predict with any confidence the relation between cause and effect. Change is emergent. History is largely unpredictable. New inter-relational processes are constantly being generated, which in turn may affect and change those already existing. Small 'butterfly' actions may have a major impact, and big ones may have very little impact.

According to Ramalingam *et al.* (2008:ix, 1, 4–5) this body of ideas aids:

> understanding of the mechanisms through which unpredictable, unknowable and emergent change happens... [and] can prove particularly useful in allowing us to embrace what were previously seen as 'messy realities'.

Ramalingam *et al.* (2008) list ten ideas around the composition of systems, adaptive change and agency (see Box 1.1).

Box 1.1   Key Ideas in Complexity Sciences Relevant to
Development Policy

i.   Systems are composed of:

* Interconnected and interdependent elements and dimensions.
* Feedback processes that promote and inhibit change within systems.
* System characteristics and behaviours that emerge often unpredictably from the interaction of the parts, such that the whole is different to the sum of the parts.

ii.   Systems change occurs via:

* Nonlinearity – i.e. when change happens, it is frequently disproportionate and unpredictable.
* Sensitivity to initial conditions – i.e. small differences in the initial state of a system can lead to massive differences later; butterfly effects and bifurcations are two ways in which complex systems can change drastically over time.
* Phase space or the 'space of the possible' – i.e. the dimensions of a system, and how they change over time.
* Attractors, chaos and the 'edge of chaos' – i.e. the order underlying the seemingly random behaviours exhibited by complex systems.

iii.   Agency is a function of:

* Adaptive agents – who react to the system and to each other.
* Self-organisation – a particular form of emergent property that can occur in systems of adaptive agents.
* Co-evolution – which describes how within a system of adaptive agents the overall system and the agents within it evolve together, or co-evolve, over time.

Source: Extracted from text in Ramalingam *et al.* (2008).

The point of departure is that systems are made of multiple elements and processes which are not only connected but inter-dependent. For example, rural livelihoods are not simply a result of adding up factors but of interactions. Longer time frames necessitate greater levels of uncertainty. Thus changes we discuss are often highly uncertain and cause is the product of a juxtaposition of factors (one could argue a demarcation of dependent and independents variable is thus problematic). What are the things one might look out for in our forthcoming discussion? First, focus on the processes of change rather than solely on outcomes. Second, focus on inter-relationships and juxtapositions producing co-evolving processes and outcomes. Third, don't forget diversity of pathways and contexts – any claims to universality need to be balanced with commentary on the outliers.

3. What is the state of global development now?

So, where are we now? What is the base-line? The MDGs are a starting point for policy-making. Conceptually, although the 2000/1 *World Development Report* accepts a multi-dimensional approach to poverty as do the OECD DAC *Poverty Guidelines* (see Chapter 1 in both), controversy remains over which dimensions deserve greater emphasis, and income measures are still more commonly used or have an implicit 'first among equals' position (Booth and Lucas, 2002:23; Kanbur and Squire, 2001:187): The number one Millennium Development Goal (MDG) is the dollar-a-day and education and health MDGs follow.

Empirically, the most recent global income poverty estimates (see Table 1.1 and Figure 1.1) are that approximately one billion people – or one in five of the world's population – live below the dollar-a-day poverty measure. Although when China is excluded the absolute number of poor people has actually risen in the last two decades, Chen and Ravallion (2004:22) have argued 1990 dollar-a-day poverty *will* be almost halved by 2015 (but largely due to future poverty reduction in China). The World Bank's dollar-a-day data has been contested for a range of reasons including the purchasing power parity (PPP) conversion, to name just one issue (for critical discussion, see in particular, Redde and Pogge, 2002; Wade, 2004). The PPP is used to compare the cost of products in different countries.

The PPP has become even more contentious recently as the International Comparison Programme (which collects price data across countries) collated actual and detailed price data from 146 countries in December 2007 for the first time since 2003 (and for the first time with China's participation). The result has thrown doubt across the dollar-a-day data for many countries as actual prices are greatly in divergence with existing PPP estimates. The net effect is a lot more poor people (using the dollar-a-day measure). Prices are higher in Asia in particular than previously thought, thus people can afford much less. For example, Milanovic (2008) calculated spending power fell by between 40% in

China and India and the Philippines and 20–30% in South Africa and Argentina. Achieving MDG 1 is thus going to be much harder as there are suddenly more poor people.[2] At time of writing there is no update on the dollar-a-day global data but it is controversial (see Ravallion *et al.*, 2008).[3] One final note is that much economic research done in the last 10–15 years may be erroneous (that which compares dollar-a-day data with economic growth, governance or globalisation for example – see Chapter 4, 5, and 6). In light of the above, Table 1.1 and Figure 1.1 cautiously present the most recent set of global poverty data of Chen and Ravallion (2007) which estimates dollar-a-day poverty from 1981–2004.

How about the other MDGs? In 2004, net primary enrolment (NPE) was 88% for all developing countries with South Asia and Sub-Saharan Africa lagging somewhat at 79.0% and 62.8% respectively (UN, 2007:11; UNESCO, 2005:293, 309). The earlier, primary school enrolment gender equality target was at 93% for developing countries in 2001. Again South Asia and Sub-Saharan Africa lagged, at 86% and 89% respectively (*ibid.:293*). Child malnutrition still affects 28% of under-fives in developing countries and one in three infants in South Asia and Sub-Saharan Africa are chronically malnourished (Vandemoortele, 2002:6). Further, it is estimated, 800 million people are malnourished globally, 1.2 billion people still lack access to 'improved' water sources, 2 billion lack access to 'adequate' sanitation and one woman dies every minute from maternal mortality.

Projections of global development in 2015 based on current rates of progress are as follows (drawing on UN, 2007):

- MDG 1: The global halving of dollar-a-day poor is projected to be met (assuming 'old' PPPs). The hunger target at current rates will be unmet. Global progress on child malnutrition remains uneven with the expectation of the target being missed by 30 million children. Sub-Saharan Africa will achieve neither the poverty target nor the hunger target. South Asia is expected to remain home to the largest number of malnourished children in the world.
- MDG 2–3: Most countries are on target for 100% NPE. The NPE targets in Sub-Saharan Africa can only be met with concerted effort – 30% of children of primary school age were out of school in 2005 in Sub-Saharan Africa. South Asia with 90% NPE in 2005 is likely to achieve the target. The bigger concern is the higher exclusion of girls than boys from education in both Western and Southern Asia. Further, absence of data from conflict-affected countries and the higher likelihood of children from the poorest families dropping out

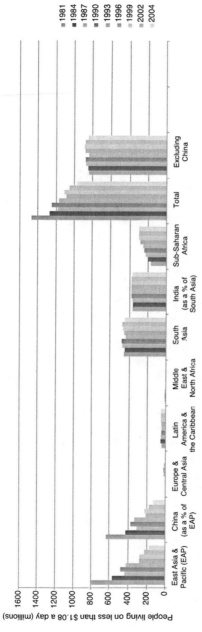

Figure 1.1 Global Poverty Estimates based on US$1.08 per day at 2005 PPP, 1981–2004

Source: Chen and Ravallion (2007)

may cast doubt over the projected achievement of the NPE target by 2015.

- MDG 4–8: No region is on track to meet the child mortality targets. The very slow progress in Sub-Saharan Africa followed by sluggish gains in South Asia in particular stand to keep the overall target off track. In terms of maternal mortality, the global trend is not encouraging with half a million maternal deaths each year. Sub-Saharan Africa and South Asia remain home to the majority of maternal deaths. Neither region will meet the target of maternal mortality reduction by three-quarters by 2015. In recent years, there has been some respite through levelling-off of HIV prevalence. However, AIDS mortality remains a very high concern in Sub-Saharan Africa. In addition, in regions of high HIV prevalence, women comprise more than half those living with the virus. Access to safe drinking water and improved sanitation targets will be missed by almost 600 million people if the trends continue. Sub-Saharan Africa and Southern Asia, with just 37% and 38% of the respective populations using improved sanitation in 2004, are most off target.

In summary, based on the current trends, the world is likely to have far fewer dollar-a-day poor by 2015 thanks to poverty reduction in China (even assuming the new PPP data). However, the uneven progress at the regional level in most MDGs is significant. The developing world stands to be divided into two distinct categories. Those countries that achieved overall poverty reduction with good progress in the non-income MDGs such as in East Asia, and those countries where despite progress in a number of sectors, income and non-income poverty remains a high concern – such as in South Asia and Sub-Saharan Africa. In light of these poverty and development projections what do we have in terms of policy narratives and ideas?

4.   Are big ideas back in fashion?

There is apparently much 'development' to do. What ideas do we have to work with? Arguably the last 'big idea' or meta-narrative for international development policy was the 'Washington Consensus' (WC), which was, as Williamson, its originator put it,

the conventional wisdom... among the economically influential parts of Washington, meaning the US government and the international financial institutions (1993:1329).

However, the term itself, 'Washington Consensus', as Naim noted, acquired a life of its own, becoming:

> a brand name known worldwide and used independently of its original intent and even of its content (2000:88).

Williamson's original WC was based on – as Beeson and Islam (2005:202) called them – 'the ten commandments' – a list of ten policies (see Box 1.2 below). The Washington Consensus was:

> a set of policy reforms which most of official Washington thought would be good for Latin America (Williamson, 1993:1334).

> the common core of wisdom embraced by all serious economists... sensible people [have] better things to do with their time than to challenge its veracity (Williamson, 1998:111).

> the WC, as practiced by the IFIs became 'state-bashing' – a wholesale attempt to dismantle the developmental state (Kanbur, 1999:2).

> privatisation, liberalisation, and macro-stability... a set of policies aimed ... minimizing the role of government (Stiglitz, 2002:1).

One might be surprised to see in Williamson's original list: progressive taxation; welfare systems (albeit non-deficit financed); and institutional reform (see Box 1.2). However, the WC, as practised by the international

---

Box 1.2   Williamson's Original Washington Consensus

1. Fiscal Discipline
2. Public Expenditure Prioritisation
3. Tax Reform
4. Financial Liberalisation
5. Exchange Rates Liberalisation
6. Trade Liberalisation
7. Foreign Direct Investment Liberalisation
8. Privatisation
9. Deregulation
10. Property Rights Establishment

Source: Williamson (1993).

financial institutions became a wholesale attempt to dismantle the developmental state (Kanbur, 1999; Stiglitz, 2006). The 'vehicle' – policy – for the IFI WC was to 'roll back the state' through privatisation, and economic liberalisation.

The WC generally assumed that markets were perfectly competitive (thus unemployed labour would relocate or retrain). Indeed there was an over-emphasis on the economic dimensions of 'development', and economic efficiency in particular, to the detriment of other dimensions, notably the dimensions of the 'social' and the 'politics'. Table 1.2 summarises. We identify points of departure (i.e. the 'world view' of the WC), forms of travel (how to progress under the WC) and points of arrival (the goals of development).

The practice of the 'WC' was largely wrapped up in Stabilisation and Structural Adjustment Programmes. These were programmes which critics argued were imposed on developing countries to ensure debts were serviced. Programmes under the remit of the IMF addressed the short term concerns of the stabilisation of inflation and the balance of payments (with an emphasis on restraining demand and consumption via such policies as currency devaluation, high rates of interest and cuts in public expenditures). Programmes also dealt with the medium term, generally under the remit of the World Bank with an emphasis on expanding supply and production and establishing the conditions for export-led growth via privatisation; trade liberalisation; FDI liberalisation and financial market liberalisation.

Easterly's (2000) assessment of 958 SAPs from 1980–1998 is sobering. It argued growth was very weak. From 1980–1998 developing countries averaged just 0.1% per year in income growth per capita (in contrast to 1960–1979 average annual income growth of 2.5% per capita).

Table 1.2   The Washington Consensus

	Point of departure	*Form of travel*	*Point of arrival*
The 'Washington Consensus' (WC) (cf. Williamson 1993; 1998 in particular)	Distortions and dysfunctional policies in post-colonial societies caused by state intervention.	WC as practised by IMF/World Bank: Anti-statist; macro-economic stability; opening economies; privatisation.	Economic growth, macro-economic stability as ends in themselves.

However, one might argue stabilisation was achieved and in some countries growth was better – the average hides a significant level of variation in country experience. That said, there are – of course – numerous critiques of SAPs on their severe social impacts (for example, Cornia *et al.*, 1987).

The context radically changed in the 1990s. When the Cold War ended in 1989 there was the emergence of a new group of 'developing' countries which became known as transition economies (in the sense of a transition from a planned to a market economy). In the early 1990s there was a triumphalist sense that capitalism – defined as neo-liberalism or the WC – had won the Cold War (symbolically marked by the establishment – without protests – of the WTO in 1994). However, the WC was to be undermined by a series of events in the mid to late 1990s. First, there was the series of crises in developing countries – in East Asia, Russia, Brazil, Argentina. The East Asian crisis was arguably the most damaging as, although hardly neo-liberal, the tiger economies were praised by the IFIs and their collapse undermined the IMF's reputation in particular at that time. The collapse was unpredicted by the IMF and arguably predicated on the gusto with which the Fund promoted financial and capital account liberalisation and exacerbated by the Fund's crisis management.

Second, even from within the IFI, Joseph Stiglitz, still then Chief Economist of the World Bank, had regular spats in the *Financial Times* with the IMF and the US Treasury on policy matters such as financial crisis management in particular.

Third, there were numerous large protests that to the point, international leaders had difficulty meeting without being fenced off. In diplomatic circles trade talks stalled and attempts at a global investment treaty at the OECD (to be, arguably, imposed on developing countries), known as the Multilateral Agreement on Investment (MAI), collapsed in autumn 1997. Finally, the resignation of Ravi Kanbur in 1999 in protest at censorship by the US treasury of his participatory WDR 2000/1 was something of a landmark.

There were then three further major changes in the early 2000s. First, the reported death of the main development paradigm: in May 2004, James Wolfensohn, then President of the World Bank, observed, 'the Washington Consensus has been dead for years. It has been replaced by all sorts of other consensuses' (Wolfensohn cited in Maxwell, 2005:1).

Second, a (related) shift towards developing countries defining their own policies via the introduction of Poverty Reduction Strategy Papers (PRSPs): in June 2005, the G8 communiqué declared, 'developing countries... need to decide, plan and sequence their economic policies to fit their own development strategies' (G8, 2005:2) and 'explicit endorsement of the PRSP by the Executive Boards of the two institutions [the IMF and the World Bank] is no longer required for PRGF [Poverty Reduction Growth Facility] lending' (IMF, 2005:1).

However, third, and with somewhat bad timing given the above, there has been talk that the development community has actually run out of 'big ideas'. There is a lack of 'meta-narratives', universal claims and development theory (Lindauer and Pritchett, 2002:1; Thorbecke, 2005:34). So where are we now? Do we have a dominant set of policy ideas? Is the WC dead? If so, what has replaced it or who are the contenders?

The initiators of the last two claims to a 'consensus' have been dismissive. Williamson (2000:251, 262) has argued that 'no consensus currently exists... the quest for a consensus is hopeless'. Stiglitz (2004:1) has more recently added: 'There is no consensus except that the WC did not provide the answer.' Others have gone as far as to suggest new paradigms – take for example, Maxwell's (2005) 'meta-narrative' (perhaps a 'New York Consensus', rather than a Washington Consensus, led as it is by the UN Millennium Declaration signed in New York) or Gore's (2000) 'Latent Southern Consensus' (see later discussion for both). Any claims to a new 'meta-narrative' are unlikely to be as grand as previous development paradigms because their need to account for wide variations in country experiences weakens any universal claims. That said, as Maxwell notes, a few general ideas might be insightful:

> The first rule of the meta-narrative should probably be that development is particular and path-dependent, and that we should beware of meta-narratives. Nevertheless, there are some general themes in the current conventional wisdom that cut across the range and variety of development experience (Maxwell, 2005:2).

Indeed, whether we need a universal paradigm applicable to all is contentious: 'What the world needs right now is less consensus and more experimentation... a 'thin' set of rules... as opposed to a 'thick' set of rules' (Rodrik, 2002:18). The unifying theme at the time was one of reconsolidation.

> After half a century of development effort, there is now widespread interest in assessing the development record – what has gone right and what has gone wrong (Meier, 2005:vii).

The last few years have been marked by a critical re-evaluation and consolidation of previous concepts and techniques as opposed to the formulation of brand new ideas per se (Thorbecke, 2005:34).

Table 1.3 compares claims to a contemporary development paradigm at that time, in terms of point for departure (i.e. where developing countries are now), form of travel (i.e. policies) and point of arrival (i.e. where developing countries want to be). Much discussion centred on the concept of a 'post-WC' driven by Stiglitz's (1998a; 1998b) work.

Table 1.3   Claims to a Contemporary Development Paradigm (2000–2005)

	Point of departure	*Form of travel*	*Point of arrival*
The Post-Washington Consensus (cf. Stiglitz)	Low-income societies characterised by poor institutions and weak governance	Quality institutions; regulatory structures; macro-economic stability; strong financial system; privatisation with competition; human capital formation; property rights; cautious integration; social safety nets; technology policy	Economic growth and multi-dimensional poverty reduction, sustainability, equity and democracy
The Millennium Meta-narrative or New York Consensus (cf. Maxwell, 2005; UNMP, 2005)	Low-level equilibrium poverty trap for low-income LDCs; inequality and poverty 'pockets' in middle-income LDCs. Both – 'governance' failures	Growth; trade openness; aid; prioritising public expenditure; good 'governance'	Attaining the MDGs
The Latent Southern Consensus (Gore, 2000)	Agrarian, low-income societies	Strategic integration; fiscal discipline; full capital and human employment; human capital formation; state facilitation of private sector-led development; agrarian reform; regional cooperation	Structural change and social transformation

The post-WC, though is primarily a critique of the WC as practised by the IFIs rather than a new paradigm. Stiglitz (1998a:34) has argued that the WC was 'incomplete' and 'misleading' and that there was a lack of understanding of economic structures (too unrealistic ontological assumptions), a narrow set of objectives (too economic) and a narrow set of policy instruments (too limited). However, many have argued that the difference between the post-WC and WC is relatively little. Perraton (2005:897) suggested the difference was 'rather less than the rhetoric suggests' and noted that Stiglitz only repudiates fiscal discipline, and liberalisation of the capital account and tight monetary policy. Elsewhere there is only caution or sequencing rather than opposition to trade and FDI liberalisation and privatisation. On the post-WC others have more radically argued it is:

> a paler, micro-contingent version of the welfarism... [akin to the] Keynesianism of the McNamara era (Fine, 2002:2006)

> a novel synthesis of the two previously dominant paradigms in development theory and practice [national developmentalism and neo-liberalism] (Öniş and Şenses, 2005:286)

> the reinvention of global neo-liberalism under the guise of an 'augmented Washington Consensus' (Beeson and Islam, 2005:199).

Rodrik (2002:1) labelled the post-WC '[u]nfeasible, inappropriate and irrelevant' and dubbed it the 'augmented-WC', arguing that it describes the desirable features of development but not how to get them, and added ten policies to Williamson's original list to form the 'augmented WC'.[4]

The point of departure for the post-WC is, in places, quite different from the IFI WC: that low-income societies are characterised by poor institutions (rather than state-induced economic chaos), weak governance and imperfect markets. The 'vehicle' is high quality institutions (but how to get them?) and regulatory structures underpinning markets, cautious international integration, and social safety nets for adjustment. The point of arrival was broader than the IFI WC. It was multidimensional poverty reduction, sustainability and democracy.

Maxwell (2005:1–2) takes the post-WC as expanding the WC but argues the post-WC is still 'incomplete' and tentatively proposes a new 'meta-narrative': 'The WC has been replaced by a new and improved orthodoxy, called here the "meta-narrative". It emphasises the Millennium Development Goals (MDGs) as an overarching framework, and lays out the link between the MDGs, nationally owned poverty reduction strategies, macro-economic policy (including trade), effective public expenditure management, and harmonised aid in support of good governance and good policies' (Maxwell, 2005:v).

For the new Millennium Meta-narrative or perhaps a New York Consensus, the point of departure is – according to the Jeffrey Sachs-led UNMP (2005:29) – for low-income LDCs, a low equilibrium poverty trap (causes: low savings rate, low-tax revenue, low FDI, conflict, brain drain, population growth, environmental degradation and low innovation), but for middle-income LDCs, inequality and poverty 'pockets' are the point of departure. Both relate to 'governance' failures (causes: limited rule of law, limited 'soundness' of economic policies, 'mis-appropriateness' of public expenditure and management). One might add the 'vehicle' is MDG-led PRSPs based on: growth; trade openness; aid; prioritising public expenditure and good 'governance' (Maxwell, 2005:2).

Gore's (2000:791) Latent Southern Consensus is another attempt at outlining 'a big idea'. It is a synthesis of East Asian developmentalism (state facilitated private sector-led development) and Latin American neo-structuralism (that stresses the importance of centre–periphery relations in delivering the conditions of national development). Gore (2000:796) identifies five groups of policies: (i) the strategic integration of the national and international economy rather than rapid liberalisation (i.e. gradual import liberalisation; promotion of exports; promotion of FDI with local linkages); (ii) growth and structural change by 'productive development policy' (reduce inflation; fiscal discipline but also full employment of capital; state facilitation of this through, for example, human resource development); (iii) a developmental state linking government and business cooperation – private sector led but government sets framework (i.e. overcoming technology imperfections); (iv) the 'managing' of distribution and growth to ensure productive employment (i.e. agrarian reform); (v) regional integration and cooperation.

Kanbur (2000) summed up contemporary policy debates as a discourse between a group from the 'mainstream' or 'orthodox' perspective labelled by Kanbur as 'finance ministry'. In opposition were a group of detractors from a 'non-mainstream'/'non-orthodox' perspective labelled by Kanbur as 'civil society'. These groups were intended as tendencies rather than specific individuals.[5] Many, notably from the civil society grouping, including UN agencies (see for example, Oxfam, 2004; UNCTAD, 2002a; 2002b; UNDP, 2001) have argued that a 'finance ministry'-type IFI WC is alive and well in contemporary policy and in the PRSPs. Academic opinion is equally damning:

> [The PRSPs are a] remorphing of neo-liberal approaches (Craig and Porter, 2003:54).

> [In the PRSPs there has been] no fundamental departure from the kind of policy advice provided under earlier structural adjustment programmes. Current policies contain all the elements of the first generation of policy reforms designed to promote the role of the market and 'get prices right'... ... financial and trade liberalisation; privatisation; public sector reform (Stewart and Wang, 2003:19–21).

Developing countries do have greater policy autonomy but the international financial institutions still have overt/covert influence over PRSPs and IFI agendas may be internalised as the Ministry of Finance takes over from the IMF as the dominant player in the process.[6] As the *Economist* (2005:12) downloaded at economist.com noted, 'the shift in fashions [to PRSPs] should not be exaggerated. Where before donors told governments what to do now governments largely tell donors what they want to hear'.

There have been a number of content reviews of PRSPs (see Stewart and Wang, 2003 cited above for example or the African country studies in the Booth, 2003 edited volume). Overall, although strict monetary and fiscal policy and privatisation are rarely absent, trade liberalisation is not included in over a quarter of PRSPs and a third do not include FDI deregulation or capital account liberalisation.[7]

Furthermore, this trend is much stronger in HIPC countries and notably African HIPC countries (not surprising as most HIPC countries are African). In HIPC counties although once again strict monetary and fiscal policy and privatisation are rarely missing, trade liberalisation is absent in well over a third; FDI deregulation is missing in half of those countries and capital account liberalisation in over two-thirds. A point to take from this is 10–20 years ago one might reasonably expect all these policies to be components of any SAPs.[8] The current paradigm seems to be as follows: a market economy but with a market-regulating state – i.e. privatisation but only with regulating institutions; economic openness but in a cautious, sequenced and orderly fashion and limited in the case of financial and capital account liberalisation; fiscal discipline but ring-fencing of education and health and other social expenditures (safety nets and social protection for example) and FDI deregulation and financial/capital account liberalisation are less fashionable in the poorest LDCs. There is less 'state-bashing' and some sense of pragmatism.

There has been, since 2005 and Wolfensohn's declaration, a new interest in meta-narratives. Indeed, over the last few years (2005/6–2007/8) in particular there has been a re-emergence of attempts at a grand-narrative. Have these made the post-WC 'complete'?

Haddad (2006:3) notes that these are largely Western narratives. He argues there is actually one meta-narrative underwriting all of these and that is what Walter Russel Mead (2007) in *God and Gold: Britain, America and the Making of the Modern World*, called the 'Whig Narrative' or an Anglo-Saxon concept of history as certainty, as irresistible capitalist progress under the guidance of 'invisible hand' rationality.

Table 1.4 compares the Collier, Easterly and Sachs books in terms of point for departure (i.e. where developing countries are now), form of travel (i.e. policies) and point of arrival (i.e. where developing countries want to be). Of the most recent books, arguably the most famous is Paul Collier's *Bottom Billion*. The book is based solely on Collier's own (largely econometric) research. For detractors his book's success is related to its catchy title, striking photograph of child with a gun and some major marketing machinery; for others it is Collier's well-told story regardless of whether or not one agrees with it or, as Maxwell (2008:1) put it, a 'master class in research to policy'. Competing titles are William Easterly's *White Man's Burden* which built upon *the Elusive Quest for Growth*. There is also the Jeffrey Sachs-led UNMP (2005) noted earlier and Sachs follow-ups, *The End of Poverty* and *Common Wealth*.

After this set there is a larger collection focusing largely on the globalisation of trade. This includes Ha-Joon Chang's *Bad Samaritans* which built upon *Kicking Away the Ladder*, Chang and Ilene Grabel's *Reclaiming Development*, Dani Rodrik's *One Economics, Many Recipes*, Joseph Stiglitz's *Making Globalisation Work* and Stiglitz and Andrew Charlton's *Fair Trade for All*. Finally, one might also note Alice Amsden's *Escape from Empire*, Wolfgang Sach and Tilman Santarius's *Fair Future* and, depending on how far to cast the net, the two *Copenhagen Consensus* books (Lomborg, 2006; 2007), respectively, *How to Spend $50 billion to Make the World a Better Place* and *Solutions for the World's Biggest Problems*.

As noted before, each author has presented a diagnosis of the 'problem'. Each has presented an entry point with most leverage for (good) change. For Collier (2007), the core problem is 58 (unnamed) countries that are 'falling behind and often falling apart' (p.3). He argues the MDGs focus is misleading because 80% of the world's poor live in countries that are making progress. We should be concerned with the bottom billion who live in the 58 countries. These countries are afflicted by one or more of four interlocking development traps: a conflict trap (especially civil war); a natural resource trap – abundance of which makes 'democracy malfunction' (p.42); a landlocked with bad neighbours trap – in the sense of poor markets – 'If you are coastal, you serve the world; if you are landlocked, you serve your neighbours' (p.57); and a bad governance in a small country trap. What should we do? We should focus on those 58 poor countries (low income, fragile states, etc) not poor people, and focus on growth not the MDGs (p.11). In other work, notably his review of the *World Development Report 2006* on inequality, Collier suggests that development policy has been distracted by poverty and inequality from a key focus on raising incomes for societies as a whole. Policy-makers should worry about growth first and have faith that, generally, poverty reduction will follow. Further, the North can be decisive in supporting the 'heroes' or 'good guys' but change must be internally driven. Collier argues globalisation is not going to solve these problems if left to itself – the bottom-billion countries need to diversify into manufacturing trade. This will not happen by removing OECD trade barriers, or through fair trade. The key is temporary protection from successful exporters in Asia in certain sectors such as textiles. Aid is a holding operation. Military intervention is useful. International laws and charters which shape behaviour and support 'heroes' are important in areas of managing natural-resource revenues; for democracy; for budget transparency; for post-conflict situations; and for investment. In sum, for Collier, it is more instruments and a focus on fewer countries. What matters is growth (more attention), governance (international charters and laws) and globalisation (trade protectionism under certain conditions).

For Easterly, the sub-title of his best-known book says it all – *why the West's efforts to aid the rest have done so much ill and so little good.* Easterly focuses on aid and argues that not only has aid done little good, it has actually harmed developing countries. Aid has removed incentives for poor states to innovate and find their own solutions. Aid has been bad because of its focus on planning (e.g. PRSPs) and its support to governments who are often undemocratic, inefficient and corrupt. The alternative is to support 'searchers' (rather than support planners). Searchers are innovative individuals who find novel solutions and 'get things done'. Incentives and markets for searchers need to be enhanced. This might all look like a somewhat simple, entrepreneurs versus bureaucrats or markets versus states. For many, Easterly's book appears nihilistic and fails to recognise little of the evidence of progress. For Easterly, what matters are incentives, markets and 'searchers'.

For Jeffrey Sachs (2005), the narrative is an extension of the UNMP (2005). The goal is the achievement of growth and the MDGs via large aid investments from the North to the South in a 'big push'. The focus is on 'quick wins' and targeting programmes to the poor. Sachs offers a different set of traps as to why countries are poor (2005:56–61) including a poverty trap (the poor are too poor to save for the future and accumulate capital), a physical geography trap (similar to Collier), a fiscal trap (limited government resources), a governance trap/failure, cultural barriers (notably on rights and gender inequality), a geopolitics trap (as a result of trade barriers), a constraining of innovation trap (due to small markets and weak incentives), and a demographic trap (as a result of high fertility). In short, poverty is a result of a lack of savings, the absence of

Table 1.4   Collier, Easterly and Sachs: New Meta-narratives?

	Point of departure	*Form of travel*	*Point of arrival*
Collier	Conflict trap; natural resource trap; landlocked trap; bad governance trap.	Governance (international charters and laws) and globalisation (trade protectionism under certain conditions).	Growth (which will lead to poverty reduction).
Easterly	Focus on planning has been the problem. Aid to date has harmed countries. Failure is due to weak accountability.	Support searchers – innovative individuals who find novel solutions and 'get things done'. Create incentives and markets for searchers. We need home-grown initiatives.	Innovation – and endogenously led development.
Sachs	A poverty trap, a physical geography trap, a fiscal trap, a governance trap, cultural barriers, a geopolitics trap, an innovation trap, a demographic trap.	Aid for agriculture inputs, investments in basic health, investments in education, power, transport and communication services, safe water and sanitation.	MDGs.

trade opportunities (due to geography), technological reversal, natural resource decline, adverse productivity shocks, and population growth (2005:54–5). The solutions include (2005:233–4) agriculture inputs, investments in basic health, investments in education, power, transport and communication services, safe water and sanitation). This being the basis of the UNMP, the Millennium Villages Project and the Global Fund for HIV/AIDS. More recently Sachs in *Common Wealth* (2008) has ambitiously set out plans for action on climate change, growth, trade, diseases, population and biodiversity based on the experiments in the Millennium Villages pilot projects.

What about others? As noted, globalisation in the form of the globalisation of trade dominate so we discuss these in detail in Chapter 6.

One final thought provoking piece worth mentioning is by another Sachs – Wolfgang Sachs. His co-edited book *Fair Future* and related article (2007), *Global Challenges: Climate Chaos and the Future of Development* discusses how we have reached the biophysical limits of growth due to climate change and now must seek convergence in resource use per unit. Wolfgang Sachs discusses the current distribution of resource use, a fair distribution of resource use and how an international agreement might be pursued. The book thus highlights a missing element of sustainability with particular reference to growth missing in much of the recent debates (see further discussion in Chapter 4).

5.   Where next?

The world is changing and there are still a lot of poor people. The world in 2015 and beyond is difficult to predict. Thinking back, who would have imagined the spread of the Internet, the collapse of the Soviet bloc or the post-9/11 world? What can we say at this stage? The increased global interconnectedness is expressing itself in a growing variety of ways. Take for example:

- volatility in global markets (i.e. food, fuel and credit);
- climate change and natural resources;
- technology (notably ICTs and industrial biofuels);
- terrorism and security.

The net outcome of all the above is a lot of change – of lifestyles and livelihoods. Larger migratory movements nationally as well as internationally are likely as is an increased potential for conflict over resources as a result of people on the move. So, the question is how can we promote pro-poor policy after the MDGs and amid all these complex changes, some of which mediate in favour of the poor, many do not?

Three policy themes emerge as a 'centre of gravity' from the discussions above (all with some considerable contextual leeway). First, 'good' or at least better governance in various dimensions is essential. Second, growth matters but we need to think about quality or the inclusiveness of growth. Third, globalisation in some form or other can be progressive. Growth is a means. Globalisation is a means. However, governance is a means but it could also be an end, as participation has intrinsic value. Cutting through all of these are the underlying core issues of multi-dimensional poverty, ill-being and inequality.

So do we have a consensus on what matters and where to focus attention for maximum impact? Not quite. The apparent common themes hide much in terms of nuance. First, on doing governance: All commentators emphasise governance matters. However, what exactly to do in practice remains somewhat unclear. How do we get good (enough) governance? We pick up this discussion in Chapter 4. Second, on doing growth: Many commentators say growth matters to varying degrees but many other disagree. Collier goes as far as to suggest growth is central and poverty reduction generally follows. It certainly matters to MDG1 – the dollar-a-day measure. How much, though, is highly contentious. We pick up discussions on growth and its relationship with poverty, inequality and sustainability in Chapter 5. Third, globalisation. All commentators say something about how globalisation (both private investment and trade and public investment in the form of aid) is not working but might somehow be made to work and thus matters. Again, what interventions are necessary is a contentious issue. We discuss these matters in Chapter 6.

In the remainder of Part I of this book we discuss a brief history of development to the present day and the role of the MDGs in the development policy architecture (Chapter 2). We then turn to consider that said architecture, options for after-2015 targets/goals/indicators and focus on the nature of policy and policy change in international development (Chapter 3).

Notes

1 This chapter draws upon and builds on discussion in Sumner *et al.* (2008b) and Sumner (2006, 2007).
2 Chen and Ravallion (2008) noted an extra 65–130 million more poor people in China alone. However, the China data focused mainly on cities, where

prices are significantly higher. A large part of the Chinese population live in rural areas, where goods are cheaper, the new survey may over-estimate the number of poor people. They also proposed a new poverty line of US$1.25.

3 This may perhaps reflect the political sensitivities of suddenly increasing the global poverty count or perhaps relate to a shortly forthcoming update of the price survey for India and presumably a debate on the appropriateness of the dollar-a-day measure.

4 These were corporate governance; anti-corruption; flexible labour markets; WTO agreements; financial codes and standards; 'prudent' capital account liberalisation; non-intermediate exchange rate regimes; an independent central bank and inflation targeting; social safety nets; targeted poverty reduction.

5 The *finance ministry* group consists of those working in finance ministries as well as economic analysts, Anglo-Saxon trained academics, economic policy managers, operational managers of the IMF and World Bank and the financial press. In contrast, the *civil society* group consists of those working in NGOs, the United Nations agencies, aid ministries in the North, social sector ministries in the South and non-economist researchers. Kanbur identified three reasons for the disagreements: differing levels of aggregation in analysis, differing time horizons and differing perspectives on market structure.

6 Additionally, in October 2005, the IMF board approved the establishment of a 'Policy Support Instrument'. This is a non-lending programme to provide advice and to *signal* to donors and markets about a country's economic policies. As such it could form a de facto 'judgment' under the IMF's article 4 consultations. For more details see http://www.imf.org/external/np/sec/pn/2005/pn05145.htm

7 See Sumner (2007) PRSP Review. The scepticism may be a reflection of recent critical cross-country studies. For sceptics' research on FDI, growth and poverty see for example, Agénor, 2002; Carkovic and Levine, 2005; Milanovic, 2002; Santarelli and Figini, 2003. For sceptics' research on capital account liberalisation, growth and poverty see Arteta *et al.*, 2001; Klein, 2003; Rodrik, 1997; 1998. On trade liberalisation, see Agénor, 2002; Hertel *et al.*, 2003; Lundberg and Squire, 2003. On privatisation see Cook and Uchida, 2001.

8 Of course although one of the objectives of PRSPs is to be comprehensive, policies may be 'missing' in the PRSP document that actually are in existence and there is also the issue of the qualitative nature of policies. For example, the extent or degree or scope of 'privatisation' or other policies.

References

Agénor, R. (2002) *Does Globalisation Hurt the Poor?* Mimeograph. Washington, DC: World Bank.

Arteta, C., Eichengreen, B. and Wyplosz, C. (2001) *On the Growth Effects of Capital Account Liberalisation*. Mimeograph. California: University of California.

Beeson, M. and Islam, I. (2005) 'Neo-Liberalism and East Asia: Resisting the Washington Consensus', *Journal of Development Studies*, 41(2):197–219.

Booth, D. and Henry, L. (2002) 'Good Practice in the Development of Poverty Reduction Strategy Papers Indicators and Monitoring Systems', Overseas Development Institute Working Paper No. 172, London: ODI.

Booth, D. (2003) *Fighting Poverty in Africa: Are PRSPs Making a Difference?* London: Overseas Development Institute.

Carkovic, M. and Levine, R. (2005) Does Foreign Direct Investment Accelerate Economic Growth?, in Moran, T.H. and Graham, E.M. (eds) *Does Foreign Direct Investment Promote Development*. Minneapolis, MN: University of Minnesota, Department of Finance Working Paper.

Chambers, R. (1997) *Whose Reality Counts? Putting the First Last*. London: ITDG.

Chang, H.-J. (2007) *Bad Samaritans*. London: Random House.

Chen, S. and Ravallion, M. (2004) How have the World's Poor Poorest Fared since the Early 1980s? *World Bank Observer*, 19(2):141–70.

Chen, S. and Ravallion, M. (2007) 'Absolute Poverty Measures for the Developing World, 1981–2004', Policy Research Working Paper Series 4211. Washington, DC: World Bank.

Chen, S. and Ravallion, M. (2008) 'The Developing World is Poorer than We Thought, But No Less Successful in the Fight against Poverty', Policy Research Working Paper Series 4703. Washington, DC: World Bank.

Collier, P. (2007) *The Bottom Billion*. Oxford: Oxford University Press.

Cook, P. and Uchida, Y. (2001) 'Privatisation and Economic Growth in Developing Countries', Centre on Regulation and Competition Working Paper Series No. 7. Manchester: University of Manchester.

Cornia, A., Jolly, R. and Stewart, F. (1987) *Adjustment with a Human Face*. New York: Oxford University Press.

Craig, D. and Porter, D. (2003) 'Poverty Reduction Strategy Papers: A New Convergence', *World Development*, 31:53–69.

Easterly, W. (2000) *The Effect of IMF and World Bank Programs on Poverty*. IMF Staff Papers. IMF, Washington, DC.

Easterly, W. (2006) *The White Man's Burden*. New York: Penguin.

Eyben, R. (ed.) (2006) *Relationships for Aid*. London: Earthscan.

Fine, B. (2002) 'Economics Imperialism and the New Development Economics as Kuhnian Paradigm Shift', *World Development*, 30(12):2057–70.

G8 (Group of 8) (2005) *Final Communiqué*. Gleneagles. June. Downloaded at http://www.g8.gov.uk

Gore, C. (2000) 'The Rise and Fall of the Washington Consensus as Paradigm for Developing Countries', *World Development*, 28(5):789–804.

Haddad, L. (2006) *Reinventing Development Research: Listening to the IDS40 Roundtables*. Paper prepared for IDS40 Conference, 'Reinventing Development Research'.

Hertel, T., Ivanic, M., Preckel, P. and Cranfield, J. (2003) *Trade Liberalisation and the Structure of Poverty in Developing Countries*. Paper prepared for 'Globalisation, Agricultural Development and Rural Livelihoods', April 11–12, Ithaca, NY: Cornell University.

IMF (International Monetary Fund) (2005) *Poverty Reduction Strategy Papers (PRSP): A Fact Sheet*. Washington, DC: IMF. Downloaded from http://www.imf.org/external/np/exr/facts/prsp.htm

Kanbur, R. (1999) *The Strange Case of the Washington Consensus: A Brief Note on John Williamson's 'What Should The Bank Think About The Washington Consensus?'* Mimeograph, Ithaca, NY: Cornell University.

Kanbur, R. (2000) }Economic Policy, Distribution and Poverty: The Nature of Disagreements', *World Development*, 29(6):1083–94.

Kanbur, R. and Squire, L. (2001) The Evolution of Thinking About Poverty: exploring the contradictions, in Meier, G. and Stiglitz, J. (eds) *Frontiers of Development Economics*. Oxford: Oxford University Press.

Klein, M. (2003) *Capital Account Openness and the Varieties Of Growth Experience*. National Bureau of Economic Research (NBER) Working Paper Number 9500. Cambridge, MA: NBER.

Kuhn, T. (1962) *The Structure of Scientific Revolutions*. Chicago: University of Chicago.

Kuhn, T. (1970) Reflections on My Critics, in Lakatos, I . and Musgrave, A. (eds) *Criticism and the Growth of Knowledge*. New York: Cambridge University Press.

Kuhn, T. (1972) Second Thoughts on Paradigms, in Suppe, F. (ed.) *The Structure of Scientific Theories*. Illinois: University of Illinois Press.

Leach, M., Bloom, G., Ely, A., Nightingale, P., Scoones, I., Shah, E. and Smith, A. (2007) *Understanding Governance: Pathways to Sustainability*. STEPS Working Paper 2, STEPS Centre. Brighton, UK: IDS.

Lindauer, D. and Pritchett, L. (2002) 'What's the Big Idea? Three Generations of Development Advice', *Economia*, 3.1, Fall.

Lomborg, B. (2006) *How to Spend $50 Billion to Make the World a Better Place*. Cambridge: Cambridge University Press.

Lomborg, B. (2007) *Solutions for the World's Biggest Problems: Costs and Benefits*. Cambridge: Cambridge University Press.

Lundberg, M. and Squire, L. (2003) 'The Simultaneous Evolution of Growth and Inequality', *Economic Journal*, 113(487):326–44.

Maxwell, S. (2005) *The Washington Consensus is Dead! Long Live the Meta-Narrative!* Overseas Development Institute (ODI) Working Paper 243. London: ODI.

Maxwell, S. (2008) 'A Master-Class in Bridging Research and Policy?', *Development Policy Review*, 26(1):113–18.

Meier, G. (2005) *Biography of a Subject: An Evolution of Development Economics*. Oxford: Oxford University Press.

Milanovic, B. (2002) *Can We Discern The Effect of Globalisation on Income Distribution?* World Bank Policy Research Working Paper. Washington, DC: World Bank.

Milanovic, B. (2008) *Developing Countries Worse Off Than Once Thought*. Mimeo. Yale University.

Naim, M. (2000) 'Washington Consensus or Washington Confusion?', *Foreign Policy*, Spring: 87–103.

Öniş, Z. and Şenses, F. (2005) 'Rethinking the Emerging Post-Washington Consensus', *Development and Change*, 36(2):263–90.

Oxfam (2004) *From 'Donorship' to Ownership? Moving Towards PRSP Round Two*. Oxford: Oxfam Publishing.

Perraton, P. (2005) Review Article: Joseph Stiglitz's Globalisation and its Discontents, *Journal of International Development*, 16(6):897–906.

Ramalingam, B., Jones, H., Reba, T. and John, Y. (2008) *Exploring the Science of Complexity: Ideas and Implications for Development and Humanitarian Efforts*. London: ODI.

Ravallion, M., Chen, S. and Sangraula, P. (2008) *Dollar-a-day Revisited*. World Bank Policy Research Working Paper Number 4620. World Bank, Washington, DC.

Redde, S. and Pogge, T. (2002) *How Not to Count the Poor*. Department of Economics Working Paper. New York: Colombia University.

Rihani, S. (2005) Complexity Theory: A New Framework for Development is in the Offing. *Progress in Development Studies*, 5(1).

Rodrik, D. (1997) *Trade Policy and Performance in Sub-Saharan Africa*, Mimeograph. Cambridge, MA: Harvard University.

Rodrik, D. (1998) Who Needs Capital-Account Convertibility?, in Fischer, S. (ed.) *Should the IMF Pursue Capital Account Convertibility?* Essays in International Finance Number 207. Princeton, N.J: University of Princeton.

Rodrik, D. (2002) *After Neoliberalism, What?* Paper presented at 'Alternatives to Neoliberalism', Washington, DC, May 23. Downloaded at http://ksghome.harvard.edu/~drodrik

Russel Mead, W. (2007) *God and Gold: Britain, America, and the Making of the Modern World*. New York: Vintage.

Sachs, J. (2005) *The End of Poverty*. London: Penguin.

Sachs, W. (2007) *Global Challenges: Climate Chaos and the Future of Development*. IDS Bulletin, 38(2):36–9.

Sachs, J. (2008) *Common Wealth*. London: Penguin.

Santarelli, F. and Figini, P. (2003) *Does Globalisation Reduce Poverty? Some Empirical Evidence for Developing Countries*. Paper presented at UNU WIDER Conference, 'Inequality, Poverty and Human Well-being', Helsinki, May 30–31.

Scoones, I. *et al.* (2007) *Dynamic Systems and the Challenge of Sustainability*, STEPS Working Paper 1. Brighton: IDS.

Senge, P. (1990) The Leader's New Work: Building Learning Organizations, *Sloan Management Review*, 32(1):7–23.

Stewart, F. and Wang, M. (2003) *Do PRSPs Empower Poor People and Disempower the World Bank, Or is it the Other Way Round?* Queen Elizabeth House Working Paper, Oxford: Oxford University.

Stiglitz, J. (1998a) *More Instruments and Broader Goals: Moving Towards the Post-Washington Consensus*. UNU WIDER Annual Lecture, Helsinki, 7 Jan.

Stiglitz, J. (1998b) *Towards a New Paradigm for Development: Strategies, Policies and Processes*. Prebisch Lecture at UNCTAD, Geneva, 19 October.

Stiglitz, J. (2002) *The Post Washington Consensus*, Initiative for Policy Dialogue Working Paper: Columbia, MA: Columbia University.

Stiglitz, J. (2006) *Making Globalisation Work*. New York: WW Norton.

Streeten, P. (1983) Development Dichotomies, *World Development*, 11(10): 875–89.

Sumner, A. (2006) 'In Search of the Post Washington (Dis)Consensus: The "Missing" Content of PRSPs', *Third World Quarterly*, 27(8):1401–12.

Sumner, A. (2007) 'Foreign Direct Investment in Developing Countries: Have We Reached a Policy "Tipping Point"?', *Third World Quarterly*, 29(2):239–53.

Sumner, A., Meija, A., Cabral, L. and Hussein, K. (2008a) 'What Factors Mediate the Participation of the Rural Poor in Policy Processes?'. Background Paper for IFAD Rural Poverty Report 2009 (forthcoming). Rome: IFAD.

Sumner, A., Giordano, T. and Wiggins, S. (2008b) 'How is the World Changing and What Does it Mean for the Rural Poor?'. Background Paper for IFAD Rural Poverty Report 2009 (forthcoming). Rome: IFAD.

Sutcliffe, B. (1999) The Place of Development Theories in Theories of Imperialism and Globalisation, in Munck, R. and O'Hearn, D. (eds) *Critical Development Theory: Contributions to a New Paradigm*. London: Zed Books.

Thorbecke, E. (2005) *The Evolution of the Development Doctrine 1950–2005*. Paper presented at UNU WIDER conference, 'The Future of Development Economics', 17–18 June, Helsinki.

UN (United Nations) (2007) The UN Millennium Development Goals. New York: United Nations. Available at http://www.un.org/millenniumgoals/ (accessed 15 June 2007).

UNCTAD (United Nations Conference on Trade and Development) (2002a) *Economic Development in Africa: From Adjustment to Poverty Reduction: What is New?* Geneva: UNCTAD.

UNCTAD (2002b) *The World Bank's PRSP Approach: Good Marketing or Good Policy?* Geneva: UNCTAD.

UNESCO (2005) *Education for All: Global Monitoring Report*. Paris: UNESCO.

UNDP (United Nations Development Programme) (2001) *UNDP Support for Poverty Reduction Strategies: the PRSP Countries*. New York: UNDP.

UNMP (United Nations Millennium Project) (2005) *Investing in Development: A Practical Plan to Achieve the Millennium Development Goals*. London: Earthscan.

Vandemoortele, J. (2002) *Are the Millennium Development Goals Feasible?* Mimeograph. UNDP.

Wade, R. (2004) Is Globalization Reducing Poverty and Inequality? *World Development*, 32(4):567–89.

Waldrop, M. (1994) *Complexity: the Emerging Science at the Edge of Order and Chaos*. London: Penguin Books.

Warner, M. (2001) *Complex Problems ... Negotiated Solutions: The Practical Applications of Chaos and Complexity Theory to Community-based Natural Resource Management*. London: ODI.

WDM (World Development Movement) (2005a). *Denying Democracy: How the IMF and the World Bank Take Power From Poor People*. London: WDM.

WDM (2005b) *Economic Policies in Poverty Reduction Strategy Papers*. London: WDM.

WDM (2005c) *One Size for All: A Study of IMF and WB PRSPs*. London: WDM.

White, H. (2002) 'Combining Quantitative and Qualitative Approaches in Poverty Analysis', *World Development*, 30(3):511–22.

White, H. and Black, R. (2003) *Targeting Development: Critical Perspectives on the Millennium Development Goals*. London: Routledge.

Williamson, J. (1993) 'Democracy and the Washington Consensus', *World Development*, 21(8):1329–36.

Williamson, J. (1998) What Should the Bank Think about the Washington Consensus? Paper prepared as a background to the World Bank's World Development Report 2000.

Williamson, J. (2000) 'What Should the World Bank Think About the Washington Consensus?', *World Bank Research Observer*, 15(2):251–64.

2
The MDGs and Beyond

> If development means good change, questions arise about
> what is good and what sort of change matters... Any develop-
> ment agenda is value-laden (Chambers, 2004:1).

1.   Introduction

'Development' has come to mean the MDGs for many – policy-makers
in particular. In this chapter we look at the evolution of the meaning
of development and its relationship with the MDGs.[1] We draw on
recent conceptual discussions regarding the evolving notion of 'wellbeing' (as opposed to poverty, deprivation and 'ill-being') and ask what
it adds and what it might contribute to a post-2015 future.

This chapter is structured as follows: Section 2 discusses the meaning
of 'development' up to the MDGs. Section 3 is then concerned with
the MDGs and how they have shaped prevailing notions of 'development'. Section 4 discusses what might happen after 2015. Section 5
concludes.

2.   A brief history of 'development' up to the MDGs

Over the last 50 years, every two decades or so one might note a 'development milestone' which steers the prevailing notion of 'development'
for better or for worse. For example, in 1949 it was, controversially to
many, the Truman Declaration (and the Marshall Plan). In 1969 one
might say Dudley Seers's *The Meaning of Development* and the work of
Paul Streeten and the ILO (and others) on *Basic Needs* played a role in
redirecting development. In the 1990s it was Amartya Sen and UNDP's
Human Development and the annual *Human Development Reports* that

were influential. The human development agenda ultimately contributed to the emergence of the MDGs via numerous UN poverty conferences in the 1990s (and an earlier incarnation of the MDGs in the OECD's International Development Targets – IDTs).

How do the MDGs fit into a history of 'development' post-World War II? Truman's declaration is associated with the deliberate efforts at progress made in the name of 'development' since World War II, particularly industrialisation or industrial transformation:

> We must embark on a bold new programme for making the benefits of our scientific advances and industrial progress available for the improvement and growth of underdeveloped areas (cited in Esteva, 1992:6).

Such a transformative view of societal change dominated the 1950s and 1960s. Industrialisation, structural societal change and economic growth mattered. However, such a perspective 'slipped from view' in the 1970s and since. As Gore (2000:794–5) notes,

> The dynamics of long-term transformations of economies and societies [has] slipped from view and attention was placed on short-term [indicators]... The shift to a historical performance assessment can be interpreted as a form of the post-modernisation of development policy analysis (Gore, 2000:794–5).

The key characteristics of such a perspective are that it is focused on processes of structural societal change, it is historical and it has a long-term outlook. This means that a major societal shift in one dimension, for example from a rural or agriculture-based society to an urban or industrial-based society (what is sometimes called the shift from 'traditional' to 'modern' characteristics), would also have radical implications in another dimension, such as societal structural changes in the respective positions of classes and groups within the relations of production for example (by which we mean the relationship between the owners of capital and labour). Hickey and Mohan (2003) take the view that the pressure on international development research to be relevant has undermined this older-established definition in favour of a more instrumental one of poverty indicators (see below). A long-term, broad view may address the big picture but it may have a limited capacity to meaningfully guide development practice, such as policy-making, which typically focuses on a shorter time period.

How did such a development outcomes focus – exemplified in the MDGs – evolve into the mainstream? The shift from development as a process to development as an outcome is intertwined with the shift from development as essentially economic in nature to development as a broader concept. In the late 1960s, Seers's *Meaning of Development* (1969) led to a rethinking of development away from reliance solely on growth in GDP per capita income alone:

> The questions to ask about a country's development are there-fore: What has been happening to poverty? What has been hap-pening to unemployment? What has been happening to inequality? If all of these three have become less severe, then beyond doubt this has been a period of development for the country concerned...
> ...If one or two of these central problems have been growing worse, especially if all three have, it would be strange to call the result 'development', even if per capita income has soared (Seers, 1969:24).

Dudley Seers (1969) launched the paradigm shift to broader under-standings of development beyond GDP per capita and into 'basic needs'. Further major contributions on 'basic needs' were made by other development economists, notably Paul Streeten (see Hicks and Streeten, 1979; Streeten, 1984) and staff at the ILO (1976; 1977). These 'basic needs' included not only income and employment but also the physical necessities for a basic standard of living such as food, shelter and public goods. This coincided with the emergence in the 1960s and 1970s of 'levels of living indicators' due to dissatisfaction with the use of income per capita as a measure of welfare and of development. The culmination of efforts was the first composite measure of standards of living – Morris's (1979) physical quality of life index (PQLI). Indeed, a continuum is discernible from the 1960s into the 1970s and then into the 1990s: the research of, ILO, Morris, as well as Baster (1979), McGranahan *et al.* (1985) and UNRISD (1970) set the foundations for Amartya Sen's work with the United Nations Development Programme (UNDP).

In the 1990s development thinking and policy were fundamentally reshaped by the work of Sen and the new annual development report, launched in 1990 by the UNDP, the *Human Development Report*. It pro-vided a new framework known as 'Human Development' or Sen's 'Capabilities Approach' and a related set of composite indicators led by the UNDP's *Human Development Index*.

Sen (see in particular 1999), Nussbaum (see in particular 2000) and UNDP (1990–2008) have argued that attention should be to the capabilities – means, opportunities or substantive freedoms – which permit the achievement of a set of 'functionings' – things which human beings value in terms of 'being' and 'doing'. Development is not, as previously conceived, based on desire fulfilment (utility or consumption measured by a proxy for income – GDP per capita) as this does not take sufficient evaluative account of the physical condition of the individual and of a person's capabilities. Income is *only* an instrumental freedom – it helps to achieve other constitutive freedoms. Sen does not ignore income; rather he argues that too much emphasis can be placed on this dimension of development. Instead,

> Development consists of the removal of various types of unfreedom that leave people with little opportunity of exercising their reasoned agency... Development can be seen... as a process of expanding the real freedoms that people enjoy... the expansion of the 'capabilities' of persons to lead the kind of lives they value – and have reason to value (Sen, 1999:xii, 1, 18).

Sen has argued that there is a broad set of conditions (including being fed, healthy, clothed and educated) that together constitute wellbeing. Individuals have a set of entitlements (command over commodities) which are created through a set of endowments (assets owned – physical and self – financial, human, natural, social and productive) and exchange (production and trade by the individual). These entitlements are traded for a set of opportunities (capabilities) in order to achieve a set of functionings (outcomes of wellbeing). Sen resolutely refused to name the capabilities although he (1999:38) did identify five basic freedoms. These are:

- political/participative freedoms/civil rights (e.g. freedom of speech, free elections);
- economic facilities (e.g. opportunities to participate in trade and production and sell one's labour and product on fair, competitive terms);
- social opportunities (e.g. adequate education and health facilities);
- transparency guarantees (e.g. openness in government and business and social trust);
- protective security (e.g. law and order, social safety nets for unemployed).

Furthermore, in the case of poverty assessment and 'basic capabilities', Sen (1992:44–5) noted that:

> [i]n dealing with extreme poverty... [capabilities might include] ...the ability to be well-nourished and well-sheltered, ... escaping avoidable morbidity and premature mortality, and so forth.

There have been numerous other attempts at constructing sets of capabilities (see for discussion Alkire, 2002). However, the actual identification of sets of 'capabilities' and 'functionings' remains unresolved after two decades. Indeed, there are now numerous 'capabilities' sets. However, this should not detract from the fact that the multi-dimensional approach to poverty 'is so common place it is easy to forget it was not always the case' (Kanbur, 2001:1085).

The 2000/1 *World Development Report*, citing Sen early on, played a central role in solidifying a multi-dimensional model of poverty. It coincided with the UN Millennium Assembly in New York, on 18 September 2000, at which all countries signed the Millennium Declaration from which the Millennium Development Goals poverty reduction targets for 2015 were derived. The Millennium Declaration is based on six 'fundamental values'. These are freedom (incorporated into MDG 1, 2, 3, 4, 5, 6); equality (MDG 2); solidarity (MDG 8); tolerance (no MDG), respect for nature (MDG 7) and shared responsibility (MDG 8). The MDGs themselves were in fact a collation of goals agreed at various UN conferences in the preceding period.

Development as the MDGs – an outcome of poverty reduction – has become the mainstream definition of development, particularly so amongst development policy-makers. Gore (2000:794) characterises an approach to development as an outcome indicator as 'performance assessment' (refer also to Saith's critique of the MDGs below). Thomas (2000; 2004) characterises this approach as 'a vision or measure of progressive change' and notes,

> 'development' is a concept which is contested both theoretically and politically, and is inherently both complex and ambiguous ... ... Recently [it] has taken on the limited meaning of the practice of development agencies, especially in aiming at reducing poverty and the Millennium Development Goals (Thomas, 2004:1, 2).

This view is narrower in definition and is technocratic or instrumental – indeed, some might argue that it is too technocratic. At its most basic level it is simply concerned with development as occurring in terms of a set of short- to medium-term 'performance indicators' – goals or outcomes – which can be measured and compared with targets (for example changes in poverty or income levels). The key feature of this perspective is that it is focused on the outcomes of change so that it has a relatively short-term outlook, leading some commentators, such as Gore, to label it as 'ahistorical'. This also raises the question of 'ownership' not so much in the context of governments or of countries but more in the context of peoples, and the poor in particular.

There is a third perspective on 'development' that has not yet been discussed here. That is the post-modern or post-development position. Hickey and Mohan (2003:38) sum it up thus:

> Post-modern approaches... see [poverty and development] as socially constructed and embedded within certain economic epistemes which value some assets over others. By revealing the situatedness of such interpretations of economy and poverty, post-modern approaches look for alternative value systems so that the poor are not stigmatized and their spiritual and cultural 'assets' are recognized.

The 'post-modern' approach is not so much a conceptualisation of development as a frontal onslaught onto the 'development industry' (including researchers, practitioners and aid institutions). Many of the post-development writers are unequivocal – for example:

> Poverty is a myth, a construct and the invention of a particular civilisation (Rahnema, 1997:158).

So far it has not been argued that for the purpose of development policy formation such a post-modern perspective is relevant. However, we return to this perspective later in this chapter when considering 'development' after the MDGs and changing policy narratives and discourses.[2]

If 'development' can be seen as a long-term process of structural societal transformation (for example, industrialisation) or as a short- to medium-term outcome of desirable targets (for example, GDP growth or the MDGs) what combinations might this lead to? What about structural transformation *with* poverty reduction? We would be looking for development which is (in whatever dimension) pro-poor (at least in the absolute sense, i.e. poverty reducing) and transformative

Table 2.1   Typology of Possible 'Development(s)' Based on Structural Change and Poverty Reduction

		Poverty reduction (individual welfare) (i.e. 'development' as a desirable outcome)	
		High	*Low*
Structural societal change (i.e. 'development' as a process)	High	Scenario i. Development – transformative and pro-poor growth	Scenario iii. Maldevelopment
	Low	Scenario ii. Poverty reduction without structural change	Scenario iv. Stagnation

Source: Adapted from Amalric (2007:138).

(in that it leads to structural societal change in economic or social structures). We can develop a typology of categories based on the process and outcomes definition which can be drawn upon and adapted (see Table 2.1).

If we assume improving individuals' welfare is the primary aim we can map four scenarios. Two are desirable: scenario i – a high level of transformation with significant poverty reduction – by whatever dimension (e.g. China? Viet Nam?) or scenario ii – a significant poverty reduction without any major transformation (e.g. Sri Lanka? Kerala? Costa Rica?). Two scenarios are not desirable: scenario iii – high structural change with low poverty reduction (e.g. India? Mexico?) and scenario iv – little structural change with low poverty reduction i.e. stagnation (e.g. the experience of parts of Sub-Saharan Africa?).

In sum, 'development' has been defined as an outcome of change or a process of change. Indeed the simplest definition of 'development' is Chambers (2004:2–3) 'good change'. However, although we might agree on the theme of change, what constitutes 'good change' and who decides remains contentious. 'Good change' for development policy has come to mean poverty reduction via the MDGs for the moment.

3.   The Millennium Development Goals

The MDGs evolved at various UN social development conferences in the 1990s, notably the Copenhagen 1995 UN World Social Summit on

Development. However, the MDGs were not formally part of the international agenda until after the 2000 UN Millennium Assembly and Declaration signed in New York.

Towards the end of the 1990s, the OECD countries adopted various pre-existing commitments under the umbrella of the 'International Development Targets' (IDTs) (Hanmer and Wilmhurst, 2000:6; UNDP, 2003:29). These were a product of a year long consultation and review by the OECD (and culminating in OECD, 1996).

Seven goals were extracted from agreements at UN conferences and the dollar-a-day measure added (although it was never agreed at a UN Conference). Subsequent expert meetings quantified the IDTs and added the 2015 deadline. The IDTs were as follows (with corresponding UN conference in parentheses):

- To halve extreme poverty (Copenhagen, 1995);
- To attain universal primary education (Jomtien, 1990; Beijing, 1995; Copenhagen, 1995);
- To attain gender equality in education (Cairo, 1994; Beijing, 1995; Copenhagen, 1995);
- To reduce by two-thirds infant mortality and under-five mortality (Cairo, 1994);
- To reduce by three-quarters maternal mortality (Cairo, 1994; Beijing, 1995);
- To provide reproductive health care for all (Cairo, 1994);
- All countries to have a national strategy for sustainable development by 2005 (Rio, 1992).

The IDTs were viewed as donor led and never adopted by developing countries or supported by civil society groups, who saw them as too minimalist (Sadasivam, 2005:31; UNDP, 2003:29). However, all the IDTs, minus the IDT on reproductive health, were incorporated into the MDGs.

In total there are eight MDGs including 18 targets and 48 indicators covering extreme income poverty and nutrition (MDG 1), universal primary education (MDG 2) the promotion of gender equality and empowerment of women (MDG 3), the reduction of child mortality (MDG 4) and improved maternal health (MDG 5), the combating of HIV/AIDS, and malaria (MDG 6), ensuring environmental sustainability (MDG 7) and global partnerships for development (MDG 8).

The main difference was between the IDTs and MDGs is the North–South solidarity/partnership expressed in MDG 8 on global solidarity/

global compact (aid, debt relief, rules-based trade and financial systems; and access to affordable drugs and new technologies).

These poverty targets have become central to policy-making since the late 1990s and especially so since 2000. The MDGs prevail across much of international development policy documentation (see for example, OECD DAC Poverty Guidelines; the Commission for Africa report; the Human Development Reports since 2000; the World Development Reports since 2000) and some bilateral agencies, notably DFID, have gone as far as to judge the value of *all* their activities on the contribution to achieving the MDGs.

However, Saith (2007) argues strongly that the MDG 'scaffolding' distorts development policy and practice and that the MDGs 'ghettoise' the problem of 'development' by locating it exclusively in the 'third world' with our agenda for 'them' based entirely on absolute deprivation/levels or standards of living.[3] Saith does though note the positive value of the MDGs, which are:

- The strength of *good intentions* framed in the Millennium Declaration;
- The strength of *solidarity and purpose* galvanising the international community;
- The strength of *instrumentality* providing a 'template of targets for the bureaucratic mind' (pp.1167–8).

The MDGs have a legitimacy and consensus rarely seen in international politics. The MDGs are useful in the sense that they have that legitimacy and are a common understanding among development actors; they are motivational; they create accountability and exert pressure for more data on wellbeing (Poston *et al.*, 2004).

Saith, broadly, critiques the MDGs as follows (pp.1173–5, 1178–9). First, a weakness in method/methodology – not only is data availability and quality weak but also many of the MDGs fail to 'capture' dimensions of wellbeing that they claim to (e.g. what do primary enrolment/completion rates really say about education?) and where are the 'new' dimensions such as governance, voice/participation and vulnerability?

Second, a weakness in theory/pathology – Saith argues that the MDGs lack attention to any theory, structural relationships, policies, pathologies or causation linking policy and outcomes and thus by default are embedded in the 'grand neo-liberal strategic agenda'. The scope of the MDGs is not beyond absolute deprivation and thus 'ghettoise' development as something that happens to 'them' in the South, neglecting global (and national) inequality/disparities and global (and national) interconnectedness.

Third, the potential distortion of policy and practice – Saith argues that there is a potential distortion of development via the diversionary impact of the MDGs on the orientation of social science research agendas much of which is dependence on externally raised funds, especially so from development agencies that are MDG driven. There is also a potential distortion of policy and practice via the behaviour of bureaucracies and governmental regimes through the 'misuse and manipulation of statistics and the misrepresentation of outcomes... perverse incentives and behaviour can result' (pp.1174–5). Saith notes widespread human rights abuses as a result of population control but also notes the likely targeting of *those nearest the poverty lines* rather than *the poorest* to maximise the apparent impact of interventions on target indicators such as headcount poverty and the switching from *non-target groups* (e.g. the disabled) to those groups more related to the MDG targets (e.g. children).

Are these comments fair? On Saith's first point, methodologically, MDG data availability has been questioned. However, there is certainly a general perception within the development community that development data is getting better (especially so with major initiatives such as the World Bank's DHS and UNICEF'S MICS, although whether the data make their way through to the MDG indicators, which are often based on official statistics, is unclear). The problem is, perhaps less so the current data and more so baseline data which is, of course, essential for assessing whether the MDGs with percentage reduction targets are met. Only a short while ago the *Human Development Report* (2003:35) noted even for some of the main MDGs, 50–100 countries had no real survey trend data (2 points, 3 years apart in the 1990s) and 20–50 countries had no data at

Table 2.2   Gaps in Selected MDG Data Availability

Selected MDGs	Number of countries lacking trends data	Number of countries with no data
Population living on less than $1 a day	100	55
Children underweight for age	100	22
Net primary enrolment ratio	46	17
Children reaching grade five	96	46
Births attended by skilled health personnel	100	19

Source: UNDP (2003:35).

all (see Table 2.2). It is fair to assume things are much better now given the data initiatives noted. It is, however, somewhat paradoxical that the poorest areas will probably have the least availability and reliability of data, because in those places the administrative support for surveying is weakest and least financially supported.

For example, on the dollar-a-day measure 100 countries had no trend data for the 1990s and 55 countries had no data at all (between 1990 and 2001). However, UNDP (2003:35) noted that relatively few countries had no child malnutrition data, no net primary enrolment data and no 'improved' water access data since 1990. Trend data (two data points between 1990 and 2001), in contrast, were not available for up to 100 countries, depending on the indicator chosen. Things are improving on data availability but if there is no 1990 baseline figure the achievement of the MDG targets will, of course, be open to question.

On data quality, things are yet more difficult. Take for example the dollar-a-day figure. There is the PPP issue referred to in Chapter 1. In addition, much data is based on surveys from the 1980s/90s. The World Bank takes the last available survey and extrapolates forward using GDP per capita, making the (highly) questionable assumption that income inequality is static (see debates triggered by Redde and Pogge, 2002). Quality is also a function of stable definitions of concepts such as 'literate', 'access' to 'clean' water, and 'adequate' sanitation, and so on.

The quality of data is open to question if it fails a basic test of consistency. Again it is a question of the baseline. Loup and Naudet (2000:11) cite a comparison of maternal mortality rates in the *Human Development Report* (HDR) and *World Development Report* (WDR) in the mid-1990s. The WDR listed 56 countries with data and the HDR listed the same countries (minus one) and a further 48. Of the 55 listed in the WDR (and in the HDR) only a quarter were within a similar range – and a half were significantly higher and a quarter significantly lower as compared with the data in the HDR.

A further issue of contention is whether proxies capture (reasonably) precisely the nature of the 'development' characteristic claimed to be captured (see Table 2.3). For example, in terms of education, enrolment can be misleading as it does not necessarily mean that daily attendance, quality teaching and resources, or that 'learning' is occurring. Also, enrolment may be over-reported through children repeating years or inaccurate records on the total number of children in age cohorts. Similarly, in terms of literacy, being 'literate' is a relative concept – there is no defined cut-off point for 'illiterate'.

Table 2.3   **Selected MDG Indicators and Selected Contentions**

MDG Indicator	*Contentions*
Dollar-a-day	– We do not know if a person can live on a dollar-a-day (although it was the average of eight countries' poverty lines in 1980 it was only close to three of those eight); – Limited account of differential experiences (especially intra-household, as typically based on the household head); – Lack of attention to public goods; – Ignores the physical condition of the individual (Sen's critique) – Highly sensitive to the construction of the poverty line and the pricing of items and basket weighting of components; – Problems with heterogeneous household sizes and compositions of households; – Comparability and consistency of national household surveys questionable due to different consumption patterns in different countries; – Lack information on the depth and severity of poverty and inequality among the poor (but there are MDGs addressing this point).
Primary school enrolment	– Does not necessarily mean daily attendance, or high quality education in terms of teaching and resources; – May be over-reported through children repeating years or inaccurate records on total number of children in age cohorts.
Adult literacy	– No definitive cut off point for 'literate'; – Self-declared or household head-declared literacy could be misleading, due to stigma in acknowledgment.
Health mortality	– Accurate birth and death records may not exist (likewise for cause of death for maternal mortality rates).
Access to water and sanitation	– No internationally accepted definition of how far facilities need to be in order to be 'accessible' and what is defined as 'improved' or 'safe' water or 'adequate' sanitation differs between countries; – Individuals may be recorded as having access to water or sanitation even when the facilities are broken or the person is physically unable to reach them.

Further, self-declared or household head-declared literacy could also be misleading, as there may be a stigma in acknowledging illiteracy or literacy may be weak. Likewise, health, nutritional and environment measures are not without problems. For example, mortality data rely on accurate birth and death records that may not exist (likewise for cause of death for maternal mortality rates) and individuals may be recorded as having access to water or sanitation even when the facilities are broken or the person is physically unable to reach them. There is also no internationally accepted definition of how near facilities need to be in order to be 'accessible' and what is defined as 'improved' or 'safe' water or 'adequate' sanitation differs between countries.

The MDGs also notably do not capture well gender equality, environment sustainability, governance, vulnerability or subjective definitions of poverty and 'ill-being' (i.e. stigma attached to being seen to be poor). Gender equality is reduced to education/literacy, share of waged non-agriculture employment and women in the national parliament. There is no mention of the Beijing target of access to reproductive health care (which was in the pre-cursor to the MDGs, the IDTs). There is *'widespread dissatisfaction at the environmental sustainability goals'* (Sadasivam, 2005:31). Access to water and sanitation, and secure tenure are relatively uncontentious in terms of what is desirable. However, what movements are deemed to be favourable in the other green indicators is open to question. Finally, many 'new' dimensions (post-2000 Millennium Declaration) of poverty are completely missing, such as governance dimensions of participation and empowerment, as well as risk and vulnerability, subjective perceptions of wellbeing and so on. In sum, the MDGs were framed at a time when a more quantitative, physiological, material consumption set of poverty measures predominated. Debates have conceptually evolved since.

4.   After the MDGs

Development to date has been largely defined as being about poverty reduction, and poverty as deficits in outcomes and the quantity or quality of:

- income or income in kind (and thus a lack of sufficient purchasing power);
- food intake (and a lack of micro-nutrients i.e fruit/vegetables, lack of proteins and heavy reliance on carbohydrates);
- schooling and education (in particular few years of schooling or low enrolment of children in primary school);
- water and sanitation (i.e. non-rain water sources and non-outdoor sanitation within 2 km);

- physical health (leading to risk of child and maternal morbidity and mortality) as a result of above and exposure to malaria, HIV/AIDS and other communicable diseases.

These multiple dimensions of deficits or deprivations are inter-linked. For example, malnourished people are less economically productive, less able to go to study at school and more likely to get ill.

The causes of poverty can be sub-divided into 'context-specific' and 'core' causes (see Table 2.4). When we refer to 'context-specific' causes of poverty we mean the broader economic, political and socio-cultural context which includes political factors such as the responsiveness of policy-makers to voices, conflict, and prevailing levels of corruption.

Economic factors relate to factors such as the pro-poorness of economic growth, income inequality and vulnerability to shocks. Socio-

Table 2.4   **Selected Causes of Poverty**

Key dimensions of poverty	Causes of poverty		
	Context-specific causes of poverty	Core causes of poverty	
	Basic causes	Underlying causes	Immediate causes
Income and education (MDG 1–3)	Political context: – political participation. – responsiveness of policy makers to citizens voices. – Legislative framework.	– low parental education attainment. – discrimination by ethnicity or gender.	– unemployment. – underemployment. – low income employment. – limited asset ownership.
Health and nutrition (MDG 1, 4–7)	Economic context: – the poverty elasticity of growth. – income inequality. – vulnerability to shocks. Socio-cultural context: – gender inequality. – age dependency ratio. – HIV infection rates.	– inadequate access to food. – inadequate care for mothers and children. – insufficient health services. – unhealthy environment.	– inadequate dietary intake. – disease.
Policy response	Overall development strategy	Indirect interventions	Direct interventions

cultural factors relate to gender equality, ageing/dependency ratios, urbanisation, and HIV/AIDS prevalence. Of course, there are numerous factors we could place in this 'context-specific' causes list.

We also have core causes of poverty that can split between 'core-intermediate' and 'core-immediate'. By 'core-immediate' we mean those causes of poverty that are direct. For example, a 'core-immediate' cause of nutrition deprivation would be inadequate dietary intake. In contrast, by 'core-intermediate' we mean those causes of poverty that are indirect or underlying causes. For example, a 'core-intermediate' cause of nutrition deprivation might be inadequate access to food. The 'context-specific' causes of poverty are addressed by analysis of a country's overall development strategy. The 'core-immediate' causes of poverty are addressed by a country's relevant direct interventions/programmes/laws. The 'core-intermediate' causes of poverty are addressed by analysis of a country's relevant indirect interventions/programmes/laws.

However, the above analysis of the causes of poverty is very much based on poverty or ill-being as largely about material consumption. As we move closer to 2015 space will open to rethink 'development' after the MDGs. One area of expansion is asking people how they define their poverty/ill-being. Arguably, the growth of interest in a more endogenous definition of development is in response to the post-modern critique of 'development' noted earlier. The post-modern approach suggests that conceptualisations of poverty and development imply that some people and countries are 'inferior' to those who construct the concept or the 'discourse' (for example, the perception of the 'backwardness' of some rural communities in agricultural production technology). Indeed, central to the 'post-modern' critique is that development has been defined as synonymous with modernity, which is presented in the discourse as a superior condition. This goes to the heart of the post-modern theorists' condemnation of development as a discourse constructed in the North as 'modernity' and applied upon the South. The 'discourse' is socially constructed and values certain assets which the South does not have. Thus the South is viewed as 'inferior'. For example, 'traditional' or non-modern/non-Western approaches to medicine or other aspects of society are perceived as 'inferior' (Hickey and Mohan, 2003:38). Instead we need to move the focus to self-defined – endogenously defined – development and wellbeing.

A focus on such 'subjective' or local definitions of poverty and of development is associated in particular with Robert Chambers (1983; 1997; 2006) who argues that the perceptions of poor people (rather than of rich people or members of the development community) should be the point of departure because top-down understandings of poverty may not correspond with how poor people themselves conceptualise changes in their wellbeing. As Harriss (2006:3–4) noted, Chambers was particularly influenced by the Indian social scientists, NS Jodha's analysis of poverty in villages in Rajasthan:

> Drawing on data and experience from over twenty years Jodha showed that while according to conventional measurement poverty had increased, according to almost all of the very many ways in which – given his understanding of these ways of thinking – village people themselves conceptualise changes in their wellbeing, they had become better off. In summary they were better off because they were more independent and relied less on particular patrons; relied less on low pay-off jobs or options; had improved liquidity and mobility; consumed a greater range of commodities; and owned more consumer durables.

We should give greater weighting to poor people's own concerns and to the qualitative, and social and psychological aspects of wellbeing. Security, respect, status, dignity, voice, and vulnerability may be more important than consumption. Kingdon and Knight argue that,

> an approach which examines the individual's own perception of wellbeing is less imperfect, or more quantifiable, or both, as a guide to forming that value judgment than are the other potential approaches (2004:1).

Participatory Poverty Assessments (PPAs) have sought to elicit such perspectives on wellbeing from poor households (albeit with the contradiction of having to use some definition of poverty to identify the poor sample beforehand). Participatory methods such as Rapid Rural Appraisals (RRAs) and Participatory Poverty Assessments (PPAs) have been utilised as techniques to elicit poor households' perspectives on wellbeing. These are:

> a family of approaches and methods to enable local (rural and urban) people to express, enhance, share and analyze their knowledge of life and conditions, to plan and to act (Chambers, 1994:1253).

The largest study to date has been the World Bank's *Voices of the Poor* (Narayan *et al.*, 1999) which included 60,000 people in more than

60 countries. The study concluded that the poor define poverty as multi-dimensional and material in nature (food security and employment were noted though) but also beyond material consumption (or objective well-being) and including subjective and relational aspects such as vulnerability, and 'voice' (being able to influence decisions made about one's life).

Vulnerability and poverty are overlapping but different concepts. Poverty itself is about deprivation in various dimensions. Vulnerability is about the risk or probability of an individual, household or community moving in or out of poverty (i.e. transient or chronic poverty by whatever definition taken of poverty) in response to shocks and fluctuations. What kinds of shocks and fluctuations? Such shocks may be environmental in nature (changes related to climate change, for example), economic or market-based (access to finance, for example), political risks (changes in workers' rights or conflict in society), social risk (changes in social protection). In short, vulnerability and risk are not just 'new' dimensions of poverty but actual causes of poverty and deprivation in themselves. Concern is with who is at risk, what are the sources of risk and how might said risk be insured against. For various reasons, some people and households move in and out of poverty over time – i.e. poverty may be a transient phenomenon. Many poor people move in and out of poverty over the course of a year (i.e. poverty is transient experience) because of factors such as seasonality in crops and weather but also ill-health, and associated health costs and lost income are major sources of poverty. Whilst for others, in either depth, severity or longevity the experience of poverty (by whatever dimension) may be a long-term (i.e. chronic) phenomenon (see for discussion Hulme *et al.*, 2001). The chronic poor are likely to include those who face:

- Life cycle deprivations – old, young, widows;
- Discrimination owing to minority religion, caste, refugee, indigenes, migrants, etc.;
- Disadvantage within households – girls, daughters-in-law, children where there are many other children;
- Chronic health and disability;
- Problems related to living in remote areas, urban ghettos, areas of conflict.

Such chronic poverty can also be inter-generationally transferred. As Sen (1999:4) notes, '...capabilities that adults enjoy are deeply conditional on their experiences as children'. For example, the priority period for nutrition is while the child is in the womb and up to

18 months of age. Malnutrition losses in this period are irreversible – they represent losses the child will carry throughout life. Of the female babies that survive, the ones that remain malnourished in adolescence are more likely, in turn, to give birth to malnourished babies. This also raises the issue of the inter-generational transmission of poverty. Poverty can be transmitted from parents to their children by assets (see Table 2.5).

Table 2.5   The Intra-Generational Transmission of Poverty

What is transmitted?	*How is it transmitted?*
Financial, material and environmental capital • Cash • Land • Livestock • Housing and other buildings • Other productive/non-productive physical assets (e.g., rickshaw, plough, sewing machine, television) • Common property resources • Debt	• Insurance, pensions • Inheritance, bequests, dispossession • Inter vivos gifts and loans • Dowry, bridewealth • Environmental conservation or degradation • Labour bondage
Human capital • Educational qualifications, knowledge, skills, coping and survival strategies • Good mental and physical health • Disease, impairment • Intelligence?	Socialisation • Investment of time and capital in care • Investment of time and capital in education and training • Investment of time and capital health, nutrition • Contagion, mother-to-child transmission • Genetic inheritance
Social, cultural and political capital • Traditions, institutions, norms of entitlement, and value systems • Position in community (i.e., family, "name," kin group, caste, race, nationality, language, physical appearance) • Access to key decision-makers, political patrons, civil society organisations and development agencies • "Culture of poverty?"	Socialisation and education • Kinship • Locality • Genetic inheritance

Source: Hulme and McKay (2003).

According to Hulme and Shepherd (2003) transmission is effected by such economic and non-economic factors as follows:

Economic factors
- Economic trends and shocks (e.g. commodification, shifts in terms of trade, hyperinflation);
- Access to and nature of markets – e.g., nature of labour market (employment opportunities for children, young people and women; labour migration as livelihood strategy); access to financial market;
- Presence, quality and accessibility of public, private, and community-based social services and safety nets.

Non-economic factors
- Norms of entitlement determining access to human capital, particularly education, health care and nutrition;
- Structure of household and family, including headship as well as gender, birth position, marital status and age of 'child' and 'parent';
- Child fostering practices;
- Education and skill level of 'parent';
- Intent/attitude of 'parent' and 'child';
- HIV/AIDS pandemic; other diseases regionally endemic; associated stigma;
- Nature of living space (e.g. security/conflict/violence, stigma, remoteness, sanitation).

However, IGT is far more complex than it might seem at first. Moore (2001:4) notes,

While the meaning of IGT poverty seems intuitively clear – the transmission of poverty from older to younger generations (especially from parents to children) – upon closer examination the concept is far less straightforward and can usefully be understood in a much broader manner.

She identifies a number of issues that can be distilled into the three areas of what is transmitted, how is it transmitted and what mediates or determines transmission:

- *what exactly is transferred* (typically thought to be capital – human, social-cultural, social-political, financial/material and environmental/natural);

- *how it is transferred* – the unit of analysis (private transmission via families versus public transmission via community, state and market), and the direction of transmission (older generation to younger or also younger to older – sick children can make parents poor, for example, and transmission jumping from grandparents to grandchildren and vice-versa);
- *what determines transmission (or not)* – and the role of economic/non-economic factors and internal/external household factors in transmission (shocks, socio-economic trends, policy interventions, resilience) and whether the transfer or not of these capitals is necessary and/or sufficient to lead to the IGT of poverty.

Researchers have focused on the latter – the factors that determine transmission – and made assumptions about what is transmitted and how, because the value-added of an IGT approach is that rather than simply identifying dimensions of poverty it identifies opportunities to break the IGT such as early childhood interventions to build assets. IGT is largely (though not completely) based on a conceptualisation of poverty and ill-being that is material consumption-based. This is limiting as poverty can be transmitted via non-material means too. IGT also implies a certain level of determinism (or fatalism) and takes little account of individual and/or collective agency of both children and adults. Again this is limiting. It is difficult to maintain the assertion that poor adults will *always* have poor children. Indeed, Corak's (2006) study of new data and review of all existing studies on nine developed countries argued that the IGT of poverty (via proxy of income) transmission is by no means certain – just far more likely in more (income) unequal countries.[4] Further, the limited account taken of agency and thus the reduction of the poor or children to passive subjects is a central critique of 'traditional' poverty understandings and thus IGT as currently constructed. However, the empirical evidence we do have is based on correlations of parental and child wellbeing – typically via income and typically in developed country contexts. This is useful but what we need to know (for public policy in particular) are the processes by which poverty cycles are reinforced or broken (Harper *et al.*, 2003:537–9). We also need this evidence for developing contexts.

For children (and women too), the intra-household allocation of income, consumption and resources is an important dimension of poverty and inequality. Much poverty analysis and data is at the household level, and assumes income and other resources are equally shared. In reality this assumption often does not hold. Gender inequality is an important issue. For example, malnutrition, illiteracy and other dimensions of poverty may be significantly worse amongst women. Children and girls in particular may suffer hidden deprivations and greater depth of deprivation. This may be hidden in the sense that 'traditional' proxy monetary measures of poverty and sources of data such as income and consumption are deeply problematic for children because:

- data is not collected from women/children themselves but male heads of household and in the case of children, carers;
- women and children's employment may be in the informal economy;
- non-market channels may be more important in shaping gender dimensions of poverty and childhood poverty;
- women and children's access to and control of income may be extremely marginal (and resources and power are distributed unequally within the household).

That vulnerability to poverty and voice (of the poor) mediate the livelihoods of the poor is not 'new' of course. As documented in the Sustainable Livelihoods (SL) approach, and in Sen's work on entitlements and endowments, (poor) people's livelihoods are shaped by household assets owned (human capital, social capital, etc.), the vulnerability context (to shocks, trends, seasonality) and the governance context (policies, institutions, etc.) that enables (or not) the accumulation of those assets.[5]

What is new is a revived interest in self- or endogenously defined development derived from that a revival of interest in politics and governance in the concept of voice. This resurgence of interest in politics raises the issues of the inter-connectedness of the 'poor' or those with ill-being and the 'rich' or those with wellbeing, and the inter-connection of the South and the North. Research focused on explanation of individual deprivation does not study the politics, i.e. the social relations and inequality in power, voice, governance and ultimately wealth. In short, studying poverty is not the same as studying the poor:

The way in which poverty is conceptualised separates it from the social processes of the accumulation and distribution of wealth, which depoliticises it – and depoliticisation is of course a profoundly political intellectual act (Harriss, 2006:5).

This also resonates with the issue that Saith noted, of the MDGs as ghettoising 'development' as something that happens in the South, i.e. the 'poor'. What about 'development' beyond developing countries – i.e. in the North and/or the inter-connectedness of poverty and wealth and 'development' in North and South? All countries are developing in some sense. There is wealth and poverty in both North and South. Many development problems and 'solutions' are neither the preserve of the North nor the South. Given international migration, wellbeing in North and South is increasingly connected via trans-national identities and wellbeing and remittances. Finally, given that many of the EPICs previously outlined are North and South problems alike (climate change and terrorism for example) their addressing also requires North–South collaboration.

An alternative approach that seeks to bring together the above dis-cussion is that of a 'Wellbeing approach'.[6] The Wellbeing and Development (WeD) group based at Bath University and partner organ-isations in Ethiopia, Bangladesh, Peru and Thailand spent five years analysing wellbeing.[7] They define wellbeing as:

> a combination of: i. what a person has, ii. what a person can do with what they have, and iii. how they think about what they have and can do...

> [It] can be conceived in terms of the interplay of i. the resources that a person is able to command; ii. what they are able to achieve with those resources, and in particular what needs and goals they are able to meet, and iii. the meaning that they give to the goals they achieve and the processes in which they engage (McGregor, 2007:317).

White (2008:5) adds:

> Perhaps the signature move of a wellbeing approach is its direction of attention not only to external 'objective' measures of welfare but also to people's own perceptions and experience of life. At a simple level, this can be seen in terms of a contrast between the familiar 'objective' indicators of income, nutrition, life expectancy etc with the 'subjective' dimension of how individuals feel about their health or economic status.

The wellbeing approach builds on Sen's 'beings' and 'doings', adding how people feel about their beings and doings and the interaction between beings, doings and feelings. In particular it expands the emphasis on the qualitative experience – on psychological and subjective, self-defined dimensions – in addition to the physiological and objective. The approach also draws on a long list of those working in and around the area including Alkire (2000), Chambers (1983; 1997; 2006), Doyal and Gough (1991), Maslow (1970), Nussbaum (1988; 1992; 2000) and Sen (notably 1993; 1999) to note but a handful of the most commonly cited references.

So, what actually determines a person's wellbeing? The WeD approach proposes three dimensions: the material, the relational and the subjective (see Table 2.6). The material concerns 'practical welfare and standards of living'. *The relational* concerns 'personal and social relations' and *the subjective* concerns 'values, perceptions and experience' (White, 2008:11). The wellbeing lens can take both the individual and the community as the unit of analysis.[8]

Is the wellbeing approach something new or simply the opposite of poverty (ill-being)? The distinction between the two concepts is perhaps overdrawn – many contemporary definitions of poverty (e.g. human development, rights-based approaches, social exclusion approaches, sustainable livelihoods) go beyond income-based definitions of poverty and include more socio-cultural and psychological dimensions of deprivation. However, the wellbeing approach does provide value-added over a 'traditional poverty' lens in at least two ways. First, its holistic nature – in particular its expanded focus on the relational and the subjective as well as the material. The approach brings together both objective (material) wellbeing and the subjective aspects of wellbeing and interactions between these. It thus addresses what people feel (their emotions and experiences) about what they can do and be, as well as what they can actually do and be. It thus expands the focus from the body/physiology to include the mind/psychology. It also emphasises areas that development has given less attention to, notably the importance of the relational or relatedness (relationships) and of autonomy, enjoyment/fun, and status. It can also be argued that the contribution of a wellbeing lens may go well beyond the simple inclusion of a subjective and relational dimension. It actually changes the way we understood the material and relational dimensions. What people feel they can do or can be plays a strong role in what people will actually be able to be and do. In turn, these feelings and perceptions are determined by people's experiences (material) as well as by the norms and values which are cultural and socially determined (relational). The subjective dimension will provide the meaning to those experiences and will decide the degree of the individual's identification with norms and values. The three dimensions are inter-connected and cannot be

Table 2.6 What Determines Wellbeing?

Level	Material – practical welfare and standards of living	Relational – personal and social relations	Subjective – values, perceptions and experiences
Individual	income, wealth and assets employment and livelihood activities education and skills physical health and (dis)ability access to services and amenities environmental quality	relations of love and care networks of support and obligation relations with the state: law, politics, welfare social, political and cultural identities and inequalities violence, conflict and (in)security scope for personal and collective action and influence	understandings of the sacred and the moral order self-concept and personality hopes, fears and aspirations sense of meaning/meaninglessness levels of (dis)satisfaction. trust and confidence
Community	vital statistics: age distribution; health status; education levels; income levels; housing quality; tenure status employment and livelihoods opportunities availability of information and communications availability/quality of services and amenities: water, sanitation, electricity, credit, shops; schools, colleges; clinics, hospitals; sports centres, play areas; places of worship… infrastructure and accessibility (eg public transport) quality of environment	community formation: main majority/minority groups; in-/out-migration; lines of solidarity/conflict; household composition/stability organisational belonging: churches, mosques, temples, clubs, sports, political parties, gangs, action groups…. informal association: where (different groups) get together relations with state – law, politics, welfare violence, crime and (in)security scope for and experience of collective action	understandings of 'a good community', 'a good society' community self-concept community fears and aspirations levels of (dis)satisfaction trust and confidence in each other sense of alienation or connectedness with wider society

understood without the others – i.e. it is not simply three domains but three co-evolving, inter-dependent and dynamically interacting domains.

Second, it can be argued that a wellbeing lens deals with the post-modernist issue of 'labelling' as stigmatising and 'Othering'. A well-being lens is more respectful as it is based on what people *can* do/be/feel, rather than *deficits* in what they can do/be/feel and thus recognition and respect issues raised in Nancy Fraser's work and related issues of stigma and labelling or 'othering' of people as the 'poor' and thus inferior to the 'non-poor'. It is also respectful or non-imposing in the sense that it is about endogenous definitions or self-determination/participation rather than those exogenously defined. Third, the wellbeing analytical lens be used across both Southern/Eastern and Northern contexts and across vastly differing contexts (in a way relative poverty can also be) but is sufficiently flexible to take account of context specificity in the subjective component.

In terms of children and women, wellbeing is particularly insightful because the nature of childhood poverty and wellbeing and gender is inherently relational and subjective as well as material. A wellbeing lens is insightful because it can emphasise the areas of childhood wellbeing that are distinct. For example, a wellbeing lens can address the relational nature of childhood poverty, the local cultural construction of childhood wellbeing and emphasise new areas particularly important to children such as enjoyment/fun and status among peers.[9]

So, what do the detractors say about a wellbeing approach? There are at least three reasons a wellbeing approach is critiqued.

First, there is a perception it is fuzzy or ambiguous as a concept. The word itself has become as maligned as globalisation and sustainability. This criticism is a bit unfair, given the perception of ambiguity is largely due to an attempt to be holistic – i.e. to include everything and thus having to appeal to definitions of conceptual rigour across various disciplines.

Second, there is a perception that a wellbeing approach is apolitical. This is again somewhat unfair. This notion is based on the idea that a wellbeing approach gives little or no account of politics, power and inequality. The development community is uncomfortable talking about 'positives' as it might seem to make poverty apolitical by ignoring the extent of misery of those in extreme poverty and suggest there is no 'problem'. Also, wellbeing explicitly takes account of individual agency and autonomy as well as collective agency and social structure. The multi-level of analysis and the focus on the relational are both inherently about politics – who has what, who can do what, who feels good about what they can have and do, who commands resources, who is able to achieve their needs and goals with those resources and who constructs meanings in terms of goals to be achieved and processes to achieve those goals. Thus we have the main conceptualisations of power synthesised within wellbeing (power as material political economy, power as discourse, power as embedded in norms, values and conventions).

Third, the operationalisation of a wellbeing approach in policy and practice. Although the wellbeing lens can used across contexts in an overall sense, the inclusion of the subjective dimension may be a disadvantage if we want to make cross-context comparisons. Further attempts to quantify (assuming the desirability of doing so) non-material dimensions are in an early stage although these can and do build on work on quantifying vulnerability to poverty and assessing social capital. The policy implications of the wellbeing perspective are discussed head-on by Copestake (2008:776) and are fourfold. He argues wellbeing offers four distinct contributions as discursive space. Wellbeing provides a common ground or 'mental map' or discursive space to discuss development across various perspectives – rights, livelihoods, exclusion, local-led development and so on.

5.   What next?

To date, there has been a rich debate on the meaning of 'development' evolving and culminating in the institutionalisation of multidimensional poverty reduction within the set of development targets of the MDGs. As we move closer to 2015 discussions will probably begin on the post-2015 development policy architecture. The MDGs have played a major role in focusing policy since their original incarnation in the 1990s and some bilateral agencies, notably DFID, have gone as far as to judge the value of *all* their activities on the contribution to achieving the MDGs. What happens when we no longer have the MDGs – what will guide policy after 2015 and how can we promote pro-poor policy after the MDGs and amid all the complex changes noted, some of which mediate in favour of the poor, many do not? Here are three options:

a. We could carry forward the same MDGs without a timeline. This might overcome the distorting effects of such targets that have been noted (for example, children in school but few books, teachers and sometimes few buildings) but the timeline has been a rallying call.

b. We could take the same MDG targets but with a new timeline. Jeffery Sachs has argued for 2025 and others for 2020. However, is just another 5–10 years enough to make progress?

c. We could have new or different kinds of targets with/without a timeline. For example, the aid effectiveness agenda is based on process targets rather than outcome targets when it calls for nationally 'owned' development strategies building on the PRSP process. This might better suit the current policy architecture and would entail much more opening up of development policy to non-state actors. These agents could participate in the formation of a national strategy leading to genuinely national development goals rather than government-owned planning subverting accountability, and/ or we might have new or different kinds of targets that go beyond the 'traditional' lens of material consumption/deprivation.

In terms of something new, a 'Wellbeing approach' is emerging as a complement – and even perhaps an alternative – to the more traditional ways of thinking about and measuring poverty and deprivation. It extends attention from what people can do and be to how people feel about what they can do and be. Wellbeing thus goes beyond the material to consider relationships and values, beliefs and behaviour. Breaking the inter-generational transmission of poverty requires not only disrupting the transmission of material deprivation via public policy such as nutrition or education programmes and projects but also the creation of progressive norms and values in terms of relationships and behaviour via public policy campaigns that seek to influence how people think. This would suggest public policy would move beyond material provision (public expenditure, growth, etc.) into areas in which policy intervention is considered at best highly controversial – values, relationships, norms and behaviour. In the remaining chapter of Part I we discuss how development policy changes (or not) before turning in Part II to our three policy arenas.

Notes

1 This chapter draws upon and builds on discussion in Sumner and Tribe (2008) and Sumner *et al.* (2009).
2 See for detailed discussion of the post-modern perspective, Sumner and Tribe (2008:11–16).
3 Instead, Saith calls for a forward-looking, rights and redistribution policy agenda arguing we should be thinking about national and international inequality and structural relationships. We should pursue a redistributionist

and universalist access to social goods with perhaps a focus on the physically and mentally disabled and handicapped and children who make up the majority of the poor.

4   These findings are consistent with the earlier Yaqub (2002) review that has a more development focus albeit with empirical literature from developed countries.

5   The SL approach is associated with the seminal paper of Chambers and Conway (1992). Further, with Scoones (1998) and DFID (1999).

6   This discussion draws upon Sumner *et al.* (2008b).

7   There is also the UNU Inequality, Poverty and Wellbeing project at the WIDER, Helsinki (see McGillivray, 2006; McGillivray and Clarke, 2006). See respectively http://www.welldev.org.uk and http://www.wider.unu.edu/ research/projects-by-theme

8   The inclusion of community wellbeing as well as individual wellbeing is important because the WeD group found that the relational and the community aspects of wellbeing were particularly emphasised in the developing countries they studied but they did not compare this with work in the developed countries. 'Relatedness' in people's lives was central for wellbeing. Further, there was often a strong moral aspect of subjective wellbeing related to collective aspects of wellbeing and the community, often relating to not just individual preferences but 'broader and shared values on what the world is and should be' (White, 2008).

9   A wellbeing lens can also seek to capture children's voice and opinions on what matters to their wellbeing via the subjective domain – while adult researchers may emphasise children's health, nutritional and scholastic outcomes, participatory research with children suggests that insufficient time to play, lack of affection from family members, feelings of social exclusion by peers, and shabby and/or dirty clothing are equally important concerns (e.g. Jones and Pham, 2005). In the Redmond (2008:1) review, when asked, children emphasised the relational in particular rather than the material: 'What concerns children is not lack of resources per se, but exclusion from activities that other children appear to take for granted, and embarrassment and shame at not being able to participate on equal terms with other children.'

References

Alkire, S. (2002) *Valuing Freedoms: Sen's Capability Approach and Poverty Reduction.* New York: Oxford University Press.

Baster, N. (1979) Models and Indicators, in Cole, S. and Lucas, H. (eds) *Models, Planning and Basic Needs.* Oxford: Pergamon.

Chambers, R. (1983) *Rural Development: Putting the First Last.* London: ITDG.

Chambers, R. (1994) 'Participatory Rural Appraisal: Challenges, Potentials, And Paradigm', *World Development,* 22(10):1437–51.

Chambers, R. (1997) *Whose Reality Counts? Putting the First Last.* London: ITDG.

Chambers, R. (2004) *Ideas for Development.* IDS Working Paper 238. Sussex: IDS.

Chambers, R. (2006) *Poverty Unperceived: Traps, Biases and Agendas*, IDS Working Paper 270. Brighton: IDS.

Chambers, R. and Conway, G.R. (1992) 'Sustainable Rural Livelihoods: Practical Concepts for the 21st Century', Discussion Paper 296. Brighton, UK: Institute of Development Studies.

Copestake, J. (2008) Wellbeing in International Development: What's New? *Journal of International Development*, 20:(5)577–97.

Corak, M. (2006) *Do Poor Children Become Poor Adults? Lessons from a Cross Country Comparison of Generational Earnings Mobility*. Discussion Papers. Institute for the Study of Labour.

DFID (1999) *Sustainable Livelihoods Guidance Notes*. London: DFID.

Doyal, L. and Gough, I. (1991) *A Theory of Human Need*. London: Macmillan.

Esteva, G. (1992) Development, in Sachs, W. (ed.) *The Development Dictionary*. London: Zed.

Gore, C. (2000) 'The Rise and Fall of the Washington Consensus as a Paradigm for Developing Countries', *World Development*, 28(5):789–804.

Hanmer, L. and Wilmhurst, J. (2000) 'Are the International Development Targets Attainable?' *An Overview Development Policy Review*, 18(1):5–10.

Harper, C., Maruc, R. and Moore, K. (2003) 'Enduring Poverty and the Conditions of Childhood. Lifecourse and Intergenerational Poverty Transmission', *World Development*, 31(3):535–54.

Harriss, J. (2006) *Why Understanding of Social Relations Matters More for Policy on Chronic Poverty than Measurement*. Chronic Poverty Research Centre, UK.

Hickey, S. and Mohan, G. (2003) Relocating participation within a radical politics of development: citizenship and critical modernism. Draft working paper prepared for conference on 'Participation: From Tyranny to Transformation? Exploring New Approaches to Participation in Development', 27–28 February 2003, University of Manchester.

Hicks, N. and Streeten, P. (1979) 'Indicators of Development: The Search for a Basic Needs Yardstick', *World Development*, 7(6):567–80.

Hulme, D., Moore, K. and Shepherd, A. (2001) *Chronic Poverty: Meanings and Analytical Frameworks*. Chronic Poverty Research Centre (CPRC) Working Paper No. 2. Manchester and London.

Hulme, D. and Shepherd, A. (2003) 'Conceptualizing Chronic Poverty', *World Development*, 31(3):403–23.

ILO (International Labour Organization) (1976) *Employment, Growth and Basic Needs: A One-World Problem*. Geneva: ILO.

ILO (1977) *Meeting Basic Needs: Strategies for Eradicating Mass Poverty and Unemployment*. Geneva: ILO.

Jones, N. and Pham, L. (2005), 'The Ethics of Research Reciprocity: Making Children's Voices Heard in Poverty Reduction Policy-making in Vietnam'. London, Save the Children, Young Lives Working Paper.

Kanbur, R. (2001) 'Economic Policy, Distribution and Poverty: The Nature of Disagreements', *World Development*, 29(6):1083–94.

Kingdon, G. and Knight, J. (2004) *Do People Mean What They Say? Implications for Subjective Survey Data*. GPRG Working Paper 3. Global Poverty Research Group.

Loup, J. and Naudet, D. (2000) *The State of Human Development Data and Statistical Capacity Building in Developing Countries*. Human Development Report Office Occasional Papers, March. Geneva: UNDP.

Maslow, A. (1970) *Motivation and Personality*. New York: Harper and Row.

McGillivray, M. and Clarke, M. (2006) *Understanding Human Well-being*. New York: United Nations University Press.

McGillivray, M. (2006) *Human Well-being: Concept and Measurement*. New York: Palgrave Macmillan.

McGranahan, D., Pizarro, E. and Richard, C. (1985) Measurement and Analysis of Socio-Economic Development: An Enquiry into International Indicators of Development and Quantitative Interrelations of Social and Economic Components of Development. Geneva: UNRISD.

McGregor, J. (2007) Researching Wellbeing: From Concepts to Methodology, in Gough, I. and McGregor, J.A. (eds) *Wellbeing in Developing Countries*. Cambridge: Cambridge University Press.

Moore, K. (2001) Frameworks for Understanding the Inter-Generational Transmission of Poverty and Well-being in Developing Countries, CPRC Working Paper 8, Manchester: Chronic Poverty Research Centre.

Morris, D. (1979) *Measuring the Condition of the World's Poor: The Physical Quality of Life Index*. London: Cass.

Narayan, N., Patel, R., Schafft, K., Rachemacher, A. and Koch-Schulte, S. (1999) *Voices of the Poor: Can Anyone Hear Us?* Washington, DC: World Bank.

Nussbaum, M. (1988) 'Nature, Function, and Capability: Aristotle on Political Distribution', Oxford Studies in Ancient Philosophy, *Supplement*: 145–84.

Nussbaum, M. (1992) 'Human Functioning and Social Justice: In Defense of Aristotelian Essentialism', *Political Theory*, 20(2):202–46.

Nussbaum, M. (2000) *Women and Human Development: The Capabilities Approach*. Cambridge: Cambridge University Press.

OECD (1996) *Shaping the 21st Century: The Contribution of Development Co-operation*. OECD: Paris.

Poston, M., Conway, T. and Christiansen, K. (2004) *The Millennium Development Goals and the IDC: Driving and Framing the Committee's Work*. London: ODI.

Rahnema, M. (1997) Towards Post-Development: Searching for signposts, a new language and new paradigms, in Rahnema, M. and Bawtree, V. (eds) *The Post-Development Reader*. London: Zed.

Redde, S. and Pogge, T. (2002) *How Not to Count the Poor*. Department of Economics Working Paper. New York: Colombia University.

Redmond, G. (2008) *Children's Perspectives on Economic Adversity: A Review of the Literature*. Unicef Innocenti Research Centre, Florence, Italy.

Sadasivam, B. (2005) 'Wooing the MDG-Skeptics', *Development*, 46:30–4.

Saith, A. (2007) From Universal Values to MDGs: Lost in Translation, *Development and Change*, 37(6):1167–99.

Scoones, I. (1998) 'Sustainable Rural Livelihoods: A Framework for Analysis', Working Paper 72, Brighton, UK: Institute for Development Studies.

Seers, D. (1969) 'The Meaning of Development', *International Development Review*, 11:2–6.

Sen, A. (1999) *Development as Freedom*. Oxford: Oxford University Press.

Streeten, P. (1984) 'Basic Needs: Some Unsettled Questions', *World Development*, 12(9):973–80.

Sumner, A. and Tribe, M. (2008) *International Development Studies: Theory and Methods in Research and Practice.* London: Sage.

Sumner, A., Giordano, T. and Wiggins, S. (2008b) How is the world changing and what does it mean for the rural poor?. Background Paper for IFAD Rural Poverty Report 2009 (forthcoming). Rome: IFAD.

Sumner, A., Haddad, L. and Gomez-Climent, L. (2009) 'Rethinking Inter-Generational Transmissions: Does a Wellbeing Lens Help?', *IDS Bulletin*, 40(1): 22–30.

Thomas A. (2000) 'Development as Practice in a Liberal Capitalist World', *Journal of International Development*, 12(6):773–87.

Thomas, A. (2004) *The Study of Development.* Paper prepared for DSA Annual Conference, Church House, London, 6 November.

UNDP (United Nations Development Programme) (1990) *Human Development Report 1990.* New York: Oxford University Press for the UNDP.

UNDP (2003) *Human Development Report.* Geneva: UNDP.

UNRISD (United Nations Research Institute on Social Development) (1970) *Contents and Measurement of Socioeconomic Development.* Geneva: UNRISD.

White, S.C. (2008) But What is Wellbeing? A Framework for Analysis in Social and Development Policy and Practice, WeD Working Paper 43, Wellbeing in Developing Countries ESRC Research Group, University of Bath.

Yaqub, S. (2002) 'Poor Children Grow into Poor Adults: Harmful Mechanisms of Over-deterministic Theory?', *Journal of International Development*, 14.8:1081C93.

3
How Does Development Policy Change (or Not)?

> Truth does not triumph by convincing its opponents and making them see the light, but rather because its opponents eventually die, and a new generation grows up that is familiar with it (Kuhn, 1962:150).

1.   Introduction

In this chapter we ask how does development policy change (or not)? And how will it change (or not) in light of the EPICs noted in Chapter 1 and their particular impact on policy and policy processes. We begin with defining policy and policy processes. We then consider models of policy change that can inform identification of the drivers of (and resistances to) policy change via actors and networks, context and institutions and policy narratives, ideas and storylines.[1] We then use this approach to assess trends in policy processes in three broad policy arenas relevant to Part II of our book – notably to growth and globalisation via global market integration, aid and public services.

The chapter is structured as follows. Section 2 discusses the meaning of policy and policy processes, both of which are becoming fuzzier. Section 3 is concerned with theories and models of policy change. Section 4 considers trends in policy processes to 2015 and beyond. Section 5 concludes.

2.   What are policy and policy processes?

Policy and policy processes have always been notoriously difficult to define. The definitions of 'policy' and 'policy process' have become fuzzier over time as informal processes, spaces and stages have become as important as formal ones. Cunningham (1963:229) famously described policy as an elephant – you know it when you see it. Illustrations of the range of definitions are as follows:

> A set of inter-related decisions concerning the selection of goals and means to achieving them within a specific situation (Jenkins, 1978:15).

> [A] broad statement of goals, objectives and means that create the framework for activity. Often taking the form of explicit written documents, but may also be implicit or unwritten (Buse *et al.*, 2005:4).

> Whatever governments choose to do or not to do (Dye, 1984:1).

> A course of actions or web of decisions rather than one decision (Hill, 2005:7).

One might think of the range of definitions of policy as expanding in breadth (see Figure 3.1). The definition extends from the explicit intentions of policy to the non-explicit, unintended and implementation of policy (or otherwise). Policy has a 'concrete' component – the actual programmes and implementation of policy – and a 'non-concrete' component such as statements of intent that may or may not be (currently) feasible. Further, policy can also be deliberate or unintended or inaction, and rarely is policy-making a specific decision made by a single decision-maker.

For example, in the case of policies on childhood poverty UNICEF (2007) makes a differentiation between policies in terms of statement of intent and implementation (see Box 3.1) and then focuses on three areas – contextual factors, macro-economic strategy, and sectoral policy (i.e. education or health). Such information would be found in current policy statements or ministerial decrees and directives from the

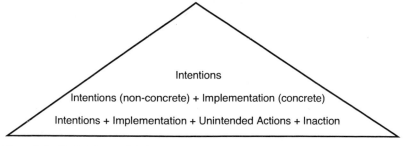

Figure 3.1   Definitions of Policy

Box 3.1   UNICEF's Policy Template

Policy consists of,

Policies [i.e. statements on intent]:

- What goals are set for improving child outcomes and progress toward gender equality in national policies, strategies or strategic plans? How are existing laws relevant to these goals?
- How much does the government spend on social programmes that impact child outcomes? What is the share of this spending in the total government budget or GDP? How much of the cost of services is borne by households, the private sector, non-government organizations or civil society actors? What evidence is there that government prioritizes child concerns?
- How well or poorly are existing interventions reaching poor and disadvantaged groups?

Outcomes [i.e. policy implementation]:

- Who are the disadvantaged children with respect to outcomes, access to and use of services and benefits (e.g. income-poor, ethic minorities, girls, residents of remote rural areas)? How large and important are differences in outcomes and service/benefit use among different groups within the country?
- How do outcomes in this area fit within the Millennium Agenda?

The above is then split into three areas.

i.   Key Contextual Factors

- The political context may include geopolitics/conflict, the nature of political participation, the responsiveness of policy-makers, the existence of public accountability mechanisms, and corruption (for example the primary channels, spaces, forums for children's voices to be heard; the responsiveness of policy makers to children's concerns; or national strategies to address corruption).

- The institutional and legal environment could include, for example, the strength of the executive branch or the judicial system as a whole, or factors that may foster or constrain legislative reform. This could also include laws for the realization of children's and women's rights (including property rights, political and social/public participation), laws that prohibit discrimination, and practical legislations required for the implementation of policies and programmes.

Box 3.1 UNICEF's Policy Template – *continued*

- Social policies (including social protection initiatives) could also be considered, as could the socio-cultural context (including the demographic situation, post-conflict or emergency issues, legal tradition, religion, gender, HIV/AIDS or health context, and urbanization). Circumstances related to climate/geography or other factors that may significantly influence the country context could also be considered.

ii. Macroeconomic Strategy

- The first issue is pro-poor growth and the extent to which concern for securing employment for the poor (e.g. those living in underdeveloped/rural areas) or for disadvantaged populations (e.g. women, youth or ethnic minorities) drives fiscal and monetary policy.
- The second issue is financing public social expenditures and the government's effort to create (additional) fiscal space for MDGs.

iii. Policy Snapshot By Sector

- Key policy objectives: This is a policy questionnaire on core national laws and policies for child outcomes and progress toward gender equality including leading/implementing government agency or partner.
- Key public expenditures: Tables in this section gather budget information to create a picture of the overall public effort in each of the five areas of child outcomes.

Source: UNICEF (2007).

---

lead government ministries responsible for income and gender equality, child protection, child nutrition, education and health, the current Poverty Reduction Strategy (PRS) or equivalent document that sets out the overall national development plan and/or national strategies for economic growth, human development, and poverty reduction, the current joint UN mission statements, the current Country Assistance Strategy (CAS) or plans of the bilateral donors, the most recent reports to treaty bodies and existing or planned relevant laws or legislative reforms.

So far, the discussion would suggest a focus solely on the outcomes of policy formation and implementation. However, there are also the actual processes – policy *processes* – that create such outcomes that require attention. We need to study such processes,

- because people care how public decisions are made;
- in order to promote greater pro-poor and/or inclusive policy-making processes;
- because the content and outcomes of policy are a function of policy processes;
- to engage with those involved in policy processes so they might also gain better understanding of what they are involved in.

In terms of such processes there are stages, spaces and levels to consider. The stages of policy-making – agenda setting, formation, decision-making, implementation and evaluation – have survived as an approach to break down the complexity of policy processes. Although discredited as too linear and unrealistic, the different stages are defended as a heuristic device (see discussion in Sabatier and Jenkins Smith, 1993) with which to compare reality.

An alternative to policy stages are 'policy spaces' (Brock *et al.*, 2001; Gaventa, 2006). These are spaces in which policy is discussed by some or all actors, depending on the space type. Grindle and Thomas define policy space as moments of intervention that throw up new opportunities, reconfigure relations or bring in new ones and set the tone for a new direction. Gaventa and others have argued spaces may be closed, invited, claimed/created, visible, hidden, and invisible in their nature, or we can identify spaces by their function in policy processes. Five types of spaces have been identified as follows (KNOTS, 2007:46):

- conceptual spaces (where new ideas can be introduced into the debate and circulated through various media);
- bureaucratic spaces (formal policy-making spaces within the government bureaucracy/legal system, led by civil servants with selected inputs from external experts);
- political/electoral spaces (i.e. formal participation in elections);
- invited spaces (consultations on policy led by government agencies involving selective participation of stakeholders);
- popular or claimed spaces such as protests and demonstrations that put pressure on governments.

Such spaces are likely to differ by sector, country and time. For example, the high level of technical expertise required to engage in trade or climate change policy debates will probably provide different sorts of dynamics for policy narratives, agents and context than policies on social protection. Policy 'asks' may be different across different policy areas (e.g. discursive changes versus increased resources versus legislative revisions versus paradigm shifts) too. Some policy issues may lend themselves to the introduction of a pro-poor institutional bias or participation of organisations of the poor whilst others mediate against these.

There are then finally, what might be referred to as 'entry-points' – places and spaces where actors may seek to influence policy. A non-exhaustive list demonstrates the breadth of policy processes and would include:

- Formal entry points such as PRSPs/national development strategies, interim-PRSPs, SWAPs, budgeting, etc.;
- Wider macro-policy entry points such as decentralisation, and treaties (e.g. NEPAD, Doha and EPAs);
- Informal and innovative entry points such as PPAs, social movements, and different roles of CSOs for example.

The net result is a multi-layered definition of policy processes (see Figure 3.2 – by stages, spaces and we can also add by level (local, national, etc.). Often policy processes transcend the national policy-making arena and critical interactions take place at local, district and regional levels.

There are various schemas for making sense of the complexity of policy processes. For example, the Gaventa (2006:24) 'power cube' draws on Lukes's (1974) three forms of power – visible (i.e. observable decision-making), hidden (e.g. setting the political agenda) and invisible (shaping meaning and what is acceptable in the discourse). These forms then need to be understood in relation to the spaces they occur – closed, invited, claimed/created – and Gaventa's levels of policy processes – global, national and local.

One might extend the Gaventa power cube for a policy cube. One might think of a 5 × 5 × 5 cube with the 5 dimensions of levels, stages and spaces. Entry points such as PRSPs are then specific points of the surfaces of the cube. We can say there are (at least) 5 notable spaces of policy processes, 5 stages of policy processes and there are (at least) 5 types of policy levels, and there are various 'entry points' on the surface of the cube – formal, wider macro-policy and informal.

If we view the above as a definitional framing of policy processes, what factors actually determine policy change (or otherwise) at such spaces, stages, levels and 'entry points'?

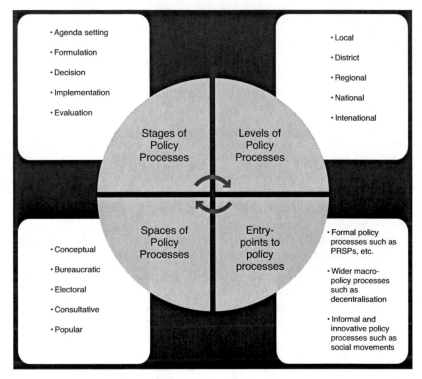

Figure 3.2   What are Policy Processes?

3.   How does policy change (or stay the same)?

There is a bewildering array of theories and analytical frameworks of how policy processes happen and analytical frameworks to guide policy process research (each with differing assumptions). These include a focus on discourse, material political economy, as well as rational/instrumental frameworks (while earlier versions have been discredited, they have been replaced by rational choice theory with an emphasis on the rationality of actors within their own contexts), addressing different questions (why do prevailing policy discourses dominate? How does research evidence shape policy processes?) with different assumptions (linear/rational versus dynamic/iterative). There are different conceptualisations and emphases in terms of actors and networks (governments, political parties, donors, civil society organisations, informal institutions), and the networks that divide and connect policy-makers and non-policy-makers, such as 'policy communities' (networks of policy actors from inside and outside government which are integrated with the policy-making process), 'epistemic communities' (networks of experts with recognised/'legitimised' policy-relevant knowledge), or 'advocacy coalitions' (groups of actors on an issue). Different conceptualisations and emphases also arise in terms of context (institutions and 'the rules of the game'; political, economic, socio-cultural), and in terms of ideas/policy narratives (the degree to which knowledge is contestable).

One could argue that policy processes are primarily concerned with power as the ability to exercise 'power over' and only secondarily, if at all, as power to, with and within.[2] If we take three non-mutually exclusive conceptualisations of the nature of 'power over' as follows:

- Material political economy (i.e. Marx) – power as held and used by individuals, actors, networks and groups (i.e. agency).
- Discourse and the socio-political construction of knowledge (i.e. Foucault) – power as embedded in ways of viewing reality or and knowledge as political. Power and knowledge are inseparable and mutually constituted.
- Habitus (i.e. Bourdieu) – power as embedded in social structures, norms, values, ways of behaving (structure or institutions for Douglas North) which creates 'habitus' or norms and conventions.

One might also add a rationalist approach to power (i.e. Lasswell) which would conceptualise power as technocratically and rationally applied in a pluralistic society by taking objective knowledge or evidence to determine decision-making.

We can then ask how have theories of policy process and analytical frameworks dealt with power? Harold Lasswell is credited with being the founder of what might be broadly called 'policy science' in the *Policy Orientation* edited by Lasswell and Lerner (1951). The birth of the area of enquiry was heavily technocratic and positivist on understandings of knowledge. The main focus was, according to Fischer (2003:3),

> bringing the necessary knowledge to the decision making table... Social Science [that] would act as a mediator between academics, government decision-makers and ordinary citizens by providing objective solutions to problems that would narrow or minimise, if not eliminate, the need for unproductive political debate.

Research relating to decision-making in public policy processes has itself evolved from Northern contexts since Lasswell in the late 1950s, expanding in the 1970s/1980s (see for examples, Etzioni, 1976; Hogwood and Gunn, 1984; Lindblom, 1959; 1979; Pressman and Wildavsky, 1973; Wildavsky, 1980). Such research has been expanded to Southern contexts over the last two decades (see for examples, Brock and McGee, 2004; Court and Young, 2003; Grindle and Thomas, 1980; Keeley and Scoones, 2003; Thomas and Grindle, 1990; Walt, 1994). Assumptions regarding policy-making processes have been challenged, particularly so in Southern contexts – notably those relating to rationality and linearity in policy processes (see for further discussion Stone *et al.*, 2001). At the same time disciplinary divergence and sectoral concentration has emerged. Socio-anthropological approaches have tended to focus on environmental, agricultural and rural policy at the social science – physical science interface (see for details, Holmes and Scoones, 2000; Keeley and Scoones, 2006; Leach *et al.*, 2005; Waldman, 2005). In contrast, material political economy approaches have tended to place an emphasis on the health sector in particular (see for example, Harpham and Tuan, 2006; Hilderbrand *et al.*, 2000; Lavis *et al.*, 2000; Moodley *et al.*, 2000; Trostle *et al.*, 1999).

First generation models in the 1950s/1960s took only a limited account of agency per se in rational and linear models that largely assume a certain kind of functioning democracy. For example, the older rational models noted (e.g. Lasswell, 1951), bounded rationality models (e.g. Simon, 1957), incrementalism and/or disjointed incrementalism models (e.g. Lindblom, 1959).

Second generation models were much more explicit and dealt with agency either in political economy terms (institutions or 'rules of the game' or formal and informal incentives and constraints, e.g. rational choice theorists such as Olson, 1965) or in discourse/ideology terms (power to frame debates, whose values count – ideological, historical and cultural influences on policy-making). There was also expansion from considering largely state actors and their political or bureaucratic interests and capacities to non-state actors and to foci on networks and a shift from linearity and stages, to iterative processes and to spaces. Examples include the middle ground or mixed scanning models (e.g. Etzioni, 1976), garbage can theories (e.g. March and Olsen, 1976), interceptor/receptor models (e.g. Hanney, 2005), the three inter-connecting streams model (e.g. Kingdon, 1984), the political economy approach of de Janvry and Subramanian (1993), the ladder of utilisation and receptors receptivity model (e.g. Knott and Wildavsky, 1980), the interactive or problem-solving/engineering models (e.g. Grindle and Thomas, 1991), the Research and Policy In Development (RAPID) research-into-policy model

(Crewe and Young, 2002), the argumentative model (e.g. Fischer and Forester, 1993), and the Structuration or KNOTS-discourse-based model (e.g. Keeley and Scoones, 2006; KNOTS, 2007).

There are some clear commonalities in frameworks. These are – broadly speaking – power relations around three interlocking domains (and three underlying assumptions) which we can take to construct a synthesis framework. The three interlocking domains are as follows,

- *Actors:* The policy actors and networks and their political interests and incentive/disincentive structures;
- *Institutions:* The context and institutions and how the socio-economic, political and cultural environment shapes policy processes and the formal/informal 'rules of the game';
- *Discourses:* The policy narrative/discourses and their underlying evidence or knowledge.

Underlying each of the three domains is an assumption. Respectively:

- There is an unclear line between those who 'make' policy and those who 'influence' policy.
- Policy processes are likely to be non-linear and highly iterative.
- 'Evidence' used in policy processes is contestable rather than positivistic.

Such assumptions resonate strongly with emerging interest in 'Complexity Science' though there has been little attempt to apply these ideas directly to the politics of policy processes. This deeper interest relates to context specificity, path dependency and 'messy realities' in a set of ideas known as Complexity Science (see for example, Ramalingam *et al.*, 2008; Rihani, 2005). In Complexity Science, one might say policy 'systems' are made of multiple elements and processes which are not only connected but inter-dependent through feedback loops, non-linear processes, and sensitivity to initial conditions. Within these systems agents are co-evolving and adaptive. Outcomes are the product of an iteration or juxtaposition of factors. So we need to focus on the processes of change rather than a focus solely on outcomes and on inter-relationships and juxtaposition of discourses/evidence, actors/networks, and context/institutions in producing co-evolving processes and outcomes. We also need to bear in mind the diversity of pathways and contexts and the nature of path dependency (i.e. sensitivity to initial conditions) and context-specificity.

In terms of describing the policy narratives and storylines, it matters to know how different discourses are shaped, communicated and legitimised. For example, we would be concerned with the extent to which there is a consensus on what should to be done, the extent of influence of international discourses on domestic policy and the extent to which policy issue is novel. In any context values shape the behaviour of actors and the structure of institutions, the key question of concern here is whether values communicate a preference for the poor. In some cases, that preference is absent, and instead discrimination or exclusion are accepted values. Actors and institutions may emerge to challenge such values, but there will be little pro-poor governance until actors, institutions, and values are aligned to privilege the poor at all stages of policy-making. We might ask what is the prevailing policy narrative? How is it framed? Whose interests does it represent? Whose are marginalised? Participation questions might include how are multiple forms of 'expertise' accommodated? What 'evidence' was presented? Whose 'evidence' prevailed – i.e. was perceived to be most credible – or prevailed in the report of the meeting?

The actors within policy processes are those individuals, groups and networks that possess a degree of agency, in that they are able, at least conceptually, to choose among various strategic options at each stage. This distinguishes actors from those whose capabilities are limited. Limited actors are constrained by regime institutions, socio-economic structures, or overarching narratives. In such cases, the actors have lost their agency, and the appropriate unit of observation is the background regime, structure or narrative. The analysis of policy actors includes those who are formally (i.e. elected) and informally (non elected, invisible) involved in the decision-making process. What matters is not only the total number of actors involved, but most importantly an understanding of what their interests are, what do they want, and what are the formal and informal powers and capabilities available to them to realise their goals. When we talk of policy actors and networks we would refer to such matters as the extent to which the ruling party is ideologically driven, the extent of 'special interests' (business, unions, etc.), the level of professionalism of the civil service, the extent of strength of civil society and the extent of influence of donors in policy-making. We might ask who is involved and how are they connected? What are their political interests and capabilities? In terms of the participation in policy processes further questions that might be asked are, who participated? Who decided who participated? Who decided the agenda and terms of discussion? Who framed the outcomes/report of the process?

We need to consider two aspects of actors in particular: their interests and their capacities. Interests can be material, in the sense of the distribution of resources, and non-material, in the sense of political power, cultural cohesion, or group norms. Both kinds of interests are closely related to the structural and ideological context from which individuals and groups emerge. What is important is to consider the way these structures and ideologies shape the contribution of actors to pro-poor governance. The second aspect of actors to consider is their capacity. Capacity refers first to technical skills, information, and resources to engage in policy-making. In policy areas in which pro-poor governance can be advanced, the technical requirements are often high. Public finance, social policy, and development strategy include highly specialised capacities. Capacity also refers to political capacity, in the sense of the power to convince others through persuasion, negotiation, pressure, or co-optation. Especially for the poor, political capacity requires organisation; by definition they lack the material resources that wealthy individuals can use to influence policy. Organisational capacity is not available in equal measure. The poor are frequently ignored within public policy, as they face significant obstacles to political organisation and communicating their interests to the public sphere.

In the case of rural actors in rural and national policy processes for example, we can identify a complex range and diversity of actors. If we take non-state actors we can identify rural civil society by primary functions of groupings as follows:

- Groups whose primary identity is by a shared source of economic livelihood – for example, agriculture co-operatives, producer organisations, trade unions, self-help groups, private sector associations, micro-credit organisations including rotating savings and credit associations and INGOs. It is important to note many of these also have a role in political representation too.
- Groups whose primary identity is by political ideology – for example, social and political interest groups, political organisations, and political parties.
- Groups whose primary identity is socio-cultural – such as religious groups and ethnicity group. These too may have a political representation role.
- Groups whose primary identity relates to community development – for example, village development associations, user groups for natural resource management, groups related to public service provision and programme implementation. These too may have a political representation role.

Often it is solidarity between civil society groups and the building of social movements that can be a major source of voice for the poor. Social movements can be particularly influential in contesting cultural politics – e.g. discourses which frame the 'deserving' and 'undeserving' poor. Movements can challenge stereotypes and be a major source of mobilisation. Social movements have become increasingly vocal as a collective, organised, sustained, and non-institutional challenge to authorities, power-holders, or cultural beliefs and practices. Social movements have shifted from 'old' social movements assumed to be class-based to 'new' social movements constituted around symbolic, informational and cultural struggles. Such movements tend to be loosely organised, actively link discontent to a certain rationale and employ extra-institutional means of protest. Resistance strategies and protest movements employ an ideology that explains the social condition that they seek to change, this 'ideology' also helps construct particular strategies of action and feeds into the formulation of the objectives of such movements. Finally, there are the government's agencies themselves – the executive branch – president/head of state, prime minister and cabinet, national ministries (including but beyond the agricultural and rural development ministry) and local government agencies as well as the legislature and the judiciary. We can then add donor agencies both bilateral and multilateral. If we focus just on global organisations relevant for agriculture, we can see the extent of the complexity and range of actors (see Table 3.1).

Institutional boundaries include and exclude potential actors, define the options that exist at any given moment, and set the likely outcomes of strategic choices. Institutions are closely related to the broader political regimes, in which democratic or authoritarian contexts severely bias institutional forms. The key points to analyse in institutions are the incentives and constraints placed on actors. Incentives make certain actions and strategies more appealing. In terms of understanding the institutions or formal rules of the game, it matters to know what they prescribe, whether institutions enjoy legitimacy from all actors, whether they are effectively or selectively enforced, and whether they have stood the test of time or are vulnerable to political and economic changes. Institutions are the rules of the game for interaction, which present actors with a series of strategic options and possible outcomes from their actions. For example, we would refer to the degree of party competition or democratic openness, the use of multi-year development plans, the level of centralisation of political decision-making, and the degree of academic and media freedom. We might ask how does the context shape policy processes? What are the formal and informal 'rules of the

Table 3.1 Types of Global Organisations Relevant for Agriculture

Sector/ Specialisation	Intergovernmental organisations	*Nongovernmental organisations and networks* *Private sector enterprises* *Organisations with mixed membership*
Specialised organisations in the agricultural sector	Food and Agriculture Organization (FAO) International Fund for Agricultural Development (IFAD) World Organization for Animal Health (OIE) World Food Programme Global Donor Platform on Rural Development	Global networks of farmers organisations (for example, International Federation of Agricultural Producers [IFAP], Via Campesina) Multinational agribusiness enterprises (for example, Monsanto, Dow Chemicals) Supermarket chains Consultative Group on International Agricultural Development (CGIAR)
Cross-sectoral organisations that include agriculture	Codex Alimentarius	Harvest Plus
Development organisations and funding agencies with agricultural programs	World Bank Group United Nations Development Programme	Private foundations and funding agencies (e.g., Rockefeller; Gates Foundation) and nongovernmental development organisations (for example, Oxfam)
Specialised environmental organisations	United Nations Environment Programme (UNEP) Intergovernmental Panel on Climate Change Global Environmental Facility	Environmental NGOs (for example, World Wide Fund for Nature, Greenpeace) International Union for the Conservation of Nature (IUCN)
Specialised organisations in other sectors	World Health Organization, World Trade Organisation, United Nations Development Fund for Women (UNIFEM)	Multinational pharmaceutical and biotechnology companies and International Organization for Standardization (ISO)
General global governance bodies	G-8 Summit and United Nations Secretariat, Assembly and Security Council	

Source: World Bank (2007).

game'? In terms of participation of the poor and their organisations, questions that might be asked are, how was the policy process initiated? What was the nature of the participation?

Incentives encourage certain kinds of strategies and behaviours. Constraints limit agency by ruling out certain options. Requirements for voting, such as literacy or property requirements, can be a highly exclusionary institutional rule that particularly discriminates against the poor. It is worth noting that institutions are both formal and informal. Formal institutions are usually written, either as legal rules or as bureaucratic requirements, and tend to be enforced with sanctions that are public and backed by state power. Changing formal rules to increase incentives to pro-poor governance is often the stuff of politics, as in adoption of international treaties and human rights legislation. Informal institutions operate on the margins and behind closed doors. These are the norms and processes by which actors modify formal rules, using informal relationships and understandings to either complement or undermine formal rules. Informality could potentially improve pro-poor outcomes, in cases in which informality allows discriminatory legislation to be ignored. Still, informal institutions are less transparent, and informality may be prejudicial to the poor.

We can propose a typology of contexts for policy processes. Moore (2001) proposes three levels of analysis for mapping political systems. First, foundational issues, relating in particular to basic political stability (i.e. territorial, resource dependence, social structure and constitutionality), e.g. does the government control the territory? Do the justice and police systems function widely? What are the main sources of government income? What extent is the government dependent on taxpayers? What is the social composition (middle class, ethnic groupings, etc.)? Does the government observe the law and constitution? Second, institutional issues – i.e. how well institutionalised are the government apparatus, policy-making processes, political parties and civil society organisations? Is political competition 'civic' and open to a broad segment of people? How is power distributed across institutions, including the military, legislature, judiciary, public enterprises, the mass media, civil society and religious organisations? Third and fourth, government capacity and accountability – i.e. does government exercise authority over the bureaucracy, military, raising public revenue, and policy-making? Is government accountable to citizens and to different parts of the state apparatus? We can then add these to types of public administration (see Table 3.2) for example, traditional, 'new' public and response governance.

Table 3.2   Typology of Governance Contexts

	Traditional public administration	*New Public Management*	*Responsive governance*
Citizen-state relationship	Obedience	Entitlement	Empowerment
Source of accountability of senior officials	Politicians	Customers	Citizens and stakeholders
Guiding principles	Compliance with rules and regulations	Efficiency and results	Accountability, transparency and participation
Criteria for success	Output	Outcome	Process
Key attribute	Impartiality	Professionalism	Responsiveness

Source: UN (2005:7).

The New Public Management approach replaced a traditional public administration model and focuses on the private sector management approaches in public agencies. Citizens are customers.

An alternative typology of contexts that has a pro-poor focus is Moore and Putzel's typology (see Table 3.3). Finally, there is also the political context in terms of the primary funding source of the state (and its impact on governance) by aid, natural resources or taxation which leads to respectively, state responsiveness to donors, the business community or citizens (Moore, 2007:12).

So, what are the current and future trends in the three interlocking domains of policy narratives, actors and institutions?

4.   Trends in policy processes up to 2015 and beyond

To assess trends in policy processes we focus in this section on three broad policy process arenas relevant to our later discussion in this book. We then use the policy actors-institutions-discourses approach above to assess trends in policy processes in those three broad policy arenas relevant to Part II of our book – notably to growth and globalisation via global market integration, aid and public services. The first arena relates to the governance of global markets and the globalisation of private capital. The second refers to the governance of globalisation via public

Table 3.3   Types of Political System and Pro-Poor Governance

Type of political system	Characteristics (examples)	Role of the poor	What can be done to promote the interests of the poor?
Collapsed states	No effective central government (e.g. Somalia)	No role – politics is dominated by force	Establish effective government
Personal rule	Rule through personalities and connections (e.g. Saudi Arabia)	No role unless poverty overlaps with political networks based on ethnicity, language, religion or location	Improved governance
Institutionalised non-cooperative states	No open competition for power (Kazakhstan)	Regimes try to control all organisations but conflicts in ruling elites may provide opportunities for popular organisations	Considerable scope to organise around demands for public services and less repressive governance
Institutionalised co-operative states	Open competition for power through programmatic political parties (India)	Scope to organise but ethnicity/ language may dominate	Very disadvantaged groups may find a voice

Source: Adapted from Moore and Putzel (2002:6).

capital – aid governance. The third relates to the governance of public services – traditionally an important avenue for poverty reduction policy. Each arena has some significant changes in narratives/ evidence, actors/networks and context/institutions (see Box 3.2).

i.   Governance trends in globally integrated markets

What exactly is changing in governance trends in globally integrated markets? Supply chains have created a number of international governance questions because they have led to a reduction in the regulatory capacity of the state due to the split between the national political structures and the international structures of production (see for

---

Box 3.2 Trends in Policy Processes: Three Arenas

i.   Globally Integrated Markets
There is changing governance via:

- The emergence of globally integrated markets.
- The proliferation of international conventions and global technical institutions.
- The emergence of (largely voluntary) supply-chain codes of conduct.
- The strengthening of producer organisations.
- The new roles of transnational CSOs in international supply chains and their collaboration with local and national social movements.

ii.   Aid
There is changing governance via:

- The Paris Declaration on Aid Effectiveness, signed in 2005.
- The IMF is reviewing its quota system.
- The emergence of new state donors amongst the BRICS.
- The emergence of large private donors.
- The emergence of stronger regional integration bodies in North and South such as EU and NEPAD and NEPAD CAADP in particular.

iii.   Public Services
There is changing governance via:

- New Public Management and Public Private Partnerships.
- Greater calls for citizens' voices in public service delivery.
- The increase in state funding from increases in aid and/or natural resource revenues.
- Global social movements responses to privatisation.
- The reduction of civil space and freedoms in many countries.
- Increased decentralisation of service delivery.

---

discussion, MacDonald, 2004; Thompson *et al.*, 2007). In terms of policy processes there are:

- New discourses and narratives: the evolution of corporate social responsibility discourses.

- New actors and roles: the rise of regional integration (i.e. NEPAD CAADP), the new roles of transnational CSOs in international supply chains and in providing support to local and national social movements.
- New contexts and institutions: the emergence of international supply chains and proliferation of international conventions and codes of conduct.

There is the emergence of (largely voluntary) supply-chain codes of conduct as a product of corporate social responsibility discourses. There are a multiplicity of such codes including corporate codes, the OECD multinationals code, industry association codes, multi-stakeholder codes and NGO-driven codes, fairtrade and other forms of consumer labelling (see for more details Keohane and Nye, 2000; MacDonald, 2004).

There is further the re-emergence of producer organisations. The liberalisation of markets that started in the 1980s led to the reduction of government support to small, especially rural producers and exposed them to fluctuations of a free market. In response there has been an increasing collectivisation of rural producers seen through emerging producer organisations like co-operatives and farmers' associations. Though co-operatives have existed for many decades, the 1990s saw renewed interest in supporting them, after a decline in funding for them in 1980s. There was a period, dating roughly from the late 1950s to the mid-1970s, when there were high hopes for farmer co-operatives – dealing specifically with marketing and input supply. Based partly on the success of some farmer co-operatives in parts of Europe, and partly on a political preference for co-operatives rather than private enterprise, many developing countries encouraged the formation of such associations with the active support of donors. Although some co-operatives were undoubtedly effective and successful, there were also many disappointments – arising above all from leadership and management that were either inefficient or corrupt or both. Consequently, enthusiasm for farmer co-operatives waned notably in the 1980s. Finally, there are the new roles of transnational CSOs in international supply chains and their collaboration with local and national social movements. There is a proliferation of transnational CSOs/NGOs involved in value-chain advocacy in solidarity with local and national social movements, trade unions and workers' groups (see for more discussion Goodwin and Jasper, 2003; Leach and Scoones, 2007).

The consequence of changes in value-chain governance suggests first, greater integration between local and global markets and second, greater linkages between transnational and local CSOs on value chains. The emergence of globally integrated markets holds potential for the poor to access those markets. At the same time, the emergence of global solidarity campaigns might provide leverage for poor people's access to governance over those markets. However, the barriers to entry may be insurmountably high and global solidarity is no guarantee of access to governance structures. Producer organisations can contribute to supporting access to markets and governance. The networking of small producers leads to more equitable negotiations with buyers on behalf of producers, facilitates increased specialisation through knowledge and resource sharing and lastly, fosters solidarity and confidence amongst small producers. There is also an issue of access of the poor to producer organisations themselves. Most smallholder co-ops and producer organisations are driven by the better-off small farmers and not the rural poor.

The NEPAD CAADP also has the potential to increase access to markets. In particular, the CAADP hopes to increase the capacity of private entrepreneurs including commercial and smallholder farmers, to promote regional and cross-country trade. These are to be realised through various measures, including the provision of information on the export market and appropriate training, promoting better farming and manufacturing technologies and removing barriers to the cross-border movement of goods.

The impact of codes of conduct and international solidarity remains to be seen. On the one hand the non-enforcement of international governance could lead to the further exploitation of workers by multinational corporations. However, mobilisation and transnational solidarity could empower workers through new forms of 'civil regulation'. Though effective in bringing about some kind of institutionalised accountability within industry, codes of conduct can devalue other emerging governance institutions as these codes are sometimes promoted by industry themselves to exercise control. Though there could be a number of reasons for the emergence of these institutions, two central ones could include the increase in the density of networks and the increased intensity of contact within networks.

ii. Governance and aid

What is changing? In terms of policy processes there are:

- New policy discourses and narratives: the evolution of the aid effectiveness and ownership discourses.

- New actors and roles: New donors such as China and the philanthropic foundations, new roles for the EU following enlargement and NEPAD.
- New contexts and institutions: The Paris Declaration on Aid Effectiveness, signed in 2005 (and reviewed and reinforced in September 2008).

The Paris Declaration on Aid Effectiveness, signed in 2005 is to be reviewed in September 2008. The Paris Declaration seeks to provide principles for donor–recipient relationships based on five principles – ownership (of partner countries), alignment (of donors and partner countries), harmonisation (of donors–donors), results-based management and mutual accountability. There is also a shift to budget support. Participation of civil society in processes has been mixed and the nature of true participation contentious. There are 12 indicators of aid effectiveness including alignment, harmonisation, and ownership

Table 3.4   The Paris Declaration: Principles and Indicators

Principle	Indicator
Ownership	1. Increase the number of countries with national development strategies.
Alignment	2. Increase the number of countries with procurement and financial systems that adhere to broadly acceptable good practice or have a reform programme in place. 3. Aid flows will be aligned on national priorities. 4. Partner country capacity strengthened by coordinated support programmes. 5. Donors will use country systems where they meet broadly acceptable good practice standards. 6. Use of parallel project implementation units to be reduced. 7. Aid disbursements will be more predictable. 8. Aid will be untied.
Harmonisation	9. Increased use of common arrangements.
Management for results	10. The increased use of shared analysis. 11. More countries will have results based frameworks for monitoring progress of national development strategies.
Mutual accountability	12. More countries will undertake mutual accountability assessments of improving aid effectiveness.

Source: Cabral (2008).

(see Table 3.4). The main indicator is that more countries will have national development strategies (for further discussion on agriculture see Cabral, 2008).

Additionally, the IMF is reviewing its quota system. Quota subscriptions generate most of the IMF's financial resources. Each member country of the IMF is assigned a quota, based broadly on its relative size in the world economy. A member's quota determines its maximum financial commitment to the IMF and its voting power, and has a bearing on its access to IMF financing. The reforms are broadly founded on the principle of extending more voice to developing countries by an increase in voting shares with a particular emphasis on African countries. The quota system will be reviewed every five years to ensure the voice of developing countries continues to grow (see for further discussion IMF, 2008; WDM, 2006).

There is then the important issue of the emergence of new donors. There is the emergence of new *state* donors amongst the BRICS+. These donors such as China, Brazil, India, China and the N11 (next 11) tend to blend aid (grants and loans) with non-aid modalities (including state-led FDI, infrastructure, trade policy and payment 'in-kind'). New donors' aid does not necessarily come with the kind of conditionalities common to aid arrangements and may not for example conform to OECD best practice standards – e.g. in terms of environmental impact and social standards. Such new (state) donors arguably also place importance on geo-political considerations in their aid relationships (see for further discussion, Kurlantzick, 2006; Lönnqvist, 2007).

There is also the emergence of large *private* donors. The influence of new philanthropic initiatives, exemplified by the Bill and Melinda Gates Foundation, is being felt increasingly. In fact there is an explosion of foundations many of which are spending large sums chanelled via CSOs rather than states. The annual budget of the Gates Foundation is greater than the Official Development Assistance of 10 of the 22 OECD Development Assistance Committee members. The foundations are redefining the 'rules of the game' of aid in at least two interrelated ways. First, the expansion of the private sector in traditionally public sector domains. Second, the increased dominance of Northern actors, as foundations often channel aid through northern NGOs, public–private partnerships, international organisations and bilateral aid programmes and tend to not favour direct grants to governments (see for discussion, Moran, 2008).

There is also the establishment of global challenge funds. This includes funds for health and the MCA. There have also been recent moves to establish a fund for African agriculture (though African governments may not be keen to see the establishment of a potential rival to NEPAD CAADP). Although it is not a challenge fund, there is also the Millennium Villages Project which argues that the most effective way to address poverty in Africa is by trying to deliver effective assistance as directly to villages as is possible.

There are stronger regional integration bodies in North and South such as the EU and NEPAD. The EU, following expansion, accounts for half of global ODA and is the largest trading partner for many developing countries (and the EC's EPAs have been highly contentious recently). The EU is likely to become more of a global player. It is likely to promote what it calls EU values – notably liberal democracy and human rights.

The NEPAD is another example of strengthening regional integration. It was ratified by the African Union in 2002 with three primary objectives: the eradication of poverty, the sustainable growth and development of African nations, and the increased empowerment of women (see for discussion, Kotzé and Steyn, 2002; Mbaku, 2004). An important component of NEPAD for rural poverty is the Comprehensive Africa Agriculture Development Programme (CAADP). CAADP aims to improve yields, improve access to agricultural markets, and increase exports. In particular, CAADP hopes to increase the capacity of private entrepreneurs including commercial and smallholder farmers, to promote regional and cross-country trade. What's special about CAADP? i. It's Africa owned. ii. It represents a re-commitment to farming, above all in the Maputo Declaration of 2003 that at least 10% of budgets should go to agriculture.

The consequence of changes in aid governance suggests more aid and more diverse aid. There will be large increases in aid from various sources and a greater diversity and new types of aid. Second, there will be more voice for national governments internationally. There is potentially more voice for the poor but this depends on national governance structures. The Paris Declaration is largely owned by central governments with participation of civil society encouraged but led/convened by national governments. The implications for CSOs is there is an entry point to influence policy processes but with a gatekeeper.

The impact on domestic governance of new donor relationships is unclear. Aid does not necessarily strengthen states but, over time, can actually weaken them. This is because the state instead of being accountable to the citizen, tends to orient itself externally. The increasing amount of Chinese debt being accumulated by some African nations is concerning. Africa already relies heavily on China for certain manufactured goods (as we all do). Africa might one day be a large market, but right now and for the next ten years the big markets are not in Africa. African exports (especially of natural resources) continue to expand, arguably leading to a form of economic growth that is not pro-poor and that may be governance-distorting. The influence of private philanthropic foundations continues to expand too. The Paris Declaration may lead to more effective aid delivery (if assessment is made on its own indicators noted above). However, how much ODA from new donors (such as China) will be within this approach?

iii.   Governance and public service delivery

What is changing? There are:

- New discourses and narratives: the NPM and PPP discourses.
- New actors and roles: the changing roles of states due to changes in state financing, the expansion of state decentralisation, the increased role of private actors in service delivery in modalities of PPP and via the emergence of new agencies under the New Public Management paradigm.
- New contexts and institutions: tension between greater calls for citizen voice in public services at a time when there are changes in democratic space and the NPM.

There are two interwoven discourses shaping much of public expenditure. The first is the New Public Management (NPM) and the second Public Private Partnerships (PPP). These new public services modalities are based on the adoption of private sector management practices in the public sector; an emphasis on efficiency; a movement away from input controls, rules and procedures toward output measurement and performance targets; a preference for private ownership, competitive tendering and contracting-out of public services; and the devolution of management control with a focus on reporting and monitoring mechanisms.

At the same time there are greater calls for citizens' voices in public service delivery. Gaventa and Valderrama (1999:2) refer to 'citizenship participation' or 'direct ways in which citizens influence and exercise control in governance'. This means that people can assert their citizenship through seeking greater accountability via participation in policy processes and claiming such activities by right rather than by invitation. This is particularly so in the case of public services. Citizens have moved 'from being simply users or choosers of public services policies made by others, to "makers and shapers" of policies themselves' (Gaventa, 2004:150). There are new arenas for citizen participation at various levels. At a local level in programmes of democratic decentralisation (i.e. planning, budgeting and monitoring of public services), at a national level (in sectoral programmes, poverty policies and PRSPs) and at a global level in policies of global governance and treaties and conventions and summits. Such trends have changed the role of states to creating an 'enabling environment' where the poor have an incentive to mobilise (for greater discussion on public services see in particular, Goetz and Gaventa, 2001).

There are also increases in state funding from aid and/or natural resource revenues. Indeed, up to mid 2008 governments' finances looked buoyant due to such additional resources from natural resources and/or aid. However, given the global economic crisis this is unlikely to be sustained.

Global social movements have evolved in response to privatisation and globalisation of public services. There is a proliferation of new actors and institutions such as transnational NGOs that are providing momentum to social movements (see for more discussion Leach and Scoones, 2007).

There is at the same time a reduction of civil space and freedoms in one-fifth of all countries. Freedom House (Puddington, 2008) noted a retreat of freedoms in 2007. (However, that means in the remaining 80% things may well be improving.) It outlines four global trends. First, '...a resurgence of pragmatic, market-oriented, or energy-rich dictatorships'. Most visibly in Russia and China, but also in other parts of the world 'rights-based governance' is deemed to be an anachronism (*ibid.*, p.4). Global governance monitoring bodies such as the UN Human Rights Council and the Organisation for Security and Cooperation in Europe are being undermined by such trends. Second, an increasing '...decline in freedom of association. As repressive regimes move to strengthen their authority and eliminate sources of political opposition, they increasingly target human rights organizations, advocates of government transparency, women's rights groups, representatives of minority groups, and trade unions' (*ibid.*, p.4). Countries in this category include a number of countries from the Middle East, Africa and the Baltic states. Third, a weakening of non-electoral governance. Freedom House notes, 'nearly two-thirds of the world's countries rank as electoral democracies, but many score poorly on government effectiveness and accountability' (*ibid.*, p.5). Corruption and lack of transparency are the causes of weak systems of governance in a number of countries in Africa, Latin America and Asia (*ibid.*). Finally, terrorism remains a critical issue, and 'while the world has been spared terrorist attacks of the magnitude of 9/11, [the] violent actions... remain an important challenge to freedom' (*ibid.*, p.5). Pakistan, Afghanistan, the Middle East are deemed to be in the grip of this phenomenon. Further, '...the threat of terrorism often provides an unjustified rationale for repressive emergency laws, torture, and the suppression of opposition political parties' (*ibid.*, p.5). NGOs and CSOs, increasingly find themselves implicated in complex legal situation due to the emergence of these counter-terrorism measures (CTMs). It is argued that many states are using increased powers under CTMs to monitor civil society.

Finally, there is increased decentralisation of service delivery. There has been a trend towards the transfer of public functions to lower tiers of the state in administrative, fiscal and political terms, the aim being to deliver better governance and public services. Over 75 countries have undertaken policies of decentralisation in the past 25 years (Ahmad *et al.*, 2005), and it is clear that more and more countries will opt for decentralised systems for service delivery. Decentralisation can involve two domains: fiscal decentralisation, entailing the transfer of financial resources in the form of grants and tax-raising powers to sub-national units of government; administrative decentralisation (sometimes referred to as deconcentration), where the functions performed by central government are transferred to geographically distinct administrative units; and political decentralisation, where powers and responsibilities are devolved to elected local governments – this form of decentralisation is synonymous with democratic decentralisation (Robinson, 2007:10).

The road to decentralisation is pretty rocky, but it can bring dividends. Decentralised government can play a useful role: locally based leaders and civil servants are more likely to be aware of local circumstances and issues than national actors. That said, experience with decentralised government has been mixed. If decentralised government is to be effective, some fairly demanding conditions have to be met. The decentralised body needs to be granted the political authority and funds commensurate with its remit; its leaders should be accountable to the electorate; and it requires sufficient administrative capacity. Decentralisation, is not a one-off reconfiguration of government. Decentralised government, and local administrations in particular, need to develop their capacity and competence. Most reviews of Bolivia's experience since 1993, when central funds were allocated directly to municipalities, report that while many of the local administrations struggled at the start, many have since learned lessons, and gained capacity, competence, and confidence. (Whitehead and Gray Molina, 2004).

The consequence of changes in public services governance suggests first, conflict between greater claims for citizen voices and decentralisation whilst voice and freedoms are retreating in many countries. Second, more finance available for public services from natural resource revenues and aid (although this is unlikely to be sustained given the global crisis) and (contentiously and perhaps also unlikely to be sustained in the current crisis) the private sector. The increase in resources available may lead to greater spending on public services although this is by no means guaranteed. NPM has the potential to deliver more efficient public services through improved public management techniques. Decentralisation may lead to better public services. However, throughout there are likely to be greater conflicts as citizens' claim to voice may sit uneasily with the retreat of freedom in a number of countries.

5.   Where next?

The world is changing fast, particularly so in governance and policy processes. Policy processes themselves are reconfiguring radically as new and changing roles of actors emerge and new and changing contexts and institutions evolve. There are some major changes in policy processes as a result of global shifts. There are new actors (China and other new donors, foundations, etc.), new contexts/institutions (decentralisation, aid architecture, urbanisation, counter-terrorism legislation, commodity price volatility shifting state funding) and newly emerging policy narratives (attention to what happens after the MDGs and 2015, the resurgence of growth narratives, citizenship, participation and rights agendas, the roles of civil society, etc.).

Amid all these meta-changes, how do we ensure pro-poor policy? Access to governance structures and participation in policy processes has both an instrumental and intrinsic value to the poor and organisations of the poor and citizens more broadly. The desired outcome we argue is pro-poor governance, by which we mean policy processes within which organisations of the poor participate and influence and achieve change through policy implementation. The exact nature of each of these is determined by the interaction of actor-specificity (interests, capacities) and context-specificity (institutions, incentives and constraints) and the policy narrative itself. The various actors involved are likely to have previously established power dynamics and networks dictated by political, economic, social and cultural interactions, which will affect the access and influence that they have to public policy processes in general, and participatory approaches specifically. The affect of participatory processes is thus likely to be greatly intertwined with the overall nature of democratic inclusiveness, political culture and accountability. We discuss these ideas in greater depth in the next chapter.

Notes

1 This chapter draws upon and builds on discussion in Schneider *et al.* (2007), Sumner *et al.* (2008a; 2008b) and Sumner and Jones (2008). We would also like to thank Aditya Bahadur, Ritika Kapur and Savitri Bobde for their work.
2 Veneklassen and Miller (2002) note four types of power: power over (domination, control), power to (agency, capacity to act), power with (solidarity, mutual support) and power within (dignity, self-esteem).

References

Ahmad, J., Devrajan, S., Khemani, S. and Shah, S. (2005) 'Decentralization and Service Delivery', *World Bank Policy Research Working Paper*, 3603. Washington, DC: World Bank.

Brock, K. and McGee, R. (2004) 'Mapping Trade Policy: Understanding the Challenges of Civil Society Participation', *IDS Working Paper*, 225. Brighton: Institute of Development Studies.

Brock, K., Cornwall, C. and Gaventa, J. (2001) 'Power, Knowledge and Political Spaces in the Framing of Poverty Policy', *IDS Working Paper*, 143. Brighton: Institute of Development Studies.

Buse, K., Mays, N. and Walt, G. (2005) *Making Health Policy*. Maidenhead: Open University Press.

Cabral, L. (2008) Accra 2008: The Bumpy Road to Aid Effectiveness in Agriculture. London: ODI.

Court, J. and Young, J. (2003) 'Bridging Research and Policy: Insights From 50 Case Studies', *ODI Working Paper*, 213. London: ODI.

Crewe, E. and Young, J. (2002) 'Bridging Research and Policy: Context, Evidence And Links', *ODI Working Paper* 173. London: ODI.

Cunningham, C. (1963) 'Policy and Practice', *Public Administration*, 41: 229–37.

de Janvry, A. and Subramanian, S. (1993) The Politics and Economics of Food and Nutrition Policies and Programs: An Interpretation, in *The Political Economy of Food and Nutrition Policies*, edited by Per Pinstrup-Anderson, Baltimore: The Johns Hopkins University Press for the International Food Policy Research Institute.

Dye, T. (1984) *Understanding Public Policy*. Englewood Cliffs, NJ: Prentice-Hall.

Etzioni, A. (1976) 'Mixed Scanning: A Third Approach to Decision Making', *Public Administration Review*, 27:385–92.

Fischer, F. and Forester, J. (1993) *The Argumentative Turn in Policy Analysis and Planning*. Durham, NC: Duke University Press.

Gaventa, J. (2006) 'Finding the Spaces for Change: A Power Analysis', *IDS Bulletin*, 37(6):23–33.

Gaventa, J. and Valderrama, C. (1999) 'Participation, Citizenship and Local Governance'. Background note prepared for workshop on 'Strengthening Participation in Local Governance', IDS, June 21–24.

Goetz, A. and Gaventa, J. (2001) 'Bringing Citizen Voice and Client Focus Into Service Delivery', Institute of Development Studies Working Paper, 138. Brighton, UK: IDS.

Goodwin, J. and Jasper J. (eds) (2003) *The Social Movements Reader*. London: Blackwell Publishing.

Grindle, M. and Thomas, J. (1980) *Politics and Policy Implementation in the Third World*. Princeton: Princeton University Press.

Grindle M. and Thomas, J. (1991) *Public Choices and Public Change*. Baltimore: John Hopkins University Press.

Hanney, S. (2005) 'Personal Interaction With Researchers or Detached Synthesis of the Evidence: Modelling the Health Policy Paradox', *Evaluation and Research in Education*, 18(1–2):72–82.

Harpham, T. and Tuan, T. (2006) 'From Research Evidence To Policy: The Case of Mental Health in Vietnam', *WHO Bulletin*, 84(8):664–8.

Hilderbrand, M., Simon, J. and Hyder, A. (2000) 'The Role of Research in Child Health Policy and Programs in Pakistan', in *Lessons in Research to Action and Policy: Case Studies From Seven Countries COHRED Working Group on Research to Action and Policy*. Geneva: The Council on Health Research for Development.

Hill, M. (2005) *The Public Policy Process*. London: Pearson Longman.

Hogwood, B. and Gunn, L. (1984) *Policy Analysis For The Real World*. New York: Oxford University Press.

Holmes, T. and Scoones, I. (2000) 'Participatory Environmental Policy Processes: Experiences from North and South', *IDS Working Paper*, 113.

Hood, C. (1991) 'A Public Management for All Seasons?', *Public Administration*, 69:3–19.

IMF (2008) *IMF Quotas*. Accessed on 01/05/2008 at http://www.imf.org/external/np/exr/facts/quotas.htm

Jenkins, W.I. (1978) *Policy Analysis*. Oxford: Martin Robertson.

Keeley, J. and Scoones, I. (2003) *Understanding Environmental Policy Processes: Cases from Africa*. London: Earthscan.

Keeley, J. and Scoones, I. (2006) 'Understanding Environmental Policy Processes', *IDS Working Paper* No. 89. Brighton: IDS.

Keohane, R.O. and Nye, J.S. (2000) 'Globalisation: What's New? What's Not? (And So What?)', *Foreign Policy*, 118:104–19.

Kingdon, J. (1984) *Agendas, Alternatives and Public Policies*. Boston: Little Brown and Co.

KNOTS (Knowledge, Technology and Society Group, IDS) (2007) *Understanding Policy Processes: A Review of IDS Research on the Environment*. Brighton: IDS.

Knott, J. and Wildavsky, A. (1980) 'If Dissemination is the Solution, What is the Problem?', *Knowledge, Creation, Diffusion, Utilization*, 1(4):537–78.

Kotzé, H. and Steyn, C. (2002) 'The African Opinion Leader Survey on NEPAD and AU-2002 Preliminary Report', Centre for International and Comparative Politics in Cooperation with Konrad-Adenauer-Stiftung. Stellenbosch.

Kuhn, T. (1962) *The Structure of Scientific Revolutions*. Chicago: University of Chicago Press.

Kurlantzick, J. (2006) 'Beijing's Safari: China's Move into Africa and Its Implications for Aid, Development, and Governance', *Policy Outlook*, No. 29, Carnegie Endowment.

Lasswell, D.H. (1951) The Policy Orientation, in D. Lerner and H. Lasswell (eds) *The Policy Sciences* (pp.3–15). Stanford: Stanford University Press.

Lavis, J., Ross, S., Hurley, J., Hohenadel, J., Stoddart, G., Woodward, C. and Abelson, J. (2002) 'Examining the Role of Health Services Research in Public Policymaking', *Milbank Quarterly*, 80:125–54.

Leach, M., Scoones, I. and Wynne, B. (2005) *Science and Citizens: Globalization and the Challenge of Engagement*. London: Zed Books.

Leach, M. and Scoones, I. (2007) 'Mobilising Citizens, Social Movements and the Politics of Knowledge', *IDS Working Paper*, 276. Brighton, UK: IDS.

Leonard, D.K. and Scott, S. (2003) *Africa's Stalled Development*. London: Lynne Rienner.

Lindblom, C. (1959) 'The Science of Muddling Through', *Public Administration Review*, 19(2):79–88.

Lindblom, C. (1979) 'Still Muddling, Not Yet Through', *Public Administration Review*, 39:97–106.

Lönnqvist, L. (2007) *China's Aid to Africa: Implications for Civil Society*. Oxford: INTRAC.

Lukes, S. (1974) *Power: A Radical View*. Basingstoke: Palgrave Macmillan.

March, J. and Olsen, J. (1976) *Ambiguity and Choice in Organizations*. Bergen: Universitetsforlaget.

MacDonald, K. (2004) Emerging Institutions of Non-State Governance within Transnational Supply Chains: A Global Agenda for Empowering Southern Workers? Paper presented at the annual meeting of the American Political Science Association, Chicago.

Mbaku, J.M. (2004) 'NEPAD and Prospects for Development in Africa', *International Studies*, 41(387).

Moodley, J. and Jacobs, M. (2000) Research to Action and Policy: Combating Vitamin A Deficiencies in South Africa, in *Lessons in Research to Action and Policy – Case Studies from Seven Countries*, ed. COHRED Working Group on Research to Action and Policy. Geneva: The Council on Health Research for Development.

Moore, M. and Putzel, J. (2002) 'Thinking Strategically about Politics and Poverty', *IDS Working Paper*, 101. Brighton: IDS.

Moore, M. (2001) 'Political Underdevelopment: What Causes Bad Governance?', *Public Management Review*, 1(3):385–418.

Moore, M. (2007) How Does Taxation Affect the Quality of Governance?, Institute of Development Studies Working Paper, 280. Brighton, UK: IDS.

Moran, M. (2008) The 800 Pound Gorilla: The Bill and Melinda Gates Foundation, the GAVI Alliance and Philanthropy in International Public Policy. Paper presented at the annual meeting of the ISA's 49th Annual Convention, Bridging Multiple Divides, San Francisco, CA.

Olson, M. (1965) *The Logic of Collective Action: Public Goods and the Theory of Groups*, Harvard University Press, 1st ed. 1965, 2nd ed. 1971.

Pressman, P. and Wildansky, A. (1973) *Implementation*. Berkeley, CA: University of California Press.

Puddington, A. (2008) *Freedom in Retreat: Is the Tide Turning? Findings of Freedom in the World 2008*. Washington, DC: Freedom House.

Ramalingam, B., Jones, H., Reba, T. and Young, J. (2008) *Exploring the Science of Complexity: Ideas and Implications for Development and Humanitarian Efforts.* London: ODI.

Rihani, S. (2005) 'Complexity Theory: A New Framework for Development is in the Offing', *Progress in Development Studies*, 5(1).

Robinson, M. (2007) 'Does Decentralisation Improve Equity and Efficiency in Public Service Delivery Provision?', *IDS Bulletin*, 38(1):7–17.

Sabatier, P. and Jenkins-Smith, H. (1993) *Policy Change and Learning.* Boulder, CO: Westview Press.

Schneider, A., Sumner, A. and Mejia, A. (2007) *Pro-Poor Governance Sourcebook.* Brighton: IDS.

Simon, H. (1957) *Administrative Behaviour.* New York: Macmillan.

Stone, D., Maxwell, M. and Keating, M. (2001) 'Bridging Research and Policy', Paper presented at DFID workshop, Warwick University, UK, 16–17 July.

Sumner, A. and Jones, N. (2008) 'The Politics of Poverty Policy: Are Pro-Poor Policy Processes Expert-led or Citizen-led?', *International Development Planning Review*, 30(4):359–76.

Sumner, A., Meija, A., Cabral, L. and Hussein, K. (2008a) 'What factors mediate the participation of the rural poor in policy processes?'. Background Paper for IFAD Rural Poverty Report 2009 (forthcoming). Rome: IFAD.

Sumner, A., Giordano, T. and Wiggins, S. (2008b) How is the world changing and what does it mean for the rural poor? Background Paper for IFAD Rural Poverty Report 2009 (forthcoming). Rome: IFAD.

Thomas, J. and Grindle, M. (1990) 'After the Decision: Implementing Policy Reforms in Developing Countries', *World Development*, 18:1163–81.

Thompson, J., Millstone, E., Scoones, I., Ely, A., Marshall, F., Shah, E. and Stagl, S.I. (2007) Agri-food System Dynamics: Pathways to Sustainability in an Era of Uncertainty, STEPS Working Paper 4. Brighton, UK: IDS.

Trostle, J., Bronfman, M. and Langer, A. (1999) 'How Do Researchers Influence Decision Makers? Case Studies of Mexican Policies', *Health Policy and Planning*, 14:103–14.

UN (2005) *Unlocking the Human Potential for Public Sector Performance. World Public Sector Report 2005.* Department of Economic and Social Affairs, United Nations, New York.

UNICEF (2007) Policy Template: Global Child Poverty and Disparity Study. New York: UNICEF.

Vene Klasen, L. and Miller, V. (2002) *A New Weave of Power, People and Politics: The Action Guide for Advocacy and Citizen Participation.* Oklahoma City: World Neighbors.

Waldman, L. (2005) *Environment, Politics and Poverty: A Review of PRSP Stakeholder Perspectives*, Brighton: IDS.

Walt, G. (1984) *Health Policy: An Introduction to Process and Power.* London: Zed Books.

WDM (World Development Movement) States of Unrest (2006) accessed on 22/6/2008 at http://www.wdm.org.uk/

Wildavsky, A. (1980) *The Art and Craft of Policy Analysis.* London: Macmillan.

World Bank (2007) World Development Report: Agriculture for Development. Washington DC: World Bank.

Part II
The 3Gs

4
Doing Governance

Without progress in governance, all other reforms will have
limited impact (Commission for Africa, 2005:133).

1. Introduction

Governance has become a central issue in international development.
Access to governance structures and 'voice' of citizens in policy
processes has both intrinsic and instrumental value to citizens and to
the poor in particular. In fact when one takes the governance and
poverty literatures, several areas are common to both such as participation and voice, rights and freedoms and access to/delivery of quality
public services for example.

The world of governance itself is changing particularly fast not only
in governance dimensions themselves (see Chapter 3) but also in terms
of the other EPICs. For example, there are major shifts in economics
(such as the rise of China *et al.* and volatility in commodity prices) that
will have an impact on governance. There are also major shifts in the
environment (such as climate change, biofuels, etc.), changes in demographic trends (such as urbanisation, migration, etc.) and major shifts
in technology and innovation (such as ICTs, biotechnology, etc). All
have governance implications and will play some role in reshaping
governance and policy processes in the future. Also, given that the net
outcome of the EPICs is a lot of change – of lifestyles and livelihoods,
larger migratory movements nationally as well as internationally and
an increased potential for conflict over resources as a result of people
on the move – governance is taking on even stronger importance.[1] As
noted previously, support for society-owned strategies and goals for
adaptation to changing circumstances are particularly important. This

chapter is structured as follows. Section 2 discusses the history of governance debates. Section 3 considers governance, poverty reduction and the MDGs. Section 4 looks to the future. Section 5 concludes.

2. A brief history of governance debates

There has been an array of governance declarations (see Box 4.1). These declarations demonstrate the range and evolution of definitions of governance which tended initially to focus on normative recommendations

---

Box 4.1   Selected Governance Declarations and Milestones

- 2000 UN Millennium Declaration and MDGs

  Millennium Development Goal 8, target 12 is to 'develop further an open, rule-based, predictable, non-discriminatory trading and financial system (including a commitment to good governance, development, and poverty reduction, nationally and internationally).

- 2002 UNDP Human Development Report: *Deepening Democracy in a Fragmented World*

  Governance is 'the system of values, policies and institutions by which a society manages its economic, political and social affairs through interactions within and among the state, civil society and private sector' (UNDP, 2004:2).

- 2005 The Commission for Africa's report, *Our Common Future*

  'Without progress in governance, all other reforms will have limited impact' (CFA, 2005:133).

- 2006 DFID's White Paper on 'Making Governance Work for the Poor'

  Good governance 'is about good politics... ...it is about how citizens, leaders and public institutions relate to each other in order to make change happen' (DFID, 2006:20).

- 2007 The World Bank Governance Strategy

  Governance is 'the traditions and institutions by which authority in a country is exercised for the common good' (Kaufmann and Kraay, 2002:5).

(regarding rule of law, rights, anti-corruption, electoral democracy, etc.) but more recently have evolved more into defining governance by its agency dimensions (i.e. citizenship, participation, representation, etc).

As Box 4.1 illustrates there is a range of definitions of governance. What are the commonalities? Governance is about the relationship(s) between governments and society. Governance is not the same as government and the solutions to poor governance are not solely in the domain of governments. Governance is not the same as management and governance is about more than just corruption (corruption is an outcome of poor governance). Governance is about who decides/who sets the rules, when and how.

Graham *et al.* (2003:1, 2) define governance as: 'the traditions, institutions and processes that determine how power is exercised, how citizens are given a voice, and how decisions are made on issues of public concern'. Hyden *et al.* (2004:5) define governance as 'the formation and stewardship of the rules that regulate the public realm – the space where state as well as economic and societal actors interact to make decisions'. They note the changing emphasis over time in Table 4.1.

Table 4.1   The Changing Emphasis of Governance

Period	Emphasis	Focus
1950s–60s	For the people	Project
1960s–70s	Of the people	Program
1980s	With the people	Policy
1990s–date	By the people	Politics

Source: Hyden *et al.* (2004:11).

Box 4.2   The World Bank's Dimensions of Governance

- Voice & accountability – political, civil and human rights;
- Political stability and absence of violence – the likelihood of violent threats to government;
- Government effectiveness – competence of the bureaucracy;
- Regulatory quality – the incidence of market-friendly policies;
- Rule of law – the quality of the police and the judiciary;
- Control of corruption – the abuse of public power for private gain.

Source: Kaufmann *et al.* (2005:4).

Table 4.2   Governance Databases

	Name	Selected Components	Scope	Source
Democratic Regimes Indices	Alvarez, Cheibub, Limongi and Przeworski, Political Regime Index	Contestation	141 countries 1950–1990	www.ssc.upenn.edu/~cheibub/data/ Default.htm pantheon.yale.edu/~jac236/ Research.htm
	Freedom House's Political Rights Index	Free and fair elections elected Rights to form political parties Autonomy and self-government	172 countries 1972–present	Freedom House www.freedomhouse.org
	Gasiorowski Political Regime Change	Competitiveness Inclusiveness Civil and political liberties	97 developing countries independence – 1992	Gasiorowski (1996)
	Polity IV/Democracy & Autocracy Indices	Competitiveness Openness Constraints on executive	161 countries 1800–2001	www.bsos.umd.edu/cidcm/polity
	Vanhanen Democratic Index/Polyarchy Dataset	Competition Participation	187 countries 1810–1998	www.svt.ntun.no/iss/data.vanhanen

Table 4.2 Governance Databases – *continued*

Name	Selected Components	Scope	Source
Governance Research Indicators Dataset (2002): Political Stability Index	Political protest Ethno-cultural, religious conflict Military coup risk Civil war Social unrest International tension Disappearance, torture Terrorism	199 countries 1996–2002	Kaufmann, Kraay and Mastruzzi www.worldbank.org/wbi/governance/govda2002/index.html
Governance Research Indicators Dataset (2002): Government Effectiveness Index	Efficiency of bureaucracies Formulation and implementation of policies Tax collection Quality of bureaucracy	199 countries 1996–2002	Kaufmann, Kraay and Mastruzzi www.worldbank.org/wbi/governance/govda2002/index.html
The Political Constraint Index (POLCON) Dataset	Independent branches of government Veto power Party composition and preferences in legislature	234 countries variable dates–2001	Witold J. Henisz www.management.wharton.upenn.edu/henisz
State Failure Problem Set	Ethnic wars Revolutionary wars Genocides	96 countries 1955–2001	State failure task force www.cidcm.umd.edu/inscr/stfail/sfdat.htm

Democratic governance indicators

Table 4.2 Governance Databases – *continued*

Name	Selected Components	Scope	Source
Weberian State Scale	Agencies generating economic policy Meritocratic hiring Internal promotion and career stability Salary and prestige	35 developing countries 1993–1996	Peter Evans and James Rausch, 'Weberian State Comparative Data Set' weber.ucsd.edu/~jrauch/webstate/

Source: Adapted from Schneider *et al.* (2007).

In the World Bank's work, governance is 'the traditions and institutions by which authority in a country is exercised for the common good' (Kaufmann and Kraay, 2002:5). Within this definition governance has six dimensions (see Box 4.2) and there are related indicators for each (see Table 4.2) available for every two years from 1996 until 2002 and including 199 countries, hundreds of indicators, and 37 separate data sources (Kaufmann *et al.*, 2005).

Indeed, there have been a number quantitative governance databases (see Table 4.2). Datasets can be clustered into three sets (see Schneider *et al.*, 2007 for deeper discussion). One group could be labelled 'minimalist' and includes basic data such as the nature of democratic regimes. Examples include the Alvarez, Cheibub, Limongi and Przeworski Regimes Index (and the Cheibub and Gandhi extension); Freedom House; Polity IV; and Vanhanen Democracy and Polyarchy Index and Dataset.

A second set expands this to democratic governance rather than regime type. These tend to be based on institutional characteristics. Examples include the World Bank Governance Indicators of Political Stability and Government Effectiveness, the Polcon Political Constraints Index, and the Weberian state scale of Evans and Rausch.

Finally, there is a grouping that relates to the way governments treat their citizens – e.g. corruption, human rights, and so on. Examples include the Freedom House Civil Liberties Index, Religious Freedom, and Press Freedom; Heritage Foundation and Wall Street Journal Index of Economic Freedom; and World Bank Governance Indicators of Voice and Accountability.

Many of these databases have become used in regression analysis. For example, Anderson and Morrissey's (2006:482) study of 126 countries found that World Bank governance indicators and infant mortality were not linked; a finding that was confirmed by the designers of the World Bank governance indicators (Kaufmann *et al.*, 2002). In contrast, researchers have more consistently found links between World Bank measures of governance and indicators of growth and economic well-being. The 1997 *World Development Report* links property rights, judicial reliability and control of corruption to investment and growth; Kaufmann *et al.* (1999; 2002) found governance positively related to per capita incomes; Knack and Keefer (1995) found better governance was associated with investment and growth; Mauro (1995) found bureaucratic efficiency associated with investment and growth; and Chong and Calderón (2000) found governance related to economic performance.[2]

What these datasets do not fully capture is the relationship between state and society and how accountable the state is to citizens. Accountability can be described as having two aspects: answerability and enforcement. Schedler (1999) states that answerability consists of accountable actors having to explain or justify their decisions; while enforceability involves accountable persons having to bear the consequences of their decision, including negative sanctions. Accountability has been categorised into three types by Newell and Wheeler (2007) although aspects of all of these tend to overlap. There is political accountability (checks and balances within the state), social accountability (checks and balances between state and citizens) and managerial accountability (financial accountability and indicators to monitor performance).

Goetz and Jenkins (2005:16) point to the beginning of a 'new accountability agenda'. This new agenda is broadly characterised by three elements: (i) a more direct role for ordinary people and their associations in obtaining accountability, using (ii) an expanded repertoire of methods, sometimes in new accountability jurisdictions, in the pursuit of (iii) a more exacting standard of social justice. They explain that while citizens and civil society have traditionally been relegated to participation in vertical channels of accountability, such as voting, they have now begun to take part in horizontal channels and the search for new roles by citizens and their associations has caused the vertical-horizontal distinction to blur.[3] In sum, governance is about who decides – who sets what rules, when and how. Such rules are no longer the preserve of the state alone. Such trends have changed the role of states to creating an 'enabling environment – an environment in which the poor have an incentive to mobilise' (Moore and Putzel, 2002:16). Indeed, the participation of the poor in defining their own priorities via participatory poverty assessments and advocating them in policy has gained considerable ground as the discourses of governance and participation have merged into what Gaventa and Valderrama (1999:2) call 'citizenship participation' or 'direct ways in which citizens influence and exercise control in governance'.

3.   Governance, poverty reduction and the MDGs

The case for a *pro-poor bias* to policy and policy processes is as follows. Voice – literally via participation in policy processes, or metaphorically via citizens' evidence informing policy processes – has both intrinsic and instrumental value to the poor. Voice (or lack thereof) in decision-making that affects one's life is a key dimension of well-being (and lack

of it poverty). In fact when one takes the governance and poverty literatures there are at least three areas of clear overlap as noted earlier. The
following are common to both and are 'new' dimensions of poverty
particularly evident since the Voices of the Poor and the World
Development Report 2000/1:

- Poverty is about a lack of participation and voice in decisions affecting one's life (in governance this is referred to under dimensions
  such as accountability, responsiveness, inclusion);
- Poverty is about a lack of rights and freedoms (relevant governance
  dimensions are labelled fairness, equity, decency, human rights, the
  rule of law, police, judiciary and the absence of violence);
- Poverty is about a lack of access or poor-quality access to public
  goods and services (in governance this is referred to as state capabilities, performance, efficiency, effectiveness, transparency, control of
  corruption, delivery of public goods and services).

In many cases, these shared dimensions are also presumed to have
a causal relationship. Improved voice and participation for the poor,
beyond their intrinsic value, are likely to reduce poverty because the
poor have a greater say in budget formation and public expenditure
priorities. As noted before, this approach is associated in particular
with Robert Chambers (1983; 1997; 2006) who argues that the perceptions of poor people (rather than of rich people or members of the
development community) should be the point of departure because
top-down understandings of poverty may not correspond with how
poor people themselves think about their well-being.

Sen (see in particular 1999), Nussbaum (see in particular 2000) and
UNDP (1990–2007) have consistently argued that development is not,
as previously conceived, based solely on desire fulfilment (utility or
consumption measured by a proxy for income – GDP per capita) as this
does not take sufficient evaluative account of the physical condition of
the individual and of a person's capabilities. Instead, 'development
consists of the removal of various types of unfreedom that leave people
with little opportunity of exercising their reasoned agency... Development can be seen... as a process of expanding the real freedoms
that people enjoy... the expansion of the 'capabilities' of persons
to lead the kind of lives they value – and have reason to value' (Sen,
1999:xii, 1, 18).

Capabilities consist of the means, opportunities or substantive freedoms which permit the achievement of a set of functionings – things

which we value 'being' and 'doing'. Although there have been numerous attempts to construct specific lists of capabilities (see for discussion Alkire, 2002), Sen resolutely refused to name them, although he did identify five basic freedoms (1999:38). These are clearly very relevant to governance concerns, notably (a) and (d) and possibly (e):

a. political/participative freedoms/civil rights (e.g. freedom of speech, free elections);
b. economic facilities (e.g. opportunities to participate in trade and production and sell one's labour and product on fair, competitive terms);
c. social opportunities (e.g. adequate education and health facilities);
d. transparency guarantees (e.g. openness in government and business and social trust);
e. protective security (e.g. law and order, social safety nets for unemployed).

Pro-poor policy processes could be either instrumentally pro-poor – i.e. a faster reduction of poverty (by whatever dimension) – or intrinsically pro-poor – a greater say in policies affecting one's life. Or one might alternatively draw on the concept of relative and absolute pro-poor growth. Absolute pro-poor policy processes would be those processes improving the standards of living of the poor. In contrast, relative pro-poor policy processes would entail the poor benefiting more than the non-poor, e.g. redistribution of public resources or power.

'Empowerment' is one of the most widespread and pervasive concepts in contemporary development discourse (World Bank, 2005:1). Indeed, 'empowering' poor people and women in particular is a common aim of projects. In the mid-1990s, Rowlands (1995:1) argued that 'empowerment' was 'often used ... but rarely defined'. Since then there have been at numerous attempts to define 'empowerment'. Recent research has evolved from Moser's (1989) power 'within, with and to' towards a wider understanding. In the most recent review of 'empowerment' Ibrahim and Alkire (2007:7–8) note 33 definitions of empowerment of which there are two types of definition. These are empowerment as the expansion of agency and empowerment as the opportunity to exert that agency fruitfully (see Box 4.3 for examples). In short, empowerment is the capacity to make a choice as well as the capacity to transform the choice into desired action/outcome.

Box 4.3   Definitions of Empowerment

The World Bank (2002:v–vi) Empowerment Source Book defines empowerment as 'the expansion of freedom of choice and action... the expansion of assets and capabilities of poor people to participate in, negotiate with, influence, control, and hold accountable institutions that affect their lives'. Such agency is a product of individual assets and capabilities (human, social capital, etc.) as well as collective assets and capabilities (voice, organisation, representation and identity).

Alsop and Heinsohn's (2005:6) definition has implicit echoes of Amartya Sen's and UNDP's 'Capabilities' or 'Human Development'. Empowerment is 'enlarging people's effective choices'. Empowerment is function of the opportunity structures – the institutional climate (information, participation, accountability, local organisational capacity) and social and political structures (openness, competition and conflict). This opportunity structure is a function of the permeability of the state, the extent of elite fragmentation and the state's implementation capacity.

Moore and Putzel (2002:13) argue it is the empowerment of poor people that matters: 'increasing the political capabilities of the poor: personal political capabilities, self-confidence, capacity for community organisation, recognition of dignity, and the collective ideas available to support effective political action'.

A particular focus on the gender dimensions of governance is also important. First, poverty and governance have gender-specific dimensions that men and women experience differently. Second, reductions in gender inequality are linked to wider poverty reduction. Women may be less able to claim their rights, enjoy fewer freedoms, participate less in decision-making than men and often suffer poorer quality of goods and services due to the 'triple burden'. Goetz (2003:29) proposes 'gender-sensitive governance' as:

> the conditions under which public affairs are managed so that women are included equally in the 'publics' served by the government, and so that gender equality is one of the goals or results.

This then has four components. First, sensitivity to gender differentials (public policy recognises and responds to the needs of individuals based on their gender so that gender inequalities reduce). Second, gender-specific interventions (reforms and services targeted at needs that only women or men face such as reproductive health services). Third, contributing to women's empowerment (reforms that seek to strengthen women's capacity to overcome gender inequalities). Fourth,

---

Box 4.4 Selected Examples of Gender-Sensitive Governance Mechanisms

Electoral Politics

- Affirmative action (quotas, reservations)
- Electoral systems
- Women's wings in political parties
- Recruitment, mentoring and leadership development in parties
- Party-independent bodies that provide financial and moral support to feminist candidates
- Women-friendly institutions (timing of meetings, type of pay, safety in travel, child support, etc)
- Gender caucuses in legislative bodies

Local Government

- Gender quorums in community meetings
- Training and support programs for local representatives
- Lengthening reservation periods

Public Administration

- Affirmative action
- Equal opportunity structures (e.g. anti-discrimination bureaus, merit protection agencies, equal opportunity commissions)
- Ministries/agencies of Gender in national and local governments
- Gender focal points
- Inter-ministerial coordinating committees
- Gender-responsive budgets
- Gender-disaggregated and sensitive monitoring indicators
- Citizen monitoring and auditing
- Performance contracts

Source: Horowitz (2007:41).

---

transformative approaches that seek to change gender relations in society as a whole by addressing attitudes and norms. There are then various gender-sensitive governance mechanisms (see Box 4.4).

It is also important to focus attention on the child dimensions of governance. Children, governance and policy processes raise a range of issues. Children in developing countries (taking the United Nations Convention on the Rights of the Child definition of people under the age of 18) account for on average 37% of the population and 49% in the least developed countries (UNICEF, 2005:12). Moreover, UNICEF estimates suggest that a disproportionately high proportion of the poor – up to 50% of those living on less than $1 per day – are children under 18 years (Gordon *et al.*, 2004:11).

A growing body of research argues that addressing childhood poverty is important not only for reducing childhood poverty but also for disrupting poverty transfers over the life-course and inter-generationally (see Chapter 2). If we take core dimensions of governance and poverty as participation and voice in decisions affecting one's life, rights and freedoms and access or poor-quality access to public goods then children's experiences are distinct and differentiated. Children generally enjoy fewer rights and freedoms than adults, have less voice and less participation in decision-making and suffer poorer public service delivery than adults. Under the UNCRC, which almost all countries are signed up to, children's participation in decision-making (article 12) which affects their lives is a key component. The UN General Assembly's Special Session on Children in 2002 (including the national and regional processes leading up to the final meeting) highlighted children's right to voice their views and be heard. Children's participation can take various forms (see Box 4.5).

However, the acceptance of the principle of children's participation is controversial on theoretical and practical grounds because it challenges traditional paternalistic models of children's needs based on adult knowledge and whether such a universal right is applicable in all contexts and whether children can articulate their ideas. The counter-argument is that at even an early age many children have complex productive, care and work responsibilities (Jones and Pham, 2007:1).

4.   The future of governance

Debates on pro-poor policy are increasingly pulled in these two potentially contradictory directions: that pro-poor policy processes are either

---

Box 4.5   Modalities of Children's Participation in Policy Processes

- Consultation (for child and/or adult decision-making),
- Research (by children and/or with children),
- Advocacy (through reports to, presentations to, and discussions with commissions, policy-makers, etc),
- Campaigning (writing emails and postcards, petitioning, art exhibitions, protests, demonstrations, media and other forms of public presentation),
- Lobbying (meeting with policy-makers as individuals or small groups),
- Programme and Project Planning, Designing, Implementing and Monitoring and Evaluating.

Source: Alfini (2006).

---

citizen-led and participatory (assuming the poor know best how to improve their lives) or expert-led or evidence-informed (assuming 'experts' know best how to reduce poverty). This section argues that neither modality is necessarily pro-poor. We explore the conditions under which each might be pro-poor and how differing conceptualisations of power in the policy process add to analysis of the politics of pro-poor policy processes.

Two modalities of pro-poor policy processes are evidence-based policy (EBP) or evidence-informed policy formation/implementation and citizen-based policy (CBP) or citizen-informed policy formation/ implementation. The former involves the 'best' research evidence to maximise poverty reduction and the latter, the direct participation of the poor and/or their organisations such as CSOs.

The former, EBP, can be defined as:

> Government(s)... mak(ing) well-informed decisions about policies, programmes and projects by putting the best available evidence from research at the heart of policy development and implementation (Davies, 2004:3).

EBP could be instrumentally pro-poor – the best use of available evidence on which to base policy and thus accelerate poverty reduction *or* it could be intrinsically pro-poor if the voices of the poor are represented in the evidence used in policy processes.

In industrialised countries evidence-based/informed policy (EBP) is increasingly viewed as an essential part of government decision-making (Shaxson, 2005; Solesbury, 2001). In developed countries the attention given to the quality of evidence has become institutionalised with the creation of both the Cochrane and Campbell Collaborations, which facilitate systematic reviews of 'high-quality' scientific evidence for health and social policy respectively (Dobrow *et al.*, 2004). In developing countries we are at an earlier stage with less debate about the quality of 'evidence' and more discussion about the use of any 'evidence' at all.

Court *et al.* (2005:169–70) argue that countries with greater democratic mechanisms and good governance (meaning accountability, transparency and responsiveness) are likely to use evidence more than others because of open and accessible public policy processes, and autocratic regimes tend to limit the use of evidence. Jones (2005:6–7), contests this, pointing out that given the diversity across democracies a more nuanced analysis is needed, and noting a range of components such as the presence or absence of: multi-year national development strategies, ideologically driven or populist parties, political and fiscal decentralisation, stable and professional civil service, media and academic freedoms, a vibrant and strong civil society, openness to international discourses and the relative novelty of an issue.

The factors that would probably increase the supply and demand of evidence include a greater influence of international discourses on domestic policy, a greater extent to which the policy is novel, a greater extent of professionalism in the bureaucracy and ability to process evidence, stronger civil society and donor influence, and greater extent of democratic openness and academic/media freedoms.

Why might EBP be not pro-poor? There are several reasons such as poor-quality evidence, low supply of evidence, ability of policy-makers to access and process evidence, etc. However, the main reason why EBP may not be pro-poor is related to Foucaultian power notions and a hierarchy of evidence. In short, whose evidence counts?

There are several forms of evidence of which research evidence is only one and evidence based on participation of the poor in knowledge generation is a relatively small part, though growing. However, the primary concern is that what constitutes 'the best' evidence is highly contentious and some kinds of 'evidence' are given more weight than others by actors in the policy-making process. For example, indigenous, participatory, or experiential 'evidence' may have lower status than mathematical modelling 'evidence'.

'Evidence' and its use in policy processes remains under-researched in international development. Nutley and Webb (2004:29) note, 'we still know relatively little about the dynamics of the policy process and how research evidence impacts on the process'. The limited research to date suggests different stakeholders in the policy process have different perceptions of what constitutes 'quality' evidence for policy-making. Case studies suggest policy-makers often see NGO research as 'suspect' and value research by the international financial institutions more highly than any form of local research, including that by their own government and local independent think tanks, and that they have 'trusted sources', whilst NGOs have an aversion to World Bank/IMF studies (Court *et al.*, 2005:162; IDRC, 2004:10; Brock and McGee, 2004:30–4). Davies (2004) too has noted there are different notions of what constitutes 'evidence' between policy-makers and researchers (listing a series of dichotomies – with policy-makers favouring the former and researchers the latter – 'contextual' vs. context-free or 'scientific'; 'reasonable' vs. 'proven' empirically; policy driven vs. theoretically driven; clear message vs. caveats/qualifications). Nutley *et al.* (2002) too have noted that policy-makers and researchers have different languages, priorities, agendas, time scales, and reward systems. The notion of 'different worlds' can be linked to different perceptions of quality 'evidence'. These differences are rendered even more complex when different sectoral interests (e.g. economic vs. social policy) and levels of policy-making (e.g. local vs. national vs. international) are considered.

In short, 'evidence' is not a neutral concept (Upshur *et al.*, 2001:94). There is a widely held perception of a 'hierarchy of evidence', especially so in such sectors as health policy for example. 'Hard' evidence is that which is seen as objective and quantitative. In contrast, 'soft' evidence is that which is subjective and qualitative.[4] Systematic reviews and randomised controlled trials are at the top of the hierarchy, and opinion and anecdotal evidence at the bottom (Davies and Nutley, 2004:480). Although what counts as 'good' evidence is contentious we can list a range of types of 'evidence' in terms of use of 'evidence' in policy processes and research policy-makers perceptions of what constitutes 'high-quality' evidence.[5]

What are the prerequisites for EBP to be pro-poor? First, the availability of evidence produced with the participation of the poor. Second, openness of policy-makers to a hierarchy of evidence based on academic rigour rather than producer or type of evidence. 'Academic rigour' is of course in itself contentious (see discussion in Sumner and Tribe, 2008). Quality is often judged by whether the results of the research are published in a peer-reviewed (refereed) journal and whether the research has been funded through a process including peer review. However, publication is a 'post-process' activity and it has been questioned whether it is any guarantee of high-quality research (Grayson, 2002).

When Becker *et al.* (2006:7–8) asked over 250 social policy researchers and users of research how they conceptualised 'quality' in social policy research they placed research publication at the bottom of the list. Indeed, Becker *et al.* (2006:7–8) argue, because traditional criteria are biased towards quantitative approaches, alternative assessment criteria should seek to be more inclusive. Thus, rather than thinking of 'truth' we could think of 'trustworthiness'; rather than thinking of 'validity' we could think of 'credibility'; rather than thinking of 'generalisability' we could think of the 'transferability' of context; rather than thinking of 'reliability' we could think of 'dependability'; and rather than thinking of 'objectivity' we could think of 'confirmability'. More broadly, we can say rigour is about approaching research, investigation or study using a number of discrete stages which follow a logical sequence – although a process of iteration may involve moving back and forth between stages as the research progresses. This 'process' is the 'research cycle'. The first essential stage is the clarification or definition of the 'research problem'. The second dimension consists of the utilisation of appropriate methodology, methods and techniques, and data/information (including 'transparent' sources) within the research process. If the research, investigation or study is undertaken systematically the conclusions, results or outcomes will follow logically.

In contrast, Citizen-Based Policy (CBP) can be defined as:

> direct ways in which citizens influence and exercise control in governance (Gaventa and Valderrama, 1999:2).

The trend is a shift from representative or formal democracy (i.e. indirect participation) towards more mechanisms for ensuring citizens' voice in the decision-making processes.

CBP could be instrumentally pro-poor – the involvement of citizens in policy processes might lead to policies that accelerate poverty reduction *or* it could be intrinsically pro-poor because the voice of the poor is represented in the policy processes and citizens are involved directly in decisions affecting their lives.

However, CBP is not pro-poor *par excellence* as 'participation' is not a neutral concept. Many refer back to Arnstein's (1969) 'Ladder of Participation' (see Figure 4.1).

Table 4.3 Quality of Evidence: Traditional and New Criteria

Traditional criteria	New criteria
Validity: the extent to which there is a correspondence between data and conceptualization.	Credibility: the extent to which a set of finding are believable.
Reliability: the extent to which observations are consistent when instruments are administered on more than one occasion.	Transferability: the extent to which a set of findings are relevant to settings other than the one or ones from which they are derived.
Replicability: the extent to which it is possible to reproduce an investigation.	Dependability: the extent to which a set of findings are likely to be relevant to a different time than the one in which it was conducted.
Generalizability: the extent to which it is possible to generalize findings to similar cases which have not been studies.	Conformability: the extent to which the researchers has not allowed personal values to intrude to an excessive degree.

Source: Becker *et al*. (2006:7–8).

Arnstein's 'Ladder of Participation' had eight rungs, which can be simplified into three stages: non-participation, tokenism and effective action. The issue is how meaningful agency is or is not exercised, or the fruitfulness of participation – does it empower or disempower? Participation is one stage on the ladder to empowerment. The question is how do we get to empowerment and/or what are the prerequisites for citizen or participatory-based policy to be pro-poor?

First, participation or access to policy processes is insufficient. Citizens need to be able to mobilise their policy narrative, gain access to policy spaces, influence policy and monitor and evaluate policy implementation to ensure pro-poor change. First, mobilising the policy narratives of poor people requires participatory techniques and an active translation process from specific local grievances to resonant policy relevant messages. Second, there is the access of the poor to policy processes – i.e. are the poor 'in the room'? Third, there is engagement in and influence of the poor in policy processes – i.e. do the poor have the capacity and skills/resources to influence? Fourth, there is achieving change – i.e. can the poor conduct monitoring and evaluation to ensure pro-poor policy change? This leads back to further mobilisation and a continuing cycle.

1. Citizen control   Citizen power

2. Delegated power

3. Partnership

4. Placation   Tokenism

5. Consultation

6. Informing

7. Therapy ('curing citizens of their pathology')   Non-participation

8. Manipulation ('illusory participation')

Figure 4.1   Arnstein's 'Ladder of Participation'

At a first stage (even before access to policy processes are considered) the mobilisation of the poor's policy narrative is required. By this we mean the self-identification of problems, ideally via various forms of participatory learning such as PPA, PRA, etc. Karl (2002:32) proposes a list of questions at this and later stages to include: what are the livelihood priorities of the poor? What policies affect the poor and their livelihoods? What kinds of policies would be supportive of poor livelihoods? At which level is policy (change) needed? Where in the policy process is the need for change most pressing – policy formulation (planning, information-gathering, analysis and decision-making), implementation, or monitoring and evaluation?

At the next stage – access of the poor to organisations of the poor (producer organisations, CSOs, etc.) and to policy processes themselves (formal and informal) is essential. Important questions to ask, again drawing upon Karl (2002:32) relate to the patterning and efficacy of democratic structures and institutions. Are there effective laws, legal frameworks and functioning legal institutions? Do political commitment to rights and the possibility to exercise these rights exist? Is there effective decentralisation that brings decision-making closer to the local level? Is there political commitment to policy reform? What mechanisms exist to influence policy through political structures? Are there existing or potential development programmes and projects that could work with government to facilitate policy reform? Are bureaucracies dominated by people from a particular disciplinary background, geographic area, academic institution, etc.? Are there particular patterns linking the bureaucracy to political parties or the private sector?

Are bureaucracies organised in such a way that cross-sectoral approaches are possible? Do bureaucracies operate transparently? Does bureaucratic capacity exist for policy reform?

In the third stage – engaging in and influence of the poor in (formal and informal) policy processes – we need to consider how the poor gain the requisite capacities to engage in policy dialogues. We could ask what groups and organisations exist at the local level (e.g. farmers' organisations, women's organisations, village associations, co-operatives)? Who do these groups and organisations represent? Are there under-represented or excluded segments of the local population (e.g. women, children and the very poor and indigenous people)? What can be done to enable the under-represented or marginalised groups to participate? What are the power relations and dynamics among and within groups and organisations? What is their political capital in relation to local, district and national government and governance institutions? What experience do they have in policy processes? What human, social and financial capital can they draw on to participate in policy-making? What skills do they possess that would enable or enhance their participation? The final stage – change via policy implementation again relates to the assets and capabilities that enable the poor to participate and thus a similar list.

What are the prerequisites for CBP to be pro-poor? There are a number of different factors that may influence the impact of participation itself. The actors involved and their interests, incentives and capacities, the institutions and context (or the 'space') in which participation occur are important. The various actors are likely to have previously established power dynamics and networks dictated by political, economic, social and cultural interactions, which will affect their access to and influence on public policy processes in general, and participatory approaches to policy reform specifically. The impact of participatory processes is thus likely to be greatly intertwined with the overall nature of democratic inclusiveness, political culture and accountability.

The conditions under which institutions are accountable vary by country and context. Key cross-cutting factors that can improve the responsiveness to the poor and marginalised groups are legal and constitutional provisions, histories of citizen engagement, democratic space, cultures of accountability and state–market relations (particularly with respect to natural resource incomes). Newell and Wheeler (2007) argue that accountability can rarely be provided from above. More effective reforms will be those that harness existing momentum within civil society, connect to existing government and citizen initiatives, and engage the private sector in a fuller debate about its responsibilities. Often these are informal, local and political in contrast with traditional approaches which tend to be national in focus, narrowly targeted at institutional reforms and regarded as technocratic interventions.

Goetz and Jenkins (2001:369) explain that citizens' accountability initiatives need to seek partnership with the state in order to be effective and have an impact beyond the local level. They suggest key conditions for making citizen–state accountability partnerships effective, as follows. First, legal standing for non-governmental observers within institutions of public-sector oversight. Second, a continuous presence for these observers throughout the process of the agency's work and well-defined procedures for the conduct of encounters between citizens and public-sector actors in meetings. Third, structured access to the flow of official documentary information, and fourth, the right of observers to issue dissenting reports directly to legislative bodies. Mahmud (2007:72) endorses this approach and adds that awareness-raising, financial support and grassroots mobilisation are also important.

> Poor people see themselves as having very limited responsibility and even less ability with respect to participation in public processes... People lack confidence in questioning government action since their knowledge about state delivery mechanisms is limited and they are unable to assess how the state operates. The realization that participation requires time and energy dampens enthusiasm and propensity for action (*ibid.*, 2007:58).

Cornwall (2007:33) captures all of these points by highlighting the importance of having an overarching political project in which there is an explicit ideological commitment to popular participation as well as legal and constitutional rights to participate, while Moore and Putzel (2002:16) argue that credibility (the poor feel that the people in question can be relied upon) and predictability (stability over time) are all key ingredients of success.

Sumner *et al.* (2008) found in 86 case studies of rural poor participation in policy processes that participation is a function of innovation, incentives and inequality. The rural poor – compared with their urban counterpart – face additional structural constraints (distance, political invisibility, weak/lack of co-ordination) for mobilising and affecting the policy process. The rural poor also face many of the issues noted previously but more acutely due to prevailing levels of poverty (take for example the role of literacy in participation and generally lower literacy level among the rural poor compared with the urban poor, or the barriers that spatial poverty imposes). At mobilisation stage enabling factors are supporting establishment and development of CSOs of the poor to articulate their demands. Grassroots ownership of CSOs of the poor via political parties, producer organisations and social movements are important too. Institutions matter in terms of the establishment of rights (and a legal framework) such as freedom of association and a history of social mobilisation and social movements can make a big difference.

At the access stage enabling factors are awareness-raising carried out with CSOs of the poor on institutional and legal processes and the political commitment/leadership on the process of participatory policy processes. Donors can be significant in opening spaces for CSOs of the poor to participate and in funding such processes (particularly in financial support to CSOs of the poor to access policy spaces and incentives for CSOs of the poor to participate). Institutions matter in terms of over-coming bureaucratic resistances to CSOs of the poor participating and the transparent establishment of rules and legal statutes promotes participation. At the influence stage enabling factors are capacity development for CSOs of the poor to engage in policy debates via training in technical, advocacy and language skills and skills in negotiation, lobbying, and communication. Also of importance is access of CSOs of the poor to information necessary to participate (policy history, etc.) and access to good evidence to support their case and the availability to CSOs of the poor of the means of communication to make the voices of the rural poor heard, and to network with other stakeholders. In terms of institutions, receptivity to voice from governance structures, bureaucracy and politicians as a result of political leadership and/or legitimacy of CSOs of the poor who are seen as credible representatives of the poor is important. Finally, at the implementation stage enabling factors are capacity development for CSOs to engage in monitoring and evaluation and built-in monitoring procedures to provide feedback to key partners periodically. Institutions matter in terms of a defined and publicised procedures for providing feedback, support in the fulfilment of roles in policy implementation and effective local and regional co-ordinating mechanisms.

5.   What next?

Policy processes are likely to be closely intertwined with the overall nature of democratic inclusiveness, political culture and accountability. The poor face structural constraints (distance, political invisibility, weak/

lack of co-ordination) for mobilising and affecting policy processes and there are also issues of technical literacy and English literacy, confidence, resources, and capacity to understand the issue, together with institutional resistances, which hinder any participation in high-level technical policy discussions.

To recap from Chapter 3, citizen and evidence-based policy can both be pro-poor (or not) depending on other factors. If we return to the commonalities in analytical frameworks already noted – the three interlocking domains of actors/networks, institutions/contexts and discourses/policy narratives – we can ask a series of questions that relate to material political economy, habitus and discourse conceptions of power. When we talk of policy actors and networks we would refer to material political economy and such matters as the extent to which the ruling party is ideologically driven, the extent of 'special interests' (business, unions, etc.), the level of professionalism of the civil service, the relative strength of civil society and the extent of influence of donors in policy-making. We might ask who is involved and how are they connected? What are their political interests and capabilities? In terms of pro-poor policy processes further questions that might be asked are, who participated? Who decided who participated? Who decided the agenda and terms of discussion? Who framed the outcomes/report of the process?

In terms of institutions and contexts we would refer to habitus conceptualisations of power and the degree of party competition or democratic openness, the use of multi-year development plans, the level of centralisation of political decision-making, and the degree of academic and media freedom. We might ask how does the context shape policy processes? What are the formal and informal 'rules of the game'? In terms of pro-poor policy processes and participation of the poor and their representative organisations, questions that might be asked are, how was the involvement of the poor in the policy process initiated (invited or claimed)? What was the nature of the participation? And did a better process translate into more pro-poor outcomes?

In terms of describing policy narratives we would refer to discourse conceptualisations of power and how different discourses are shaped, communicated and legitimised. Whose evidence counts in evidence-based policy? We would be concerned with the extent to which there is a consensus on what should be done, the extent of influence of international discourses on domestic policy and the extent to which a policy issue is novel or counters conventional wisdom. In any context values shape the behaviour of actors and the structure of institutions;

the key question of concern here is whether values communicate a preference for the poor. In some cases, that preference is absent, and instead discrimination or exclusion are accepted values. Actors and institutions may emerge to challenge such values, but there will be little pro-poor governance until actors, institutions and values are aligned to listen to and address the concerns directly via participation in policy processes or indirectly via evidence from the poor informing policy processes at all stages of policy-making. We might ask, what is the prevailing policy narrative? How is it framed? Whose interests does it represent? Whose are marginalised? 'Participation' questions might include, how are multiple forms of 'expertise' accommodated? What 'evidence' was presented? Whose 'evidence' prevailed – i.e. was perceived to be most credible – or prevailed in the report of the meeting?

Notes

1 This chapter draws upon and builds on discussion in Schneider *et al.* (2007), Sumner and Jones (2009) and Sumner *et al.* (2008a; 2008b).
2 There are three issues of contention worth noting. First, much of the data is based on perceptions, i.e. data based on subjective opinions of surveys of business people. Second, it is extremely difficult to apply quantitative measures in exactly the same way in different places and at different times. Third, quantitative indicators occasionally measure what is observable rather than what is conceptually valid. For example, instead of evaluating the process of governance (is trade policy decided democratically, transparently, etc.), policy outputs, such as trade openness, are easier to observe, and therefore measure. Yet, trade openness is a policy output, reflecting a certain kind of liberal economic policy, and it may not be a reflection of the process or concept of governance itself.
3 Accountability mechanisms may function along either a 'vertical' or a 'horizontal' axis. Vertical accountability involves external mechanisms used by citizens and non-state actors to hold policy-makers to account. Along this axis, there is also 'downward' accountability where those with less power may hold those with more power (i.e. those 'higher up') to account for their actions and decisions. Horizontal accountability involves institutional oversight, checks and balances internal to the state.
4 See for discussion (Martson and Watts, 2003:150). Upshur *et al.* (2001:94) proposed a model of evidence with four distinct but related types of evidence in four quadrants for what kind of research is seen as credible in different disciplines. The vertical axis is methodology (meaning to measurement) and the horizontal axis is context (particular to general context). The four were qualitative personal (concrete/historical), qualitative general (concrete/social), quantitative personal (personal/mathematics) and quantitative general (impersonal/mathematics). They argued that each of these dominated in different disciplines: the first in clinical medicine, the second in social sciences, the third in clinical epidemiology and the fourth in economics and political science.

5   Davies (2004:7) argues there are six types of evidence (research evidence; systematic reviews; single studies; pilot studies and case studies; expert's evidence and Internet evidence) and seven types of research evidence (attitudinal evidence – surveys, qualitative; statistical modelling – linear and logistic regression; impact evidence – experimental, quasi-experimental, counter-factual; economic and econometric evidence – cost-benefit, cost effectiveness, cost utility, econometrics; ethical evidence – social ethics and public consultation; implementation evidence – experimental, quasi-experimental qualitative, theories of change; and descriptive analytical evidence – surveys, admin data, comparative and qualitative).

References

Alfini, N. (2006) *Child Participation in Policy and Academia.* Brighton: IDS.

Alsop, R. and Heinsohn, N. (2005) *Measuring Empowerment in Practice: Structuring Analysis and Framing Indicators.* Washington, DC: World Bank.

Alkire, S. (2002) *Valuing Freedoms: Sen's Capability Approach and Poverty Reduction.* New York: Oxford University Press.

Anderson, E. and Morrissey, O. (2006) 'A Statistical Approach to Identifying Poorly Performing Countries', *Journal of Development Studies,* 42:3:469–89.

Arnstein, S.R. (1969) 'A Ladder of Citizen Participation', *Journal of the American Institute of Planners,* 35:216–24.

Becker, S., Bryman, A. and Sempik, J. (2006) 'Defining "Quality" in Social Policy Research: Views, Perceptions and a Framework for Discussion'. Suffolk, UK: Social Policy Association.

Brock, K. and McGee, R. (2004) 'Mapping Trade Policy: Understanding the Challenges of Civil Society Participation', Brighton, Institute of Development Studies, *IDS Working Paper,* 225.

Chambers, R. (1983) *Rural Development: Putting the First Last.* London: ITDG.

Chambers, R. (1997) *Whose Reality Counts? Putting the First Last.* London: ITDG.

Chambers, R. (2004) 'Ideas for Development', *IDS Working Paper,* 238. Sussex: IDS.

Chambers, R. (2006) *Poverty Unperceived: Traps, Biases and Agenda.* IDS Working Paper 270.

Chong, A. and Calderón, C. (2000) 'Causality and Feedback Between Institutional Measures and Economic Growth', *Economics and Politics,* 12(1):69–81.

Commission for Africa (CFA) (2005) *Our Common Interest.* London: CFA.

Cornwall, A. (2007) Democratising the Governance of Health Services: The Case of Cabo De Santo Agostinho, Brazil, in Cornwall, A. and Coelho, V. (eds) *Spaces for Change: The Politics of Citizen Participation in New Democratic Arenas.* London: Zed Books.

Cornwall, A. and Guijt, I. (2007) 'Shifting Perceptions, Changing Practices in PRA: From Infinite Innovation to the Quest for Quality', *Participatory Learning and Action,* 50.

Court, J. and Young, J. (2003) 'Bridging Research and Policy: Insights From 50 Case Studies', *ODI Working Paper,* 213, London: ODI.

Court, J., Hovland, I. and Young, J. (2005) 'Bridging Research and Policy in International Development: Evidence and the Changing Process'. London: Intermediate Technology Development Group (ITDG).

Court, J., Mendizabal, E., Osborne, D. and Young, J. (2006) 'Policy Engagement: How Civil Society Can be More Effective', Research and Policy in Development Programme (RAPID), Overseas Development Institute.

Davies, P. (2004) Is Evidence Based Government Possible? Paper presented at the 4th Annual Campbell Collaboration Colloquium, Washington, DC. 19 February.

Davies, H. and Nutley, S. (2004) Healthcare: Evidence to the Fore, in Davies, H., Nutley, S. and Smith, P. (eds), *What Works? Evidence-based Policy and Practice in Public Services*. Bristol, UK: The Policy Press.

Dobrow, M., Goel, V. and Upshur, R. (2004) 'Evidence-Based Health Policy: Context and Utilisation', *Social Science and Medicine*, 58(1):207–17.

Gasiorowski, M. (1996) *An Overview of the Political Regime Change Dataset Comparative Political Studies*, 29(4):469–83.

Gaventa, J. (2004) Participatory Development or Participatory Democracy? Linking participatory approaches to policy and governance, *Participatory Learning and Action*, 50:150–9.

Gaventa, J. and Valderama, C. (1999) 'Participation, Citizenship and Local Governance', Background note prepared for workshop on 'Strengthening Participation in Local Governance', IDS, June 21–24.

Goetz, A.M. and Jenkins, R. (2001) 'Hybrid Forms of Accountability: Citizen Engagement in institutions of Public-sector Oversight in India', *Public Management Review*, 3(3):363–84.

Goetz, A.M. and Jenkins, R. (2005) *Reinventing Accountability: Making Democracy Work for Human Development*. Basingstoke: Palgrave Macmillan.

Gordon, D., Nandy, S., Pantazis, C., Pemberton, S. and Townsend, P. (2003) *Child Poverty in the Developing World*. Washington, DC: UNICEF.

Graham, J., Amos, B. and Plumptre, T. (2003) *Principles for Good Governance in the 21st Century*. Ottawa: Institute on Governance.

Grayson, L. (2002) Evidence Based Policy and the Quality Of Evidence: Rethinking Peer Review. ESRC UK Centre for Evidence Based Policy and Practice Working Paper Number 7. London: Queen Mary, University of London.

Hyden, G., Court, J. and Mease, K. (2004) *Making Sense of Governance: Empirical Evidence from Sixteen Developing Countries*. Boulder: Lynne Rienner.

Ibrahim, S. and Alkire, S. (2007) 'Agency and Empowerment: A Proposal for Internationally Comparable Indicators', *Oxford Development Studies*, 35(4): 379–403.

IDRC (International Development Research Centre) (2004) *Making the Most of Research*. Ottowa: IDRC.

Jones, N. (2005) 'Reflections on Young Lives 2000–2005: Bridging Research, Policy Analysis and Advocacy to Tackle Childhood Poverty', *Young Lives Working Paper*, 17. London: Save the Children.

Jones, N. and Pham, L. (2005) 'The Ethics of Research Reciprocity: Making Children's Voices Heard in Poverty Reduction Policy-making in Vietnam', *Young Lives Working Paper*. London: Save the Children

Jones, N., Lyytikäinen, M., Mukherjee, M., Gopinath Reddy, M. (September 2007) 'Decentralization and Participatory Service Delivery: Implications for Tackling Childhood Poverty in Andhra Pradesh, India', *Journal of Children and Poverty*, 13(2):207–29.

Karl, M. (2002) Participatory Policy Reform from a Sustainable Livelihoods Perspective: Review of Concepts and Practical Experiences. FAO, Livelihood Support Programme Working Paper Number 3. Rome: FAO.

Kaufmann, D., Kraay, A. and Zoido-Lobatón, P. (1999) *Aggregating Governance Indicators*. World Bank Policy Research Working Paper No. 2195. Washington, DC: World Bank.

Kaufmann, D. and Kraay, A. (2002) *Growth without Governance*. Washington, DC: World Bank.

Kaufmann, D., Recanatini, F. and Biletsky, S. (2002) *Assessing Governance: Diagnostic Tools and Applied Methods for Capacity Building and Action Learning*. Washington, DC: World Bank.

Kaufmann, D., Kraay, A. and Mastruzzi, M. (2005) *Governance Matters IV: Governance Indicators for 1996–2004*, Policy Research Working Paper, 3630. Washington, DC: Wold Bank.

Knack, S. and Keefer, P. (1995) 'Institutions and Economic Performance: Cross-Country Tests Using Alternative Institutional Measures', *Economics and Politics*, 7(3):207–27.

Mahmud, S. (2007) Spaces for Participation in Health Systems in Rural Bangladesh: The experience of Stakeholder community groups, in Cornwall, A. and Vera Schattan and Coelho, P. (eds) *Spaces for Change: The Politics of Citizen Participation in New Democratic Arenas*. London: Zed Books.

March, J. and Olsen, J. (1976) *Ambiguity and Choice in Organizations*. Bergen: Universitetsforlaget.

Martson, G. and Watts, R. (2003) Tampering With the Evidence: A Critical Appraisal of Evidence-Based Policy-Making. *The Drawing Board: An Australian Review of Public Affairs*, 3(3):143–63.

Mauro, P. (1995) 'Corruption and Growth', *Quarterly Journal of Economics*, 110:681–712.

Moore, M. and Putzel, J. (2002) 'Thinking Strategically about Politics and Poverty', *IDS Working Paper*, 101. Brighton: IDS.

Moser, C. (1989) 'Gender Planning in the Third World: Meeting Practical and Strategic Needs', *World Development*, 17(11):1799–825.

Newell and Wheeler (2007) Show Me the Money: New Approaches to Accountability. ID21. Brighton: IDS.

Nussbaum, M. (2000) *Women and Human Development: The Capabilities Approach*. Cambridge: Cambridge University Press.

Nutley, S., Davies, H. and Walter, I. (2002) 'Evidence Based Policy and Practice: Cross Sector Lessons from the UK', Paper presented at a Seminar on 'Evidence-Based Policy and Practice', organized by the Royal Society, Wellington, New Zealand.

Nutley, S. and Webb, J. (2004) 'Evidence and the Policy Process', in Davies, H., Nutley, S. and Smith, P. (eds) *What Works? Evidence Based Policy and Practice in Public Services*. Bristol, UK: The Policy Press.

Rowlands, J. (1995) 'Empowerment Examined', *Development in Practice*, 5(2):101–7.

Schedler, A. (1999) Conceptualizing Accountability, in *The Self-Restraining State: Power and Accountability in New Democracies*. London: Lynne Rienner.

Schneider, A., Sumner, A. and Mejia, A. (2007) *Pro-Poor Governance Sourcebook*. Brighton: IDS.

Sen, A. (1999) *Development as Freedom*. Oxford: Oxford University Press.

Shaxson, L. (2005) 'Is Your Evidence Robust Enough?', *Evidence and Policy*, 1(1):101–11.

Solesbury, W. (2001) 'Evidence-Based Policy: Whence It Came and Where It's Going', ESRC UK Centre for Evidence Based Policy and Practice Working Paper, 1. London: Queen Mary, University of London.

Sumner, A. and Tribe, M. (2008) *International Development Studies: Theory and Methods in Research and Practice*. London: Sage.

Sumner, A., Meija, A., Cabral, L. and Hussein, K. (2008a) 'What Factors Mediate the Participation of the Rural Poor in Policy Processes?', Background Paper for IFAD Rural Poverty Report 2009 (forthcoming). Rome: IFAD.

Sumner, A., Giordano, T. and Wiggins, S. (2008b) How is the World Changing and What Does It Mean for the Rural Poor? Background Paper for IFAD Rural Poverty Report 2009 (forthcoming). Rome, IFAD.

Sumner, A. and Jones, N. (2009, forthcoming) 'The Politics of Poverty Policy: Are Pro-Poor Policy Processes Expert-Led Or Citizen-Led?', *International Development and Planning Review*.

Upshur, R., VanDen Kerkhof, E. and Goel, V. (2001) 'Meaning and Measurement: An Inclusive Model of Evidence in Health Care', *Journal of Evaluation in Clinical Practice*, 7(2):91–96.

World Bank (2002) *Empowerment and Poverty Reduction: A Sourcebook*. Washington, DC: World Bank.

World Bank (2005) *Measuring Empowerment*. Washington, DC: World Bank.

5
Doing Growth

> I do not share the discomfort with growth... the problem of
> the bottom billion has not been that they have had the wrong
> type of growth, it is that they have not had any growth
> (Collier, 2007:11).

1. Introduction

Economic growth was perceived to be central to development policy
formation in debates from the 1950s to the late 1980s. The issue of
policy concern was the quantity of growth and how to produce it. From
the late 1980s onwards growth was to a certain extent knocked off the
policy 'top spot' by poverty reduction and subsequently debates shifted
to discuss the quality rather than just the quantity of growth. Indeed,
although it actually emerged as a concept in the 1970s as 'redistribution
with growth', 'pro-poor growth' (in various guises) has been an important part of the post-WC and debates of the 1990s.[1] Throughout there
has also been the underlying issue of growth and environmental sustainability too. This is likely to become increasingly important in light
of the EPICs outlined in earlier chapters, most notably climate change,
but one might also note demography and growth links too.

In this chapter we consider growth.[2] This chapter is structured as
follows. Section 2 gives a brief history of growth debates. Section 3 is
concerned with the relationship between growth and the MDGs and
poverty reduction. Section 4 then looks to the future and focuses on
growth and environmental sustainability. Section 5 concludes.

2. A brief history of growth debates

In the 1950s, Arthur Lewis (1955:9–10) argued that, for economists, the
subject matter was growth, and inequality was not a concern whilst

135

Simon Kuznets, writing at the same time, argued it was the growth-inequality relationship that was central to economics.[3] Fifty years on, Kanbur and Squire (2001:183) argued that poverty reduction 'lies at the heart' of Development Economics but Dollar and Kraay (2002:27) posited 'anyone who cares about the poor should favour... growth'. Where are we now? Collier has argued strongly that the importance of growth has been underplayed and development policy has been distracted by inequality and poverty. He has argued that policy-makers should worry about growth first and have faith that, generally, poverty reduction will follow. For Collier the growth arguments in *The Bottom Billion* can be reduced to two key positions. First, growth matters and has been neglected. It should be our central concern. Second, growth is generally good for poor people. The quantity of growth (or lack of it) is the problem – not the quality of growth. Collier does 'not share the discomfort about growth' felt by many people caring about development, he argues that the problem of the Bottom Billion is that 'they have not had any growth', rather than the 'wrong type of growth' and he claims that 'growth usually does benefit ordinary people' (Collier, 2007:11). Although he does add, 'I am definitely not arguing we should be indifferent to how an economy grows', his diagnosis is clear: 'the failure of the growth process in these societies simply has to be our core concern, and curing it the core challenge of development' (p.11).

Is Collier right? Crucial to the idea that growth benefits the poor is the relationship between growth and inequality. This relationship was the attention of much work in the 1950s–1970s. It gave birth to one of the most famous and controversial theories in Development Economics, the Kuznets curve. It is worth noting at the outset that there are actually at least two debates on inequality and growth. The first, the relationship Kuznets hypothesised from growth-to-inequality. The second, a trade-off that Kuznets implied on inequality-to-growth.

Simon Kuznets (1955; 1963) argued, in his presidential address to the 1954 American Economic Association and in later articles, a relationship based on a 'hypothetical numerical exercise' of which Kuznets noted 5% was empirical information and 95% was speculation (cited in Kanbur and Squire, 2001:192). Kuznets postulated an inverted U-shape relationship between income and inequality. Kuznets predicted an increase in inequality in the early stages of development and a reduction in inequality in subsequent periods. This was formulated using the Lewis dual economy model.[4] Kuznets argued that agricultural economies (i.e. developing countries) are initially relatively equal societies with low average income. As the economy develops, the population migrates to non-agricultural sectors, where average incomes are higher, as is inequality. Thus initially, inequality worsens because of the higher proportion of national income in the industrial sector and the higher proportion of profits in national income. The early benefits of economic growth go to those with control over capital and better education. In time, as more of the population move out of the traditional, rural, agricultural sector to the modern, urban, industrial sector and real wages in industry begin to rise, income inequality decreases.[5] What Kuznets implied on the inequality-to-growth linkage was that there is a trade-off: inequality is a short-term price worth paying for long-term economic development and that growth would eventually lead mechanistically to poverty reduction through the 'trickle down' effect (Bourguignon *et al.*, 2003:4).

In spite of numerous attempts, no systematic association from growth-to-inequality has been reported in the recent empirical work (Adams, 2003; Deininger and Squire, 1998; Dollar and Kraay, 2002; Easterly, 1999; Ravallion and Chen, 1997).[6] The dominant view is that inequality is not an outcome of growth but plays a role in determining the pattern of growth and poverty reduction (Bourguignon, 2003:12). This does not necessarily mean that growth has no impact on distribution, rather there are too many country specifics to make a generalisation.[7] However, most studies have focused not on growth-to-inequality but

Table 5.1 Summary of Empirical Work on Inequality-to-Growth Relationship

	Positive association	No association	Negative – associated with lower future growth
The impact of initial inequality on future growth	*Early studies:* Adelman and Morris (1973) Ahluwalia (1976) Ahluwalia *et al.* (1979) Paukert (1973)	Bruno *et al.* (1998) Deininger and Squire (1996) Knowles (2005) Li *et al.* (1998) Lopez (2005)	Alesina and Rodrik (1994) Birdsall *et al.* (1995) Clarke (1995) Easterly (2002) Perotti (1996)
	Later studies: Deutsch and Silber (2004) Forbes (2000) Li and Zhou (1998)		*Asset inequality:* Birdsall and Londoño (1997) Deininger and Squire (1998)

Note: Unless stated inequality refers to income/expenditure inequality.

on the inequality-to-growth trade-off (see Table 5.1). A number of studies in the 1970s initially supported the contention that initial inequality had a positive impact on subsequent growth.

However, in 1990s a series of new studies led by Anand and Kanbur (1993a; 1993b) found a non-inverted U shape questioned this. Some argued there was no empirical relationship between initial inequality and growth or that greater inequality actually reduced subsequent economic growth.[8]

Most recently, the empirical literature has become somewhat contradictory probably due to methodological issues. Some have reaffirmed the positive impact of inequality on growth whilst others have found the exact opposite using asset inequality in contrast to income inequality (see Table 5.2). More convincing are others who have posited that the inequality–growth relationship depends on the level of economic development (Barro, 2000; List and Gallet, 1999) or differs in democratic and non-democratic countries (Deininger and Squire, 1998; Perotti, 1996) or that any change (up or down) in inequality reduces future growth (Banerjee and Duflo, 2003). Those who have considered gender issues have found that high gender inequality, especially in education, is harmful to growth (Klasen, 1999; Knowles *et al.*, 2002). Indeed, there is the impact of economic growth on non-income inequality. For example, the literature is evolving into human capital inequality and economic growth (see for example, Castello and Domenech, 2000).

Many of the discrepancies between studies could be due to aggregation and heterogeneity in country specifics (Forbes, 2000; Lopez, 2005). Table 5.2 outlines some of the major methodologically deterministic issues.[9]

Most notable is that of the raw datasets used. The original Kuznets curve was based on historical data for the first half of the 19th century for three developed countries (USA, UK and Germany) although some reference was made to India, Ceylon (now Sri Lanka), Prussia and Puerto Rico. The 1970s studies were primarily based on cross-sectional not time series data (problematic for estimating inter-temporal relationships) and many of the 1990s studies were based on the new, larger, 'high quality' dataset constructed by Deininger and Squire.[10] Additionally, as Knowles (2005:139) notes, studies based on short-run 'spells' find that the Kuznets inequality-to-growth trade-off is supported (for example, Forbes, 2000; Li and Zhou, 1998) but long-run studies do not (for example, Alesina and Rodrik, 1994; Birdsall *et al.*, 1995; Easterly, 2002).[11]

However, conceptual (re)thinking has also played a role. There has been new conceptual thinking on how initial inequality reduces

Table 5.2   'Technical/Data' Issues in the Empirical Research on
Inequality-to-Growth

	General characteristics of studies that find initial inequality and growth positively associated	General characteristics of studies that do not find initial inequality and growth positively associated
Country sample	Sample of mainly OECD countries	Sample including developing countries
Type of data	Cross-sectional	Time series
Database	Old, 'low-quality' dataset	New, larger, 'higher-quality' dataset
Time between data 'spells'	Short-run 'spells'	Long-run 'spells'
Measurement of inequality	Gross inequality/ income inequality	Net inequality/expenditure inequality

Sources: Collated from commentary in Deininger and Squire (1998) Knowles (2005).
Note: It is intended that the table represents tendencies in the empirical literature not absolutes.

subsequent growth.[12] These 'new' theories are inter-related to the 'technical/ data' issues above: of the 'new' theories, the Kuznets trade-off would be more visible in the long run than the short run, more evident in net inequality than gross inequality data and in household data than national accounts (Knowles, 2005:139).

The first 'new' theory has been labelled the 'redistributive political-economy model' (see Rehme, 2001). This is based on the idea that unequal societies create redistributive pressures leading to distortionary fiscal policy that reduces future growth.[13]

Second, a 'socio-political instability' theory (see Alesina and Perotti, 1996): that income inequality creates socio-political instability and thus reduces investment and hence future economic growth.

Third, an 'imperfect credit markets' theory (see Ravallion, 1998): that in unequal societies there is a high density of credit-constrained people and thus less investment (especially human capital) and hence growth.

In sum, an 'old', formerly strong consensus (see for example, *World Development Report*, 1990) that inequality is good for growth has been tentatively replaced by a weaker 'new' consensus (see *World Development Report*, 2000/1 and 2006) that inequality is probably bad for growth overall, but this has not been proved conclusively and there is no empirical evidence for a systematic association from growth-to-inequality.[14] As Kanbur (2004:6) has noted, 'the jury is still out'.

3. Growth, poverty reduction and the MDGs

The influence of the Kuznets hypothesis/trade-off extended into the analysis of the relationship between growth and poverty: if economic development, in the early stages at least, leads to an increase in inequality then the implication was that poverty may take many years to fall as the benefits of growth to the poor are reduced by the increase in inequality.

Consistent with the 1970s studies that supported the Kuznets trade-off a series of studies at the same time argued that, as new data became available, economic growth did not benefit the poor. Chenery *et al.* (1974:xiii) argued that a decade of growth had bypassed with 'little or no benefit' a third of the population in developing countries and Adelman and Morris (1973:189–93) wrote of hundreds of millions 'hurt' by economic development.

Since the late-1990s a small craft industry has emerged in the econometrics of the poverty elasticity of growth, mushrooming following the controversy over Dollar and Kraay's *Growth is Good for the Poor* (see Box 5.1).[15] Most of these studies have argued that growth is good for the poor in the sense that the income of the poor rises one-for-one in line with average income (Dollar and Kraay, 2002; Gallup *et al.*, 1999; Roemer and Gugerty, 1997) and the poverty headcount ratio declines significantly with growth (Bruno *et al.*, 1998; Ravallion, 1995; 2001; Ravallion and Chen, 1997). The conventional wisdom is that growth is the most important and maybe the easiest driver of poverty reduction. *But* small reductions in inequality can also be important (Kalwij and Verschoor, 2007; Ravallion, 2001). While it has been strongly asserted that on average growth is matched by proportionate reductions in poverty, more recent evidence challenges this view, suggesting rather that the incomes of the poorest may increase less than proportionately with growth (Besley and Cord, 2006; Grimm *et al.*, 2007).

The averages hide large variations across countries and across measures of poverty, questioning both the relevance of the global average and whether growth responds differently to different kinds of (chronic and transient) income poverty (Bhalla, 2002; Cord *et al.*, 2003; Eastwood and Lipton, 2001; Epaulard, 2003; Kalwij and Verschoor, 2004; Mosley, 2004). For example, growth has been associated with *increases* in poverty in much of Sub-Saharan Africa, Russia and much of Eastern Europe

Box 5.1   Dollar and Kraay's 'Growth is Good for the Poor'

Dollar and Kraay's 'Growth is Good for the Poor' claimed to provide 'evidence' (the word was used 37 times in the study) that not only is growth good for the poor but that the policies pursued by the IMF and World Bank were good for the poor because they led to growth. It could have equally been called 'growth is good for the rich' because the incomes of the poorest quintile may grow one-for-one but so do the richest quintile. Although the paper faced sustained methodological criticism few have disagreed with the main finding that the income of the poor rises proportionally with average per capita income growth. However, as Kanbur noted, no one had ever claimed economic contraction was good for the poor.

In 'Growth is Good for the Poor', Dollar and Kraay used data for 92 countries covering four decades. The paper's findings were as follows: (a) economic growth is good for the poor – the income per capita in the poorest expenditure quintile rises one-for-one (1.07) with overall per capita growth – thus implying that there is no need to worry about pro-poor growth, as growth itself is enough and this relationship has not deteriorated in recent years; (b) the standard 'pro-growth' policies (of the Fund/Bank) are good for the poor – macroeconomic stability, fiscal discipline, good rule of law, low inflation and trade openness – but there is no evidence that public spending on health and education are 'pro-poor'; and (c) globalisation is good for the poor – trade openness raises the income of the poor in line with average income and there is no evidence that capital account liberalisation is 'anti-poor'.

Nye *et al.* note that for many of the countries in the Dollar and Kraay sample, the factor of proportionality was either significantly more or significantly less than one and few countries are on the one-for-one mark (pointing to Dollar and Kraay's Figure 1). Furthermore, when Bhalla estimated poverty elasticities of growth (using a slightly different methodology), the average for developing countries excluding China and India was as low as 0.64, with the extremes being East Asia at 1.17 compared with 0.54 in Latin America. In fact, the one-for-one finding is of limited relevance because of the role of initial inequality in mediating the growth-poverty relationship: if the initial share of the poor in national income is small then they capture a small share of the growth increment. For example, at current income distributions, Mexico would have to grow at twice the rate of Indonesia or Uganda to achieve the same rise in the income of the poorest quintile and Brazil at as much as five times the rate of Vietnam.

Box 5.1   Dollar and Kraay's 'Growth is Good for the Poor'
– *continued*

Dollar and Kraay's study has been methodologically criticised, too, for using cross-country data and making little use of cross-temporal data to investigate a temporal relationship (only India, Mexico and Sri Lanka had time series data); for treating all countries the same regardless of their level of development i.e. for not differentiating between developing countries and developed countries; for using data from the 1970s and 1980s (before liberalisation and global-isation accelerated); for findings that were statistically insignificant (with the exception of the one-for-one growth-poverty finding); for using the bottom expenditure quintile as a proxy for the poor and for not questioning why, in a surprisingly high 1 in 7 cases, poverty actually rose with growth. Easterly noted that in only 10 of the 81 cases were quality of life indicators positively linked to economic growth. The finding that education does not raise the incomes of the poor has also been questioned.

Sources: Amann *et al.*, 2002; Bhalla, 2003; Easterly, 2001; Garuda, 2000; Gundlach *et al.*, 2001; Kanbur, 2002; Nye *et al.*, 2002; Oxfam, 2002; Przeworski and Vreeland 2000; Weisbrot *et al.*, 2001.

(Epaulard, 2003; Mosley, 2004) and the poverty elasticity of growth ranges widely – between 0.79 and 1.23 using relative measures (East-wood and Lipton, 2001) and 0.6–4.3 using absolute poverty measures (Ravallion, 2004).[16]

Why do countries differ so markedly? As Mosley (2004:7) has noted there are a large number of potential independent variables to choose from. Initial inequality has most commonly been identified as deter-ministic in the heterogeneity of country experience: a higher level of inequality leads to less poverty reduction at a given level of growth (Deininger and Squire, 1998; Hanmer and Naschold, 2001; Kraay, 2004; Ravallion, 1995; 1997; 2001; 2004; Ravallion and Chen, 1997; Son and Kakwani, 2003; Stewart, 2000).[17] The heterogeneity of country experience has also been linked to changes in inequality over time due to geographical differences (urban–rural); the sectoral pattern of growth; the composition of public expenditure; labour markets; social capital endowments and the variance in actual rates of growth (Fields, 2001; Kraay, 2004; Mosley, 2004; Mosley *et al.*, 2004; Ravallion, 1995; Ravallion and Chen, 1997).[18]

There are also methodological reasons for different findings.[19] Studies that use time series data, or are based on samples of non-OECD countries and/or use national accounts tend to be less optimistic about the extent of the benefits of growth to the poor. However, the most deterministic issue is the measure of poverty taken. Studies based on absolute poverty are more optimistic than those based on relative poverty definitions because relative poverty measures do not capture the distribution effects of growth impacts on poverty (Kalwij and Verschoor, 2004:2).[20]

What about growth and the non-income MDGs? It is important to understand the relationship of growth to key ultimate outcomes, an issue on which there is still relatively little evidence. Human development indicators such as education and health are generally positively related to growth but often less strongly, or over a longer time horizon, than income poverty (Gross *et al.*, 2005). For instance, mortality rates are correlated with income levels of countries, but income levels are far from being the only factor influencing recent improvements in life expectancy; other factors include public health care systems, nutrition and immunisation programmes and maternal education levels, any of which might or might not improve independently of growth.

Take for example, hunger. Economic growth, while crucial for reducing malnutrition, will not take care of malnutrition quickly enough – the two are not as tightly wedded as many imagine (Haddad *et al.*, 2006). Projections show that by 2015 only 3 out of 12 countries will halve their 1990 malnutrition rates despite projections reliant on 25 years of historically unprecedented income growth. Few studies have tried to address changes in multi-dimensional poverty versus economic growth although there have been studies on whether static per capita income 'translate' into 'Human Development' (see for example, Barro and Lee, 1997; Barro and Sala-I-Martin, 1995; McGillivray, 2003; Pritchett and Summers, 1995).

In sum, the 'conventional wisdom' is that 'growth is the most important and maybe the easiest driver of poverty reduction' *but* one might add tentatively that small changes in inequality can also be important (Maxwell, 2005:2, 4). This is a point outlined in the *World Development Report* 2000/1 (World Bank, 2000:45–59) and the DAC Guidelines (OECD, 2001:18). Even the *Human Development Report* has noted the importance of growth in achieving the MDGs (UNDP, 2003:67–84), as does the 'Monterrey Consensus' and *the Millennium Project Report to the United Nations Secretary-General* (UNMP, 2005:4–9).

Growth is important, but we also need to be concerned with the nature of that growth. We cannot just assume that growth will usually translate into broad-based improvements in ultimate outcomes. To echo Sen (1999), income is *only* an 'instrumental' freedom (i.e. it helps to achieve other 'constitutive' freedoms such as being healthy or being well fed). The key question then is how growth relates to these ultimate ends. If we consider that ultimate ends are concerned with human development, reduction of vulnerability, participation, psychological well-being, etc., then we need to understand how the growth process interacts with these. There are serious gaps in knowledge on these questions. Growth is clearly not an end in itself, but rather a means to other ends. Growth definitely does supply essential resources for the attainment of these ends, through both private and public channels, if the benefits of growth can be sufficiently widely shared.

4.   The future of growth

Concern with the impacts of economic growth and development on depletion and degradation of the natural environment emerged in the 1970s. This attention culminated in the World Commission on Environment and Development (WCED) and the later Rio Earth Summits. Over the last few years such concerns have started to take on a new impetus in light of climate change discussions. However, attempts to bring sustainability dimensions into policy-making have been plagued by one basic question – what to sustain?

The World Bank's (2002b) *World Development Report 2003 – Sustainable Development in a Dynamic World: Transforming Institutions, Growth and Quality of Life* noted (p.14) that although there are thousands of definitions of sustainable development (SD), the most often cited definition is still that of the WCED (1987:43) which identifies SD as meeting the 'needs' of the present without undermining the ability to meet the 'needs' of the future. However, this definition, although the most often used, is of little practical use. What exactly it means in policy is not clear: what is to be sustained – consumption at current levels (for future generations' 'needs' to be met) or sustain the environmental resources themselves (for future generations to meet their self-defined 'needs')?

Neumayer (2003:2–3) argues that the measurement of well-being (social and economic progress) and sustainability should remain conceptually separated because what affects the former is not necessarily the same as what affects the latter and vice versa. Additionally, the first refers to total *current* capital stock whilst the latter to the total *future* capital stock. For this reason, Neumayer rejected attempts at amalgamating social development and sustainable development completely.[21] This is not to say the concepts are not linked – poverty related to current well-being and SD to future well-being; but the first is not about the future flow of well-being and the latter is not concerned with the current stock of well-being.

Pearce *et al.* (1989) temporarily addressed the question of what to sustain with the concepts of *strong sustainability* and *weak sustainability* based on the infinite substitutability (weak) or non-substitutability (strong) of natural capital. *Weak sustainability*, also known as *utility-based sustainability* or *Solow sustainability* (see below), is based on the work of neo-classical economists such as Hicks (1939). Within this framework of inter-generational equity, Solow (1974; 1986) and Hartwick (1977) argued that SD is sustaining the utility of future generations and that this is possible if the *Solow-Hardwick rule* is followed: to maintain constant consumption over time, resource-dependent countries must reinvest all rents from natural resource extraction in productive capital (assuming an initial endowment of natural resources adequate for a certain standard of living). Economic growth is sustained as the scarcity of one resource (natural capital) can be compensated (substitution) by the availability of another (man-made or produced capital).

In contrast, Daly (2002:1) argued that *strong sustainability* or *throughput-based sustainability* is based on sustaining the entropic physical flow from nature and back to nature as non-declining. In order to do this there has to be zero economic growth and zero population growth – known as a *steady-state* because natural capital is infinitely non-substitutable. One resource (natural capital) cannot be compensated (substitution) by the availability of another (produced capital). Daly (2002:7) went so far as to argue Gross Domestic Product (GDP) growth might be *un*economic growth, because environmental depletion and GDP growth generate not only wealth but *illith* – John Ruskin's term for the opposite of wealth.

Beckerman's (1994) devastating critique undermined both *weak* and *strong sustainability*. He argued that *weak sustainability* took debates not much further than the current model of economic welfare maximisation and *strong sustainability* was morally unacceptable and totally impractical. There then followed a game of back-and-forth debates – notably in the pages of *Environment Values* (see for details, Beckerman, 1995; Common, 1996; Daly, 1995; Dower, 1994; El Serafy, 1996; Common, 1996). The weaknesses of *weak sustainability* were largely agreed, but no such consensus was reached on the 'moral injunction' on *strong sustainability* – whether considering something to be absolutely or relatively more or less sustainable than other options confers a moral imperative or not.

The inability of the main measure of economic development and development more generally – GDP – to address environmental concerns is well documented (see, for example, Daly, 1996; Hamilton and Lutz, 1996). GDP was never intended as a measure of well-being nor was it ever intended as a sustainable development indicator (SDI). Principle criticisms of GDP as a measure of progress focus on the limited incorporation in national economic accounts of environmental inputs, such as natural resource usage, and environmental outputs, such as pollution and waste.

In measuring SD, two competing schools and indicators have emerged – one economic and one non-economic. The first, *economic measures*, are based largely upon defining SD as a flow – sustaining (non-declining) future consumption (utility) at current levels and measured through adjusting national economic accounts. This being weak sustainability. The second, *non-economic measures*, define SD as a stock and measured through sustaining the environment (natural capital) itself, and is an example of strong sustainability. The first shows the current outward-orientated liberalisation-led economic growth development model to be sustainable (i.e. it will sustain future consumption) because of its methodology. In contrast, the non-economic clustering shows current outward-orientated liberalisation-led growth to be unsustainable (i.e. it will not sustain the environmental capital) because of its methodology.

Table 5.3 compares and contrasts *economic* and *non-economic measures* of sustainable development. *Economic measures* can be traced to the *weak sustainability* position and SD as sustaining consumption. Such SDIs have been pioneered by the World Bank's Environment Department (see, for example, World Bank, 1995; 1997) and are published annually in the World Bank's *World Development Indicators* and *Little Green Data Book*. The most commonly known are (a) *Adjusted Net National Product;* (b) *Genuine Savings* – also known as *Net Adjusted Savings;* and (c) *Wealth Estimates.*

The first, *Adjusted Net National Product (ANNP)*, is also known as *Approximate Environmentally Adjusted Net National Product (AENP)* or *Green GDP*. This indicator takes the standard national economic income accounts measure of Net National Product (NNP) and adjusts this for estimated values of environmental depletion or degradation. *Genuine Savings* (GS) is somewhat similar but more directly addresses future generations' welfare stock rather than the current stock (as used in

Table 5.3 Comparison of Selected Sustainable Development Indicators

Indicator	*Components and calculation*	*Definition of 'sustainable development'*
Economic measures		
Adjusted Net National Product	Output minus total capital stock depreciation	If resultant value is less than consumption
Genuine Savings	Investment minus total capital stock depreciation	If resultant value is positive
Wealth Estimates	The value of total capital stock	If resultant value is increasing
Non-economic measures		
Ecological Footprint	Biological space needed to support average per capita consumption	If average per capita consumption requires less than 1.6 hectares
Living Planet Index	Trends in number of species	If number of species is non-declining
Economic and non-economic measure		
Resource Flows	Weight per capita of material taken from and returned to the environment	No conclusion on what is 'good' or 'bad'

Source: Sumner (2004).

ANNP/AENP). It is a measure of total investment minus the total depreciation of all capitals. The standard national accounts measure of gross domestic savings is taken and deductions made for the depreciation of natural and non-natural capital. Both ANP and GS deduct an estimate for the depletion of energy reserves, minerals and forest. Values for these are calculated as the prevailing international market price of the commodity minus its average cost of extraction and the result multiplied by volume extracted. After this, a value for carbon dioxide emissions is subtracted at US$20 per metric tonne emitted (from the methodology of Fankhauser, 1995) and an addition is made for spending on education (the rationale being that natural resources have been reinvested in human capital, at least notionally). If NNP minus depreciation of capital stock is less than consumption in any year, development can be said to be 'sustainable'. If genuine savings are positive then development is sustainable – a modification of the Hartwick rule.[22] Finally, *Wealth Estimates* provides a calculation of the total commercial monetary value, at a moment in time, of a country's natural, produced and human capital. If a country's wealth estimate is increasing development is 'sustainable'.[23]

Non-economic Measures have been largely pioneered by NGOs (see for example, WRI, 1997; WWF, 2002). The most commonly known are (a) the *Ecological Footprint* and related measures, and (b) the *Living Planet Index*. Additionally, a measure that mixes economic and non-economic measures is *Resource Flow*.

The *Ecological Footprint* (EF) originated from the work of Rees (1992) and Wackernagel (1994) and is now produced yearly by the NGO World-Wide Fund for Nature (WWF) in the *Living Planet Report*. The *Ecological Footprint* measure is an area-based measure of 'sustainability'. It expresses the total biologically productive space (land and sea) in hectares, necessary to support average per capita national consumption of food, shelter and transport.[24] For example, national consumption of food is taken and the total area per capita necessary to graze animals, grow food and harvest fisheries is added to the energy needed to process and transport food (using data from the United Nations Food and Agriculture Organisation). Under this measure, sustainability is achieved if the average consumption of productive space is less than the 1.6 hectares per person globally available (for greater detail see Rees and Wackernagel, 1994; 1995). The *Living Planet Index* is produced yearly by the WWF and is a measure of biodiversity. It is an aggregate of sub-indices for three ecosystems – forests, freshwater and marine. Each index and the aggregate index is set at 1.0 for 1970. Respectively, these assess trends in 282, 195 and 217 animals for each ecosystem (for greater detail see WWF, 2002). It thus provides a 'thermometer' of the health of the planet in supporting life. Development is sustainable if the number of species is non-declining.

Finally, *Resource Flow* (RF) indicators are a system of accounts that assess resource and environmental inputs and outputs in the economy. It could be argued that this measure is neither strictly an economic nor a non-economic SDI. It makes some use of the national economic income accounts, and is produced by the NGO and think-tank *World Resources Institute* (WRI), based in Washington DC, USA. The analysis seeks to track 'material flow' – the flow of materials from nature, through the economy and back to nature, in a cycle. The physical flow of natural resources is followed through extraction, production, fabrication, use and recycling, and final disposal, accounting for losses on the way. Matthews *et al.* (2000:1) used the metaphor of the economy as a living organism: the industrial economy 'ingests' raw materials, which are then 'metabolised' to produce goods and services, and finally waste is 'excreted'.

Earlier work (WRI, 1997) considered resource inputs – Total Material Required (TMR), so as to include not only the resources taken from the environment (and accounted for in GDP), but also 'hidden flows' or externalities in production. Later, resource outputs were considered with two more measures: Total Domestic Output and Domestic Processed Output.[25] Total Domestic Output (TDO) is the aggregate measure which can be compared to GDP. It represents the total amount of domestically processed output (material outflows from the economy) and material displacement within a country. Domestic Processed Output (DPO) per capita can be seen in parallel with GDP per capita. DPO compromises the total weight (in tonnes) on a per capita basis of materials extracted from the domestic environment and imported from other countries, as well as solid wastes, liquid discharges and gas emissions. 'Gateway flows' are then the share of DPO or TDO exiting the economy in the gateways of water, air and land. By calculating these measures, the environmental depletion and degradation per capita is more evident.

How instructive are these SDIs? They can all be praised for their contribution to greater commitment towards and interest and awareness in SD, for stimulating data collection in the area, and have certainly moved SDIs forward but into something of a dead-end. What do they actually tell us about SD? Unfortunately, only a limited and fragmented amount, because major components of the environment – and what needs to be sustained – are not accounted for: none includes arguably the most common environmental hazard in developing countries which affects an estimated 700 million people – indoor pollution from cooking (World Bank, 1992:50). Pollution values only refer to commercial carbon dioxide emissions by fossil fuel and cement manufacture. Measures are biased in favour on non-renewable resources – although forests are included, there is only limited account of most renewables – for example, depletion of fisheries, water pollutants and soil degradation. In fact, the most important natural capital for sustaining human life, land, is not fully incorporated (with the exception of some inclusion in the EF and RF) even though it amounts to perhaps 80% of the natural capital in developing countries (World Bank, 1997:27).

How useful are the SDIs as signals for policy? Equally as damning as their omissions is the fact that the methodology of both clusters determines what is sustainable or not. The methodology of *economic measures* is likely to lead to the conclusion that the current outward-orientated liberalisation-led economic growth development model is always *sustainable* because of the use of international market prices for the value of environment depleted or degraded.[26] If the market value of an international commodity, such as coal, falls – as it does through world-wide liberalisation and the current world-wide push for export growth – then increasing depletion can become more sustainable. Furthermore, are international market prices satisfactory for natural resources that cannot be replaced? The assumption that natural and non-natural capital are substitutable is questionable. In fact, the market value may differ from that required to support constant utility anyway, because the only value placed on the environment is commercial exploitation. Environmental resources provide functions beyond purely commercial value, which are of importance to life support. Forests, for example, also provide a source of carbon sequestration, watershed protection, and a supply of non-timber products.

In contrast, the methodology of *non-economic measures* is likely to lead to the conclusion that the current outward-orientated liberalisation-led growth development model is always *unsustainable* because outward-orientated liberalisation-led economic growth necessitates a greater resource usage and resource flow per person through an increase in production (this is also likely to have an impact on the species in the ecosystems), unless production makes significant gains in the efficient use of resources which are unlikely in the short term. In fact, according to data in WWF (2002), usage is showing a trend towards becoming less efficient.

Where does this leave debates? None of the measures gives a clear unambiguous message of what is or is not 'sustainable'. This is because they have not overcome their weak conceptual basis and suffer from omissions of what is needed to be sustainable – a full incorporation of natural capital. An important issue is whether a currently sustainable trajectory is as much an artefact of methodology as fact – potentially leading to perverse policy signals.

The central problem is that SD is an unbounded or unlimited concept, unlike (consumption) poverty, which is a relatively more bounded (by physiology) concept related to the minimum daily nutrition intake for a human being. This is not uncontentious though, and neither is the conflict between economic and non-economic poverty measurement (see Chapter 2). The final goal of SD is then completely intangible and boundless, unlike (arguably) consumption poverty, which is that no one lives on less than 2100 calories per day. Furthermore, the current conceptualisation of SD is rather static when, by definition, SD must be dynamic because nature is in a constant state of change.

One way forward then could be to move from this unbounded and static conceptualisation of SD towards a more bounded, dynamic conceptualisation, as has been seen in the evolution of poverty measurement debates. Poverty measurement has moved not only to a bounded concept but also from a static to a dynamic concept in the measurement of the vulnerability to poverty – this recognises that households move in and out of poverty over time rather than regarding poverty as static over time.[27] 'Bounding' in SDIs might be provided, in parallel to the physiology of the 2100 calories poverty line, through *safe minimum standards* (Hanley, 1999:39–42). These would identify what would be the minimum components for each natural capital. However, this is still not a dynamic conceptualisation. Alternatively, a conceptualisation used in poverty analysis – the *poverty elasticity of growth* – might provide some insight and could incorporate Daly's (2002) concept of *un*economic growth – identifying environmentally good and bad growth.

In short, there are two highly imperfect and unsatisfactory (but not necessarily completely, mutually exclusive) definitions of SD – sustaining *economic* factors – sustaining consumption/utility for future generations versus sustaining non-economic factors – sustaining natural capital for future generations. The conceptualisation used in poverty analysis of the poverty elasticity of growth (noted earlier) might provide some insight and could incorporate Daly's uneconomic growth – identifying environmentally good and bad growth. The central concern is the interaction of economic growth and the environment within which it takes place. How might the economy and the environment be conceptually linked? A green Kuznet's curve has been hypothesised based around the thesis that the environment deteriorates at the early stages of development. For example, as income rises carbon dioxide emissions rise – and then improve – as inequality does in Kuznet's income inequality curve (see, for details, Shalizi and Kraus, 2001). In a similar vein, a 'threshold hypothesis' has been posited (Max-Neef, 1995:117). This states that in every society economic growth brings an improvement in the quality of life, but only up to a point. This is the threshold point. Beyond this point the quality of life may decline.

To recap from the earlier discussion, the poverty elasticity of growth (PEG) represents the relationship between (consumption) poverty and economic growth. A high poverty elasticity of growth is more desirable than a lower poverty elasticity of growth, because at any given growth rate poverty will be reduced by a greater amount. The concern should not be with the numerical value of the PEG but with what policies (or initial conditions) increase or reduce the PEG? And what are the commonalties between countries with high and low PEGs? If we reapply this to SD we might consider a *green elasticity of growth*. This would consider the relationship between the environment variables and economic growth. In contrast to the PEG, a higher green elasticity of growth would be less desirable than a lower or negative green elasticity of growth because at any given growth rate an environmental variable would be improving by a greater amount. Additionally, a negative green elasticity of growth would be Daly's (2002) economic growth in contrast to a positive green elasticity of growth that would represent Daly's *un*economic growth. Although the green elasticity of growth goes some way to reconciling the two definitions of SD and the interaction between sustaining consumption (economic growth) and the environment, there are a number of problems with the green elasticity of growth that are evident immediately – many similar to contentious issues with the poverty elasticity of growth. The most important problem concerns the definition of poverty or environment taken as deterministic.

A *green elasticity of growth* has seen some development in the OECD's (2002:1) concept of 'de-coupling', which refers to breaking the link between economic growth automatically leading to worse environmental indicators. 'De-coupling' occurs when the growth rate of an environmentally relevant variable is less than the GDP growth rate. The policy target then is to de-couple each indicator. Within this framework, relative 'de-coupling' occurs when the growth rate of an environmentally relevant variable is positive, but less than the GDP growth. This would be *weak sustainability* or *un*economic growth. Absolute 'de-coupling' occurs when the growth rate of the environmentally relevant variable is zero, or ideally negative.[28] This would be *strong sustainability* or Daly's economic growth.

5. What next?

If we say the objective is reducing poverty/ill-being and increasing well-being what growth-related policies are associated with this objective? First, redistributive and transformative public expenditures to break the inter-generational transmission of poverty. Policy can redistribute the benefits of growth through pro-poor public expenditure. Growth is a major potential source of government revenue to finance public expenditure, which can be designed to be explicitly pro-poor, for example through broad-based expenditure on education and health. This provides an important opportunity for the benefits of growth to be more widely shared, and in a manner which is not likely to have major disincentive effects that would crowd out future growth. On the contrary, increased spending on education, nutrition and health, as well as key items such as infrastructure, is likely to be an important basis for future growth. As part of this, investment in young children and their families, via nutrition, health or education programmes for example, in order to break the widespread inter-generational transmission of poverty, potentially offers very high returns. It remains, though, always a major challenge to make sure that public spending is not captured by the rich.

Second, by increasing the rate of job creation from growth. It is also important that growth is associated with significant job creation to provide opportunities to people to benefit from higher education levels and move out of agriculture. But the record of employment creation with growth has been very weak in many countries. How can policy increase the job creation from growth? Increased levels of private sector investment is one important part of the story, and one that is likely to require substantial financial sector development. There is also potential for job creation through more informal channels by reducing formal entry requirements and rules on informal sector trading, as well as investment in small-scale infrastructure.

Third, broad-based sectoral growth, particularly supporting food crop agriculture. Job creation may not benefit the poorest directly. Therefore, it is highly desirable to have a pattern of growth which is broad-based in terms of its coverage of sectors, regions or population, including the agricultural sector if that is the sector in which the poor are disproportionately represented. Investment in market development, research, infrastructure and value-added processing activities may all be important. Fast agricultural growth may also form a basis for transformative growth with the sectoral composition of growth shifting towards manufacturing and services. Investment in social protection (measures to reduce vulnerability to poverty) can also potentially play a major role by reducing the vulnerability of small farmers and the poor in general.

What can be concluded from the discussion on growth and sustainability? Three points can again be noted. First, although innovative and, to date, useful in focusing debate, and even though imperfect, SDIs have hit a dead-end because of the lack of an SD definition underpinning them. They have no clear conceptual 'launch-pad' from which operationalisation is possible. SDIs have been attempts to make bounded and static an unbounded and dynamic reality. Second, SDIs to-date have been something of a red herring. Not only have SDIs omitted much of what is necessary to SD (natural capital and notably renewables for example), they are also guilty of methodological determinism. Third, in light of the above, what can be done? The transposition of a poverty concept (*the poverty elasticity of growth*) has been proposed and *de-coupling* work by the OECD has a strong resonance with a new concept out-lined above (the *green elasticity of growth*). Although by no means a solution as yet, this would at least bring a more bounded and dynamic conceptualisation to the SD and SDI debates and provide a way forward.

Notes

1   This chapter draws upon and builds on Sumner (2004) and McKay and Sumner (2008). 'Pro-poor growth' emerged as a synthesis of 'growth with redistribution', 'broad-based growth' and 'growth with equity'. 'Pro-poor growth' has been defined in numerous ways, but two groupings can be out-lined by outcomes: those that are based on whether the poor have benefited in an absolute way – the headcount falls or the incomes of the poor rise – and those based on the poor benefiting in a relative sense that implicitly entails reductions in inequality. For further discussion see in Ravallion (2004) or Kakwani and Pernia (2000).

2   This chapter extends the discussion in McKay and Sumner (2008).

3   Lewis, though, had previously noted that growth and distribution were organically connected and their evolution intertwined (Fields, 2001:4).

4   Lewis, however, did not assume a rise in inequality to be inevitable.

5   For greater elaboration and a review of theoretical literature on the Kuznets curve see, in particular, Deutsch and Silber (2004).

6   In the late 1990s, many studies argued that, year-to-year, intra-country inequality does not change a great deal (Deininger and Squire, 1998; Gallup *et al.*, 1999; Li *et al.*, 1998; Ravallion, 2001; Roemer and Gugerty, 1997; Trimmer, 1997). However, over time, for example, 10–20 years, notable increases in the Gini co-efficient have been observed in a number of countries.

7   Economic growth can have an impact on inequality through various channels including modification to the distribution of resources across sectors, relative prices, factor rewards and factor endowments. Deininger and Squire note (1998:279) failure to find the Kuznets curve relationship overall does not mean it does not exist for individual countries. In 4 countries of their 49-country sample the Kuznets hypothesis was supported.

8   Additionally, other studies found redistribution was good for growth (Easterly and Rebelo, 1993; Perotti, 1996).

9   For a detailed review see Knowles (2005).

10   The Deininger and Squire (1996) 'high quality dataset' was built on three criteria. To be included the data had to be from household surveys not national accounts; representative of the whole population not just urban or

rural; and a measurement of income or expenditure that incorporated self-employment, non-wage employment and non-monetary income. This database has since been extended by the United Nations University, World Institute of Development Economics Research (WIDER)/United Nations Development Programme (UNDP) into the *World Income Inequality Database* (WIID). Details and downloadable database at http://www.wider.unu.edu/wiid/wiid.htm

11 One could also note the measure of inequality used: gross inequality (pre-tax) and income inequality measures are more likely to find an association than net inequality (post-tax) and expenditure inequality measures. Different inequality measures give different weights to different segments of the income/expenditure distribution, and sometimes reveal the diversity within the growth–inequality relationship. Finally, well-known issues in econometric methodology include the instrumental variables used for endogeneity – disentangling causality; the direction of causation and the simultaneity bias – the isolation of effects; controlling for country-specific effects and omitted variables.

12 For greater detail see Aghion *et al.* (1999).

13 Empirical evidence is mixed though (see for a range of views Clarke, 1995; Deininger and Squire, 1998; Perotti, 1996).

14 Although the *World Development Report* 2000/1 was clear in dismissing the economic growth arguments for inequality, the outline of the 2006 *World Development Report* (on inequality) argues there is no general relationship between inequality and growth (World Bank, 2005:11).

15 By poverty elasticity of growth we mean the proportionate change in the measure of poverty chosen divided by the proportionate change in mean per capita household income/expenditure. A high elasticity implies growth is 'enough', a low elasticity implies that that inequality matters. For reviews of the growth–poverty relationship see Eastwood and Lipton (2001) or Fields (2001).

16 Some limited empirical work has argued that agricultural growth is the most important sectoral growth for poverty reduction and increases in agriculture productivity the most effective for the reduction of poverty (Bourguignon and Morrisson, 1998; Gallup *et al.*, 1999; Timmer, 1997; Thirtle *et al.*, 2001). Similarly, labour-intensive growth is more poverty reducing because the poor's main asset is labour. Adelman (2000) has argued that the factor intensity of growth determines the distribution of benefits. Natural resource growth and/or capital intensive growth are unequalising because such factors are unequally distributed. Capital intensive growth raises the share of income in the wealthy group because they are the capital owning class.

17 A number of studies have separated the poverty reduction due to the 'growth effect' (the change in average income) and the 'distribution effect' (the shift in the Lorenz curve holding average income constant) using Datt and Ravallion's (1992) methodology. Bourguignon (2003) argued that overall, half of poverty reduction was due to growth effects and half to distribution. White and Anderson (2001) found, in a quarter of 143 growth 'episodes', the distribution effect was stronger than the growth effect. Relatively few studies have focused on country studies (See for example, on India, Ravallion and Datt, 1999 and on China, Ravallion and Chen, 1996).

18   Given that the range of country experience seems to be so wide, interest is moving to the 'outliers' and 'looking beyond averages'. Milanovic (2002) and Agénor (2002) have argued that only above a certain income per capita is growth from 'openness' broad-based. This issue over heterogeneity also raises deeper epistemological questions within development economics. For a general critical discussion on growth regressions see Kenny and Williams (2001); on technical reasons to question growth regressions see Lindauer and Pritchett (2002); on 'data-mining' reasons to question growth regressions see White (2002); on multiple equilibria and achieving the same two outcomes from opposite policies, and on 'going beyond averages' see in particular Ravallion (2001; 2005).

19   For a review of 'technical/data' issues in analysis of the poverty elasticity of growth see, in particular, Bhalla (2002) or Kalwij and Verschoor (2004) or Eastwood and Lipton (2001).

20   However, absolute poverty measures are not totally satisfactory either because the elasticity is very sensitive to clustering around the poverty line; although this can be addressed (see for example, Bhalla, 2002; Foster and Székely, 2002). With relative poverty measures the problem is that, taking the bottom quintile for example, the methodology treats poor people in different countries at very different levels of income as the same (Cord *et al.*, 2003:8).

21   There have been several attempts at composite measures that aimed to challenge the primacy of GDP (incorporating social, economic and environment components) such as the GPI – the *Genuine Progress Indicator* and the ISEW – the *Index of Sustainable Economic Welfare*. For greater detail on these see, for example, Moffatt *et al.* (1996).

22   For greater detail on this point and *Genuine Savings* see Hamilton (2000), Hamilton and Clemens (1998). For greater detail on *ANNP* see Hamilton (1994; 1996).

23   For greater detail see Arundhati *et al.* (1998), Serageldin (1996).

24   Related to the *Ecological Footprint* are the *Net Primary Product Relative to Consumption* (NPPRC) and *Environmental Space* measure. Both relate to carrying capacity of the environment. The NPPRC is concerned with energy demands and energy availability. For any country, the NPPRC shows the maximum population that can be supported from net primary production at current consumption, whereas *Environmental Space* is an indicator of whether a country is consuming its 'fair share' of global resources (for greater detail see Moffatt *et al.*, 1996).

25   Other measures used are Domestic Hidden Flows (DHF) and Net Additions to Stocks (NAS). DHF are the total weight in tonnes of materials moved or mobilised in the domestic environment over the course of producing commodities for the economy which do not themselves enter the economy but are in some way disturbed. NAS are the weight (in tonnes) of new construction materials used in buildings and other infrastructure material, or incorporated into new durable goods, added to a county's total physical stocks. For greater detail see Matthews *et al.* (2000).

26   The UN (1993) guidelines on green accounting argue the value of the environment lost should be the replacement cost. Natural resources are valued at international prices (US$) minus average local cost of extraction.

Prices should be at the marginal cost of extraction and not the average cost, but this is generally not available. It is also contentious to assume that international prices are the same as local prices and that the purchasing power parity conversion and discount rate for future values are not highly problematic – given a constant discount rate, the level of consumption must eventually fall over time. For greater discussion see Dasgupta (1995).

27 See, for more detail, Kamanou and Murdoch (2002); Pritchett *et al.* (2000).

28 One issue is – of course – which green indicators to use. The OECD (2002) has its own list of *Core Environmental Indicators*. They relate to five 'policy arenas' – climate change, air pollution, water quality, waste management and natural resources usage. There are ten measures in total. The UNCSD (2001) has a set of 134 SDIs. The sub-set of environmental indicators covers five themes: (1) atmosphere, (2) land, (3) oceans, seas and coasts, (4) fresh water and (5) biodiversity.

References

Adams, R. (2003) Economic Growth, Inequality and Poverty: Findings from a new data set. World Bank Working Paper Number 2972. Washington, DC: World Bank.

Adelman, I. and Morris, C. (1973) *Economic Growth and Social Equity in Developing Countries*. Stanford, CA: Stanford University Press.

Adelman, I. (2000) Fifty Years of Economic Development: What Have We Learnt? Paper presented at the Annual Bank Conference on Development Economics-Europe, Paris, 26–28 June.

Agénor, P. (2002) Does Globalisation Hurt the Poor? Mimeograph. Washington, DC: World Bank.

Aghion, P., Caroli, E. and Garcia-Peñalosa, C. (1999) 'Inequality and Economic Growth: The Perspective of the New Growth Theories', *Journal of Economic Literature*, 37.

Ahluwalia, M. (1976) 'Inequality, Poverty and Development', *Journal of Development Economics*, 3:307–42.

Ahluwalia, M., Carter, N. and Chenery, H. (1979) 'Growth and Poverty in Developing Countries', *Journal of Development Economics*, 6:299–341.

Alesina, A. and Rodrik, D. (1994) 'Distributive Policies and Economic Growth', *Quarterly Journal of Economics*, 109:465–90.

Alesina, A. and Perotti, R. (1996) 'Income Distribution, Political Instability and Investment', *European Economic Review*, 40:1203–28.

Amann, E., Aslanidis, N., Nixson, F. and Walters, B. (2002) Economic Growth and Poverty Alleviation: A Reconsideration of Dollar and Kraay. Paper prepared for the Annual Conference of the Development Studies Association, University of Greenwich, London, 9 November.

Anand, S. and Kanbur, R. (1993a) 'Inequality and Development: A Critique', *Journal of Development Economics*, 41:19–43.

Anand, S. and Kanbur, R. (1993b) 'The Kuznets Process and the Inequality-Development Relationship', *Journal of Development Economics*, 40:25–52.

Arundhati, K., Hamilton, K., Dixon, J. and Clemens, M. (1998) Estimating National Wealth: Methodology and Results. World Bank Environment Department Paper No. 75, Environment Economics Series. January, Washington DC: World Bank.

Banerjee, A. and Duflo, E. (2003) 'Inequality and Growth: What Can the Data Say?', *Journal of Economic Growth*, 8(3):67–299.

Barro, R. and Lee, J. (1997) *Determinants of Schooling Quality: A Cross Country Empirical Study*. Cambridge, MA: Massachusetts Institute of Technology (MIT) Press.

Barro, R. and Sala-I-Martin, X. (1995) *Economic Growth*. New York: McGraw-Hill.

Barro, R. (2000) 'Inequality and Growth in a Panel of Countries', *Journal of Economic Growth*, 5:5–32.

Beckerman, W. (1994) 'Sustainable Development: Is it a Useful Concept?', *Environmental Values*, 3:191–209.

Beckerman, W. (1995) 'How Would You Like Your 'Sustainability', Sir? Weak or Strong? A Reply to My Critics', *Environmental Values*, 4:169–79.

Besley, T. and Cord, L. (eds) (2006) *Delivering on the Promise of Pro-poor Growth: Insights and Lessons from Country Experiences*. Basingstoke: Palgrave Macmillan.

Bhalla, S. (2002) *Imagine There's No Country: Poverty, Inequality, and Growth in the Era of Globalisation*. Washington, DC: Institute for International Economics.

Bhalla, S. (2003) Imagine There's No Country: Poverty, Inequality, and Growth in the Era of Globalisation. Washington, DC: Institute for International Economics.

Birdsall, N. and Londõno, J. (1997) 'Asset Inequality Matters: An Assessment of the World Bank's Approach to Poverty Reduction', *American Economic Review*, 87(2):32–7.

Birdsall, N., Ross, D. and Sabot, R. (1995) 'Inequality and Growth Reconsidered: Lessons from East Asia', *World Bank Economic Review*, 9:477–508.

Bourguignon, F. and Morrisson, C. (1998) 'Inequality and Development: The Role of Dualism', *Journal of Development Economics*, 57:233–57.

Bourguignon, F. (2003) The Growth Elasticity of Poverty Reduction: Explaining Heterogeneity Across Countries and Time Periods, in Eicher, T., Turnovsky, S. (eds) *Inequality and Growth: Theory and Policy Implications*. Cambridge, MA: Massachusetts Institute of Technology (MIT) Press.

Bruno, M., Ravallion, M. and Squire, L. (1998) Equity and Growth in Developing Countries: Old and New Perspectives on the Policy Issues, in Tanzi, V. and Chu, K. (eds) *Income Distribution and High Quality Growth*. Cambridge, MA: MIT Press.

Castello, A. and Domenech, R. (2000) 'Human Capital Inequality and Economic Growth: Some New Evidence', *Economic Journal*, 112 (478):187–200.

Chenery, H., Ahluwalia, C., Bell, J., Duloy, J. and Jolly, R. (1974) *Redistribution with Growth*. Oxford: Oxford University Press for the World Bank.

Clarke, G. (1995) 'More Evidence on Income Distribution and Growth', *Journal of Development Economics*, 47(2):403–27.

Collier, P. (2007) *The Bottom Billion*. Oxford: Oxford University Press.

Common, M. (1996) 'Beckerman and His Critics on Strong and Weak Sustainability: Confusing Concepts and Conditions', *Environmental Values*, 5:83–8.

Cord, L., Lopez, H. and Page, J. (2003) 'When I Use the Word...' Pro-poor Growth and Poverty Reduction. Mimeograph. Washington, DC: World Bank.

Daly, H. (1995) 'On Wilfred Beckerman's Critique of Sustainable Development', *Environmental Values*, 4:49–55.

Daly, H. (1996) *Beyond Growth*. Boston MA: Beacon Press.

Daly, H. (2002) *Sustainable Development: Definitions, Principles and Policies*. Invited address, April 30, Washington DC: World Bank.

Dasgupta, P. (1995) Optimal Development and the Idea of Net National Product, in Goldin, I. and Winters, A. (eds) *The Economics of Sustainable Development*. Cambridge: Cambridge University Press.

Datt, G. and Ravallion, M. (1992) 'Growth and Redistribution Components of Changes in Poverty Measures: A Decomposition with Applications to Brazil and India in the 1980s', *Journal of Development Economics*, 38:275–95.

Deininger, K. and Squire, L. (1996) 'Measuring Inequality: A New Data Base', *World Bank Economic Review*, 10(3):565–91.

Deininger, K. and Squire, L. (1998) 'New Ways of Looking at Old Issues: Inequality and Growth', *Journal of Development Economics*, 57(2):259–87.

Deutsch, J. and Silber, J. (2004) 'Measuring the Impact of Various Income Sources on the Link between Inequality and Development', *Review of Development Economics*, 8(1):110–27.

Dollar, D. and Kraay, A. (2002) 'Growth is Good for the Poor', *Journal of Economic Growth*, 7:195–225.

Dower, N. (1994) 'Worth Sustaining?', *Environmental Values*, 3:159–60.

Easterly, W. and Rebelo, S. (1993) 'Fiscal Policy and Economic Growth: An Empirical Investigation', *Journal of Monetary Economics*, 32(3): 417–58.

Easterly, W. (1999) Life during Growth. Mimeograph. Washington, DC: World Bank.

Easterly, E. (2001) The Effect of IMF and World Bank Programs on Poverty. Mimeograph. Washington DC: World Bank.

Easterly, W. (2002) Inequality Does Cause Underdevelopment. Centre for Global Development Working Paper Number 1. Washington, DC: Centre for Global Development.

Eastwood, R. and Lipton, M. (2001) Pro-Poor Growth and Pro-Poor Growth Poverty Reduction. Paper presented at 'Asia and Pacific Forum on Poverty: Reforming Policies and Institutions for Poverty Reduction', Manila: Asian Development Bank.

El Serafy, S. (1996) 'In Defence of Weak Sustainability: A Response to Beckerman', *Environmental Values*, 5:75–81.

Epaulard, A. (2003) Macroeconomic Performance and Poverty Reduction. International Monetary Fund (IMF) Working Paper. Number 72. Washington, DC: IMF.

Fankhauser, S. (1995) *Valuing Climate Change: The Economics of the Greenhouse*. London: Earthscan.

Fields, G. (2001) *Distribution and Development: A New Look at the Developing World*. Cambridge, MA: Massachusetts Institute of Technology (MIT) Press.

Forbes, K. (2000) 'A Reassessment of the Relationship Between Inequality and Growth', *American Economic Review*, 40(4):869–87.

Foster, J. and Székely, M. (2002) Is Economic Growth Good for the Poor? Tracking Low Incomes using General Means. Paper presented at United Nations University World Institute for Development Economics Research (UNU/WIDER) conference, 'Growth and poverty', Helsinki, May 25–26.

Gallup, J., Radelet, S. and Warner, A. (1999) Economic Growth and the Income of the Poor. Consulting Assistance on Economic Reform II Discussion paper number 36. Harvard, MA: Harvard Institute of International Development.

Garuda, G. (2000) 'The Distributional Effects of IMF Programmes: A Cross-country Analysis', *World Development*, 28(6):1031–51.

Grimm, M., Klasen, S. and McKay, A. (2007) *Determinants of Pro-Poor Growth: Analytical Issues and Findings from Country Cases*. Basingstoke: Palgrave Macmillan.

Gross, M., Klasen, S. and Harttgen, K. (2005) Measuring Pro-Poor Growth with Non-Income Indicators. Ibero America Institute for Econ. Research (IAI) Discussion Paper, Number No. 132. Ibero-America Institute for Economic Research.

Gundlach, E., de Pablo, J. and Weisert, N. (2001) Education is Good for the Poor. Paper presented at World Institute for Development Economics Research (WIDER) conference on economic growth and poverty reduction, WIDER, Helsinki, May 25–26.

Haddad, L., Rowsell, H., Gee, C., Lindstrom, J. and Bloom, M. (2006) Mapping Development Research among UK Organizations and Their Partners. Report To The ESRC. Sussex: IDS.

Hamilton, K. and Clemens, M. (1998) *Genuine Savings in Developing Countries*. Mimeo, August. Washington DC: World Bank.

Hamilton, K. and Lutz, E. (1996) Green National Accounts: Policy Uses and Empirical Experience. World Bank Environment Department Paper, Number 39, Environment Economics Series, July. Washington DC: World Bank.

Hamilton, K. (1994) Green Adjustments to GDP. *Resources Policy*, 20(3):155–68.

Hamilton, K. (1996) Pollution and Pollution Abatement in the National Accounts. *Review of Income and Wealth*, 42(1):13–33.

Hamilton, K. (2000) Genuine Savings as a Sustainability Indicator. World Bank Environment Department Paper No. 77, Environment Economics Series, October. Washington DC: World Bank.

Hanley, N. (1999) *Macroeconomic Measures of 'Sustainability'*, Mimeo, Edinburgh: University of Edinburgh.

Hanmer, L. and Naschold, F. (2001) 'Attaining the International Development Targets will Growth be Enough?', *Development Policy Review*, 18:11–36.

Hartwick, J. (1977) 'Intergenerational Equity and the Investing of Rents of Exhaustible Resources', *American Economic Review*, 67(5):972–4.

Hicks, J. (1939) *Value and Capital*. Oxford: Clarendon Press.

Kakwani, N. and Pernia, E. (2000) 'What is Pro-Poor Growth?', *Asian Development Review*, 19(1):1–16.

Kalwij, A. and Verschoor, A. (2004) How Good is Growth for the Poor? The Role of Initial Income Distribution in Regional Diversity in Poverty Trends. Paper prepared for United Nations University World Institute of Development Economics Research (UNU/WIDER) Conference, 'Sharing global prosperity', Helsinki, September 6–7.

Kalwij, A. and Verschoor, A. (2007) 'Not by Growth Alone: The Role of the Distribution of Income in Regional Diversity in Poverty Reduction', *European Economic Review*, 51(4):805–29.

Kamanou, G. and Murdoch, J. (2002) Measuring Vulnerability to Poverty. World Institute for Development Economics Research (WIDER) Discussion paper 2002/58. Helsinki: WIDER.

Kanbur, R. and Squire, L. (2001) The Evolution of Thinking About Poverty: Exploring the Contradictions, in Meier, G. and Stiglitz, J. (eds) *Frontiers of Development Economics*. Oxford: Oxford University Press.

Kanbur, R. (2002) Trade and Growth: The Last Redoubt, Mimeograph. University of Colombia.

Kanbur, R. (2004) Growth, Inequality and Poverty: Some Hard Questions. Mimeograph. Ithaca, NY: Cornell University.

Kenny, C. and Williams, D. (2001) 'What Do We Know about Economic Growth? Or, why don't we know very much?', *World Development*, 29(1):1–22.

Klasen, S. (1999) Does Gender Inequality Reduce Growth and Development? World Bank Policy Research Working Paper Number 7. Washington, DC: World Bank.

Knowles, S., Lorgelly, P. and Owen, P. (2002) Are Educational Gender Gaps a Break on Economic Development: Some Cross-country Empirical Evidence. *Oxford Economic Papers*, 54:118–49.

Knowles, S. (2005) 'Inequality and Economic Growth: The Empirical Relationship Reconsidered in Light of Comparable Data', *Journal of Development Studies*, 41(1):135–59.

Kraay, A. (2004) When is Growth Pro-Poor? Cross-Country Evidence. World Bank Working Paper Number 3225. Washington, DC: World Bank.

Kuznets, S. (1955) 'Economic Growth and Income Inequality', *American Economic Review*, 45(1):1–28.

Kuznets, S. (1963) 'Quantitative Aspects of the Economic Growth of Nations: VIII, Distribution and Income by Size', *Economic DEvelopment and Cultural Change*, 11(2):1–80.

Lewis, A. (1955) *The Theory of Economic Growth*. Homewood IL: Irwin.

Li, H., Squire, L. and Zou, H. (1998) 'Explaining International and Intertemporal Variations in Income Inequality', *Economic Journal*, 108:26–43.

Lindauer, D. and Pritchett, L. (2002) 'What's the Big Idea? The Third Generation of Policies for Economic Growth', *Economíca*, 3(1):1–39.

List, J. and Gallet, C. (1999) 'The Kuznets Curve: What Happens after the Inverted-U?', *Review of Development Economics*, 3:200–6.

Lopez, J. (2005) Pro-Poor Growth: A Review of What We Know (and What We Don't) Mimeograph. Washington, DC: World Bank.

Matthews, E., Amann, C., Bringezu, S., Huttler, W., Kleijn, R., Moriguchi, Y., Ottke, C., Rodenburg, E., Rogich, D., Schandl, H., Schutz, H., Van der Voet, E. and Weisz, H. (2000) *The Weight of Nations: Material Outflows from Industrial Economies*. Washington DC: World Resources Institute.

Max-Neef, M. (1995) 'Economic Growth and Quality of Life: A Threshold Hypothesis', *Ecological Economics*, 15:115–18.

Maxwell, S. (2005) The Washington Consensus is Dead! Long Live the Meta-Narrative. Overseas Development Institute Working Paper. London: ODI.

McGillivray, M. (2003) Capturing Non-Economic Dimensions of Well-being. Paper prepared for WIDER Conference, 'Inequality, Poverty and Human Well-being', Helsinki, May 30–31.

McGillivray, M. (2003) 'Aid Effectiveness and Selectivity: Integrating Multiple Objectives in Aid Allocations', *DAC Journal*, 4(3):23–36.

McKay, A. and Sumner, A. (2008) Economic Growth, Poverty and Reduction and Inequality: Doess Pro-Poor Growth Matter. IDS In focus Issue, 3.

Milanovic, B. (2002) Can We Discern The Effect of Globalisation on Income Distribution? World Bank Policy Research Working Paper. Washington, DC: World Bank.

Moffatt, I., Hanley, N., Wilson, M. and Faichney, R. (1996) 'A Time Series Analysis of Indicators of Sustainability for Scotland', 1980–1993', *Ecological Economics*, 28:55–73.

Mosley, P., Hudson, J. and Verschoor, A. (2004) 'Aid, Poverty Reduction and the New Conditionality', *Economic Journal*, 114:214–43.

Mosley, P. (2004) Severe Poverty and Growth: A Macro-Micro Analysis. Chronic Poverty Research Centre (CPRC) Working Paper. Number 51. Manchester, UK: CPRC.

Neumayer, E. (2003) Sustainability and Well-being Indicators. Paper presented at United Nations University/WIDER Project meeting on 'Social development indicators'. Helsinki. 29 May.

Nye, H., Reddy, S., Watkins, K., Dollar and Kraay (2002) 'Trade, Growth and Poverty: A Critique', Mimeograph, Columbia University.

OECD (Organisation of Economic Co-operation and Development) (2001) Development Assistance Committee Poverty Guidelines. Paris: OECD.

OECD (Organisation for Economic Co-operation and Development) (2002) *Indicators to Measure De-coupling of Environmental Pressure from Economic Growth*. Paris: OECD.

Oxfam (2002) Rigged Rules and Double Standards: Trade, Globalisation and The Fight Against Poverty. Oxford: Oxfam Publishing.

Paukert, F. (1973) 'Income Distribution at Different Levels of Development', *International Labour Review*, 108:97–125.

Pearce, D., Markandya, A. and Barbier, E. (1989) *Blueprint for a Green Economy*. London: Earthscan.

Perotti, R. (1996) 'Growth, Income Distribution and Democracy: What the Data say', *Journal of Economic Growth*, 1(2):149–87.

Pritchett, L. and Summers, L. (1995) 'Wealthier is Healthier', *Journal of Human Resources*, 31(4):841–68.

Pritchett, L., Surayadi, S. and Sumarto, S. (2000) Quantifying Vulnerability to Poverty: A Proposed Measure, with Application to Indonesia. Social Monitoring and Early Response Unit (SMERU) Working Paper. Jakarta: Social Monitoring and Early Response Unit.

Przeworski, A. and Vreeland, J. (2000) 'The Effect of IMF Programs on Economic Growth', *Journal of Development Economics*, (62)2:385–421.

Ravallion, M. and Chen, S. (1996) 'Data in Transition: Assessing Rural Living', *China Economic Review*, 7:23–56.

Ravallion, M. and Chen, S. (1997) 'What Can New Survey Data Tell Us about Recent Changes in Distribution and Poverty', *World Bank Economic Review*, 11(2):357–82.

Ravallion, M. and Datt, G. (1999) When is Growth Pro-Poor? Evidence from the Diverse Experiences of India's States. World Bank Working Paper 2263. Washington, DC: World Bank.

Ravallion, M. (1995) Growth and poverty: evidence for developing countries in the 1980s. *Economic Letters*, 48:411–17.

Ravallion, M. (1997) 'Can High-Inequality Developing Countries Escape Absolute Poverty?', *Economic Letters*, 56:51–7.

Ravallion, M. (1998) 'Does Aggregation Hide the Harmful Effects of Inequality on Growth?', *Economics Letters*, 61:73–7.

Ravallion, M. (2001) 'Growth, Inequality and Poverty: Looking Behind the Averages', *World Development*, 29(11):1803–15.

Ravallion, M. (2004) Measuring Pro-Poor Growth: A Primer. World Bank Working Paper 3242. Washington, DC: World Bank.

Ravallion, M. (2005) Looking Beyond Averages in The Trade And Poverty Debate, World Bank Working Paper Number 3461. Washington, DC: World Bank.

Rees, W. and Wackernagel, M. (1994) Ecological Footprints and Appropriate Carrying Capacity: Measuring the Natural Capital Requirements of the Human Economy, in Jansson, A.M., Hammer, C. and Folke, C., Costanza, R. (eds) *Investing in Natural Capital: The Ecological Economics Approach to Sustainability*, pp. 362–90. Washington DC: Island Press.

Rees, W. and Wackernagel, M. (1995) *Our Ecological Footprint: Reducing Human Impact on the Earth*. Philadelphia PA: New Society Publishers.

Rees, W. (1992) 'Ecological Footprints and Appropriate Carrying Capacity: What Urban Economics Leaves Out', *Environment and Urbanisation*, 4(2): 121–30.

Rehme, G. (2001) Redistribution of Personal Income, Education and Economic Performance Across Countries. Mimeograph. Darmsdadt, Germany: Technische Universitat Darmsdadt.

Roemer, M. and Gugerty, M. (1997) Does Economic Growth Reduce Poverty? Consulting Assistance on Economic Reform II Discussion Paper Number 4. Harvard: Harvard Institute of International Development.

Sen, A. (1999) Development as Freedom. New York and London: Oxford University Press.

Serageldin, I. (1996) Sustainability and the Wealth of Nations: First Steps in an Ongoing Journey. World Bank Environmentally Sustainable Development Studies and Monograph Series No. 5. Washington DC: World Bank.

Shalizi, Z. and Kraus, C. (2001) *Globalisation, Openness and the Environment*. Washington DC: World Bank.

Solow, R. (1974) 'Intergenerational Equity and Exhaustible Resources', *Review of Economic Studies*, 29–46.

Solow, R. (1986) 'On the Intertemporal Allocation of Natural Resources', *Scandinavian Journal of Economics*, 8:141–9.

Son, H. and Kakwani, N. (2003) Poverty reduction: Do Initial Conditions Matter? Mimeograph. Washington, DC: World Bank.

Stewart, F. (2000) Income Distribution and Development. Queen Elizabeth House (QEH) Working Paper. Oxford University, Oxford: QEH.

Sumner, A. (2004) 'Measuring Sustainable Development in the Era of Globalisation – Can it be Done and What Way Ahead?', *World Review of Science, Technology and Sustainable Development*, 1(2):116–28.

Thirtle, C., Irz, I., Lin, L., McKenzie-Hill, V. and Wiggins, S. (2001) The Relationship between Changes in Agricultural Productivity and the Incidence of Poverty in Developing Countries. Department for International Development Report No.7946. London: Department for International Development.

Timmer, P. (1997) How Well did the Poor Connect to the Growth Process? Consulting Assistance on Economic Reform II Discussion paper Number 17. Harvard: Harvard Institute of International Development.

UN (United Nations) (1993) *Handbook of National Accounting: Integrated Environmental and Economic Accounting*. New York: United Nations Statistical Division.

UNCSD (United Nations Commission on Sustainable Development) (2001) *Indicators of Sustainable Development: Framework and Methodologies*. Geneva: United Nations Commission on Sustainable Development.

UNDP (United Nations Development Programme) (2003) Human Development Report. Oxford: Oxford University Press.

UNMP (United Nations Millennium Project) (2005) Investing in Development: A Practical Plan to Achieve the Millennium Development Goals. London: Earthscan.

Wackernagel, M. (1994) *The Ecological Footprint and Appropriate Carrying Capacity: A Tool for Planning Towards Sustainability*. Unpublished Ph.D. Thesis, University of British Columbia School of Community and Regional Planning (UBS SCARP). Vancouver: UBC SCARP.

WCED (World Commission on the Environment and Development) (1987) *Our Common Future*. Oxford: Oxford University Press.

Weisbrot, M., Baker, D., Naiman, R. and Neta, G. (2001) 'Growth May be Good for the Poor – But are the IMF and World Bank Policies Good for Growth?' Center for Economic Policy and Research Working Paper.

White, H. (2002) 'Combining Quantitative and Qualitative Approaches in Poverty Analysis', *World Development*, 30(3):511–22.

White, H. and Anderson, E. (2001) 'Growth versus Distribution: Does the Pattern of Growth Matter?', *Development Policy Review*, 19(3):267–89.

World Bank (1990) *World Bank Development Report*. Washington DC: World Bank.

World Bank (1992) *World Development Report*. Washington DC: World Bank.

World Bank (1995) *Monitoring Environmental Progress*. Washington DC: World Bank.

World Bank (1997) Expanding the Measure of Wealth: Indicators of Environmentally Sustainable Development. Environmentally Sustainable Development Studies and Monographs Series No. 17. Washington DC: World Bank.

World Bank (2000) *World Development Report 2000/1*. Washington DC: World Bank.

World Bank (2002b) *The Millennium Development Goals and the Environment*. World Bank: Washington DC.

World Bank (2005) *World Development Report 2006*. Outline (draft). World Bank: Washington DC. Downloaded from www.worldbank.org on 1 February 2005.

WRI (World Resources Institute) (1997) *Resource Flows*. Washington DC: World Resources Institute.

WWF (World-Wide Fund for Nature) (2002) *Living Report*. Geneva: World-Wide Fund for Nature.

6
Doing Globalisation

These are conclusions which are based on evidence, a careful look at the evidence, and particularly the evidence of the last 20 years. It's very important to emphasize this based on evidence because all too much of the discussion of globalization takes place in a zone which is largely free of evidence. And what we've tried to do here is to set out carefully the analysis of what the evidence really tells us (Stern, 2001:1).

1. Introduction

Globalisation – via both trade and private investment (i.e. market or private-capital/trade-led globalisation) *and* via public investment in the form of aid (i.e. non-market or public capital-led globalisation) – has re-emerged as a major area of contention. Amongst scholars, international trade, investment and aid have produced perhaps tens of thousands of journal articles, books and conference papers. Furthermore, it has triggered large-scale demonstrations, not only at international meetings in the North (Seattle, Prague and Genoa) but also, a surprising number of smaller-scale protests, dubbed 'IMF-riots' in the South (see WDM, 2003). Globalisation has numerous interactions with the EPICs perhaps most notably with market EPICs (the rise of China *et al.*, as both donors and private investors) but also with demography and migration (via remittances and urbanisation for example), and also with technology EPICs (the expansion of information and communication technologies in particular).

This chapter is structured as follows. Section 2 provides a brief history of globalisation debates in terms of market or private-capital/trade-led globalisation and non-market or public capital-led (i.e. aid) globalisation.

Section 3 addresses globalisation, poverty reduction and the MDGs. Section 4 looks to the future. Section 5 concludes.

2.   A brief history of globalisation debates

2a.   Private capital/trade-led globalisation

In economic form at least, there is some consensus on defining market or private-capital/trade-led globalisation from the positions of both 'proponents' and 'sceptics'. It is largely accepted that contemporary globalisation can be defined as global economic integration and 'open' economies in terms of current and capital accounts (see, from a 'proponent' view, World Bank, 2002:23 and, from a 'sceptic' perspective, George, 2001:11; Khor, 2001:7). The current account is international trade. The capital account is private capital flows (i.e. foreign investments) and public capital flows (i.e. aid).

Although the basic definition of economic globalisation is conceptually clear and largely accepted, there has been a divergence in the operationalisation and quantification of the point of departure. Two perspectives are evident in the conceptualisation (each with a different quantification): globalisation as economic liberalisation versus globalisation as economic internationalism. The former (economic liberalisation) is a process of 'opening' and a policy input or series of policy changes enacted by governments. However, the latter (economic internationalism) is a policy output, an end outcome of 'openness', over which governments have no direct control. The former leads inevitably to the latter, but the latter may also be achieved through diametrically opposed policy processes. In short, globalisation is possible with or without liberalisation and a country can be experiencing globalisation as liberalisation or globalisation as internationalism or both.

Economic development in East Asia is a useful illustration of the demarcation between globalisation as liberalisation and globalisation as internationalism. Most, if not all, East Asian regimes in trade, finance and production were relatively restrictive until the mid-1980s; however, international trade and investment composed large percentages of GDP (for details see, for example, Amsden, 1989; Bhattacharya and Pangestu, 1993; Chang, 1994; Salleh *et al.*, 1993; Sakong, 1993). The period to the mid-1980s could be labelled globalisation as internationalism rather than globalisation as liberalisation. Trade was global but not liberal, finance was global but financial repression was evident, and production was globalised though foreign direct investment but many sectors had restricted access (Wade, 1990; World Bank, 1993). In contrast, the time period from the late 1980s to the mid-1990s saw entry to the General Agreement on Trade and Tariffs (GATT) of many East Asian countries, the development of the Association of South-East Asian Nations (ASEAN) and sweeping liberalisation programmes (for details see, for example, Hill, 1996; Johnstone *et al.*, 1997; Jomo, 1998). The latter period could be labelled globalisation as liberalisation *and* globalisation as internationalism (demonstrating the concepts in practice are not mutually exclusive): trade was global and liberal, as were finance and, to a certain degree, investment. Table 6.1 outlines the characteristics of globalisation as liberalisation (East Asia after the mid-1980s). The table also shows the characteristics of globalisation as internationalism (East Asia prior to the mid-1980s). The former, globalisation as liberalisation, is a policy input, a process of 'opening'. The latter, globalisation as internationalism, is a policy output, an outcome of 'openness'.

Globalisation as liberalisation is measured by reductions in trade barriers or capital controls, whereas globalisation as internationalism is measured by trade or capital volumes. In general, trade and capital volumes are good measures of internationalism because they can assess the percentage of economy that is internationally orientated, but are bad measures of liberalisation because they can increase under liberal and non-liberal policies. Trade barriers and capital controls are good measures of liberalisation because they are based on quantifying changes

Table 6.1   Conceptualisation and Quantification of Globalisation: Liberalisation and Internationalism

	Globalisation as liberalisation	*Globalisation as internationalism*
Conceptualisation of globalisation		
Policy input or output?	Input	Output
Policy process or outcome?	Process of 'opening'	Outcome of 'openness'
Quantification of globalisation		
Integration of current account	Reduction in trade barriers	Increase in trade volumes
Integration of capital account	Reduction in capital controls	Increase in capital volumes

in liberal policies, but bad measures of internationalism because they provide no information on the level of international integration.

In detail, the actual quantification is not a straightforward matter by any means. In the case of trade, the most common measures are trade volumes (the share of trade in GDP) and average trade tariffs and/or non-tariff barriers. The former is a measure of internationalism, 'openness' or a policy outcome and the second a measure of liberalisation, a policy input, 'opening' or process. Trade volumes are more popular because the data is readily available for a longer time period and arguably less contentious to quantify and aggregate than tariff and non-tariff measures.[1] Other measures of the globalisation of trade fall into the two camps: internationalism or 'openness' and liberalisation or 'opening' measures. Liberalisation measures include the *Sachs-Warner index* which is an index of 0 (open) or 1 (closed) based tariffs, non-tariff barriers, state export monopolies, black market premiums and whether the country is a socialist country; and the IMF's *trade restriction index* composed of average tariffs, non-tariff coverage and export taxes and measures of price distortion – the deviation of price levels from values expected by purchasing power parity adjusted for income levels (this assumes trade restrictions raise prices). Internationalism measures include the *trade distortion index* and *related structure-adjusted trade intensity measure*. These are assessments of the deviation of trade volumes from the expected value based on theory (the former) and structural factors (the latter) and the *Black Market Premium* which measures the deviation of the exchange rate from its market level (as measured by [black market rate/official rate] – 1).

In terms of quantifying globalisation of the capital account, there are again measures of liberalisation and internationalism. Internationalism or 'openness' is more popular in the literature because, as with trade volumes, capital volumes data is readily available and perceived as less problematic than policy measures, although this assertion can be questioned.[2] Liberalisation or 'opening' measures are, in general, derived from the IMF's Annual Report on Exchange Arrangements and Exchange Restrictions (AREAER). This includes data on the number of, and intensity of, official restrictions on capital transactions reported to the IMF by national authorities, from which indicators of on/off restrictions or their intensity can be calculated. 'Openness' measures include capital flows/ gross capital formation or capital stock/GDP, the broad money aggregate, M2/GDP (strictly speaking a measure of financial development); stock market capitalisation as a percentage of GDP or the estimated gross stock of foreign liabilities as a share of GDP.[3]

Different studies have used different measures covering both internationalism and liberalisation leading to different results (see below).

2b. Public capital-led globalisation

If private capital/trade-led globalisation is ambiguous, what do we know about a more public-capital-led globalisation? i.e. aid? The various modalities of aid have made for a 'messy' debate. The debates on aid and growth can be traced back to the Marshall Plan in 1947. The optimism of replicating the success of the Marshall Plan in developing countries was premised on the following conceptualisation of the aid–growth relation. Developing countries were poor because of their poor investment capacities. Poor investment capacity was a result of low domestic savings and insufficient foreign exchange. Foreign aid could plug this gap by augmenting domestic savings and/or foreign exchange reserves. This would boost investment, which in turn would spur growth. Over a period the need for aid would cease to exist as the growth would become self-sustaining (McGillivray *et al.*, 2006).

The simplistic linear thinking noted above became the foundation for much of the research on aid in developing countries in the 1950s. The two-gap Harrod-Domar growth model dominated. The underlying assumption was more aid would imply more savings and that within the Harrod-Domar framework implied more growth. The thinking complemented the ideas put forward by development theorists at that time such as Lewis (1954) and Nurkse (1953). The role of economic growth was considered paramount for development. The empirical studies conducted over the next two decades yielded very different outcomes (see Table 6.4) The investigations deployed both the savings gap and the foreign exchange gap (Chenery and Bruno, 1962; Chenery and Strout, 1966). Later, Bacha (1990) and Taylor (1990) added the third gap by taking into account the limited revenue-raising capacity of developing country governments. The early research of the 1960s assumed an increase of one dollar in savings and investment with every dollar of aid. The models have been contested for clustering all types of foreign capital flows and foreign aid as well as omitting some variables. The assumption that foreign aid leads to a one-to-one increase in savings was challenged by Griffin (1970) and Griffin and Enos (1970). Griffin amongst others (Rahman, 1968; Weisskopf, 1972) empirically showed a negative association between capital flows and domestic savings using cross-country data. The first model to disaggregate foreign capital flows into aid, investment and other flows was put forward by Papanek (1973). In doing so, he found a strong positive association between aid flows and growth rates in the recipient countries. Mosley (1987) using sub-periods and samples of developing countries in fact found no statistically significant relationship between aid and growth. Boone's (1996) investigation of aid effectiveness provided a new dimension of political regimes into the aid debate. Boone studied the data for 91 countries for the period 1971–1990. He broadened the study by including consumption, measures of well-being and whether aid effectiveness was conditional on political regimes. The results showed an increase in the levels of government consumption. In addition, Boone found significantly lower infant mortality in liberal political regimes than in non-democratic governments.

The research on the links between aid and economic growth up to the mid-1990s became a subject of further scrutiny by a number of researchers – Cassen *et al.* (1994) and White (1992) amongst others. Both studies point to the inconclusive evidence on the positive or the negative relationship between aid and savings and aid and growth. The results were shown to be influenced by the country groupings and the selection of time periods. The macro-economic impact of aid in particular remained ambiguous and unexplained. The literature on aid effectiveness that emerged post mid-1990s was distinct from the pre-mid-1990s studies in a number of aspects. First, the gap models were replaced by the general equilibrium growth models. Second, the endogeneity of aid – dependence of aid on the circumstances in the recipient country – was acknowledged and given due importance. Third, recipient countries' economic policies and institutional infrastructure together with the non-linear effects of aid became embedded in the aid analysis (see discussion below for findings).

3.   Globalisation, poverty reduction and the MDGs

3a. Private capital/trade-led globalisation

The 'conventional wisdom' is that private capital/trade-led globalisation is 'an engine of growth and poverty reduction: economies need to be open' *but* one might tentatively add there are winners and losers (Maxwell, 2005:2, 4). This is reflected in the OECD DAC Guidelines, the *World Development Report* 2000/1; *Human Development Reports* and *the Millennium Project Report to the United Nations Secretary* (OECD, 2001:96; UNDP, 2003:154; UNMP, 2005:211–22; World Bank, 2000:179–88).

That openness to trade in particular is good for development has become 'one of the most widely held beliefs... something upon which Nobel prize winners of both the left and the right agree' (Dollar and

Kraay, 2004:1). It has even become 'a fundamental article of faith among... policy analysts' (Kanbur, 2001:2). Kanbur has argued that free trade has taken on a further significance for the Bank and the Fund in light of the fact that the institutions have conceded much of the 'Washington Consensus' (in particular, the full freedom of capital movements, wide-ranging cuts in public spending and full-scale privatisation), so that free trade has now become the remaining 'line in the sand'.

Table 6.2 characterises the features of selected recent globalisation studies on the internationalism versus liberalisation split. The 'proponents' base much of their work on globalisation as internationalism or 'openness', i.e. trade volumes or capital flows. The 'sceptics' tend to assess globalisation as liberalisation or 'opening' or reductions in trade tariffs and non-tariff barriers and capital controls. The former group are pro-globalisation and the latter find little or no evidence of the benefits of globalisation. Examples of studies are listed in the table.

Not surprisingly, a limited number of notable exceptions exist (see for example Box 6.1). For example, pro-globalisation studies not based on internationalism entirely (such as Dollar and Kraay, 2001; Edwards, 1998; Quinn, 1997; Mbabazi *et al.*, 2002) and 'sceptics' research not based on

Table 6.2   Characterisation of Selected Recent Literature on Globalisation and Growth

	'Proponents'	*'Sceptics'*
Conceptualisation of globalisation	Globalisation as internationalism	Globalisation as liberalisation
Quantification of globalisation	Studies generally based on outcomes and 'openness' (trade or capital volumes)	Studies generally based on policy and 'opening' (trade tariffs or capital controls)
Examples of studies on integration of current account	Dollar and Kraay (2002; 2003) Frankel and Roemer (1999) Irwin and Tervio (2002)	Hertel *et al.* (2003) Greenaway *et al.* (1997) Rodrik (1997)
Examples of studies on integration of capital account	Alfaro *et al.* (2000) Dollar and Kraay (2001) Lensink and Morrissey (2001)	Arteta *et al.* (2001) Klein (2003) Rodrik (1998)

Box 6.1   Dollar and Kraay's 'Trade, Growth and Poverty'

Dollar and Kraay's 'Trade, Growth and Poverty' study was in the spotlight during the period around the Prague (September 2000) and Genoa (July 2001) (anti-) globalisation protests to defend two of the protestors' targets – free trade and multinational companies. In *Trade, growth and poverty*, Dollar and Kraay took data for 73 countries (1985–97 for trade tariffs and 1975–97 for trade volumes). The study catergorised 'globalisers' and 'non-globalisers' based on 'openness' to trade (measured by tariffs and trade volumes) thus somewhat controversially 'weeding' the 'good' from the 'bad' countries. The paper argued that (a) 'globalisers' grew at 5% a year on average in the 1990s in comparison with 'non-globalisers' that grew at just 1.4% per year on average in the same decade; (b) a 1% increase in foreign direct investment (FDI) inflows/GDP led to 10–13% increases in average incomes over a decade; and (c) there was no evidence that globalisation (using the proxy of trade volumes) leads to rising intra-country inequality.

The main criticisms were as follows. The headline: 'globalisers' grew faster (5% per year) than 'non-globalisers' (2.9% per year) is misleading. When population-weighted data is used it is indeed the case that 'globalisers' grew faster than 'non-globalisers' However, if population-unweighted data is utilised 'globalisers' grew an average of 1.5% a year in the 1990s versus the 'non-globalisers' average annual growth of 1.4% in the same decade (i.e. a marginal difference). Further, almost half of the 'globalisers' grew at less than 1% and one-third of 'globaliser' countries recorded average growth at less than the 'non-globalisers' group. The difference that population weighting makes demonstrates how deterministic China's and India's categorisation are, given their population weightings. Dollar and Kraay labelled both as 'globalisers' despite the fact that both still retain significant trade (and investment) barriers/regulatory controls. Milanovic argued that there is some irony in using a communist country where one-third of output is produced by state-owned companies – virtually the highest in the world – to justify a market-led liberalisation strategy. The headline: 'globalisers' grew faster than 'non-globalisers' can be further questioned if absolute trade tariffs are used. While it is true that average tariffs were reduced by a greater amount in relative terms in the 'globalisers' (22% compared with only 11% in the 'non-globalisers'), in absolute terms Dollars

Box 6.1 Dollar and Kraay's 'Trade, Growth and Poverty' – *continued*

and Kraay's 'globalisers' actually had higher tariffs (57% falling to 35%) than the 'non-globalisers' (31% falling to 20%). Higher absolute tariffs are then linked to faster growth even in Dollar and Kraay's study. This is not acknowledged in the study. A number of methodological 'rigour' issues have also been raised. In particular, the categorisation of 'globalisers' and 'non-globalisers' (i.e. the quantification of globalisation). In fact, Dollar and Kraay mix the conceptually differing proxies – tariffs and volumes – and do so over different time periods. Tariff data is not available for the earlier period, meaning comparisons can only be made on trade volumes.

Sources: Milanovic (2002), Oxfam (2002), and Rodrik (2000).

liberalisation (such as Carkovic and Levine, 2003; Nair-Reichert and Weinhold, 2001). However, the general pattern is: those studies that find globalisation is good for growth are based on globalisation as internationalism, quantified as trade or capital volumes, and the majority of studies, which are sceptical about whether globalisation is good for growth, are based on globalisation as liberalisation, quantified in trade barriers or capital controls. The evidence linking growth to internationalism is strong whereas that associating growth to liberalisation is mixed.

If we focus solely on the FDI literature we can see the extent of contention. The 'old wisdom' or the message/policy narrative of the 1990s was simple – FDI is good (for development – growth, jobs, and so on). The simplicity of this 'old wisdom' may be open to question as academic literature shifts. Take, for example, a recent study of 28 LDCs which concluded,

> in the vast majority of countries FDI has no statistically significant long-run impact on growth. In very few cases, FDI indeed contributes to economic growth both in the long and the short run. But for some countries, there is also evidence of growth-limiting effects of FDI in the short or long term (Herzer *et al.*, 2006:1).

There is a large body of empirical literature on the impact of FDI on aggregate economic growth, but relatively little is known about growth in per capita incomes, poverty, and inequality. An underlying assumption is often that what is good for growth is good for the poor, although the growth–poverty relationship is far more contentious than this would suggest (see previous chapter). While there are strong conceptual reasons for believing FDI is good for aggregate economic growth (with some question marks over poverty reduction), the evidence from more than 30 years' data is rather inconclusive overall. These mixed findings may demonstrate a number of methodological and conceptual factors, including heterogeneity in both FDI policy environments (especially performance requirements), and FDI characteristics (mode of entry, function, sector, and financing), and host-country factors – all hidden in average trends of cross-country research. Additionally, data comparability and consistency as well as controversies related to the methodology of cross-country econometric studies are a further complication.

Table 6.3 summarises selected cross-country research on FDI and aggregate growth, GDP per capita growth, income poverty and domestic investment. Many of the benefits of FDI are either unclear or determinant on prerequisites such as levels of human capital, levels of per capita income (as a proxy for economic development) or levels of financial development or policy regimes, which may not exist in many countries.

Broadly, research is supportive of the notion that FDI leads to aggregate economic growth. However, most studies add dependent factors for the benefits of FDI, many of which are missing in the majority of developing countries – for example, a high level of financial market development (Alfaro *et al.*, 2000) or trade volumes (Balasubramanyam *et al.*, 1996; de Mello, 1999) or human capital (Borenzstein *et al.*, 1998) or the level of economic development (Blomstrom and Kokko, 1994) or a combination or two or more of the above (Balasubramanyam *et al.*, 1996). The cross-country research on FDI and changes in per capita income, poverty and inequality is limited (see Table 6.3). Carkovic and Levine (2002) found no causal link between FDI and per capita income. However, Dollar and Kraay (2001) argue that a 1% increase in FDI inflows/GDP leads to a 10–13% increase in average incomes over a decade. Soto (2000) argues similarly that a 10% increase in FDI/GNP raises per capita income by 3%. However, Agénor (2002) found no robust link between FDI and poverty, and Milanovic (2002) found no association between income per capita growth and FDI at any level of income, while Santarelli and Figini (2003) argue that greater openness measured by FDI inflows/gross capital formation, although not statistically significant, tends to be linked to higher levels of poverty.

Table 6.3 Selected Cross-Country Research on FDI

	Years covered	Countries in sample	Findings
Impact of FDI on aggregate economic growth			
Herzer *et al.* (2006)	1970–03	28	FDI has no statistically significant long-run impact on growth. For some countries, there is evidence of growth-limiting effects of FDI
Hansen and Rand (2006)	1970–2000	31	+ve. FDI has a lasting impact on GDP
Alfaro *et al.* (2000)	1981–97	39–49	+ve but dependent on level of financial market development
Lensink and Morrissey (2001)	1975–97	88	+ve
Nair-Reichert and Weinhold (2001)	1971–95	24	Highly heterogeneous. Higher in more open economies
Reisen and Soto (2001)	1986–97	44	+ve
UNCTAD (1999b)	1970–96	39	Only +ve in Asia
De Mello (1999)	1970–91	5	+ve but dependent on trade volumes
Balasubramanyam *et al.* (1996)	1970–85	46	+ve but dependent on domestic market size, competition and human capital
Borenzstein *et al.* (1998)	1970–89	69	+ve but weak correlation and dependent on human capital
Balasubramanyam *et al.* (1996)	1970–85	46	+ve but dependent on trade volumes and an export orientation
Blomstrom and Kokko (1994)	1960–85	101	+ve but dependent on level of economic development not human capital
Impact of FDI on per capita income or income poverty			
Carkovic and Levine (2002)	1960–95	72	No causal link between FDI and GDP per capita
Santarelli and Figini (2003)	1970–98	54	-ve; but not statistically significant to higher levels of poverty
Agénor (2002)	1988–98	11	FDI not correlated to poverty
Milanovic (2002)	1985–97	89	No association between FDI and income growth at any level of income

Table 6.3   Selected Cross-Country Research on FDI – *continued*

	Years covered	Countries in sample	Findings
Dollar and Kraay (2001)	1975–97	73	+ve; a 1% increase in FDI inflows/GDP leads to 10–13% increase in average incomes over a decade
Soto (2000)	1986–97	44	+ve and a 10% increase FDI/GNP raises per capita income by 3%
Impact of FDI on domestic investment			
Kumar and Pradhan (2002)	1980–99	83	+ve and –ve. CO in 29 countries, CI in 23 countries. CI most likely in market seeking FDI
Agosin and Mayer (2000)	1970–96	32	+ve and –ve but dependent on regulation. CI in Asia and CO in Latin America. Africa one-for-one. CI if economic sector is underdeveloped and CO if domestic firms already developed
UNCTAD (1999b)	1970–96	39	+ve and –ve. CO in 19 countries, CI in 10. No CI in 12 Latin American countries and no CO in 12 Asian countries
Bosworth and Collins (1999)	1978–95	58	+ve and one-for-one relationship US$ FDI and US$ domestic investment
Borenzstein *et al.* (1998)	1970–89	69	+ve and one-for-one relationship US$ FDI and US$ domestic investment
De Mello (1997)	1970–90	33	+ve but dependent on complementarity of FDI and domestic investment

Notes: +ve = positive; -ve = negative; CO = crowding-out of domestic investment; CI = crowding-in of domestic investment.

Crucial to growth and poverty impacts is the impact of FDI on inequality – does FDI lead to increases in intra-country inequality? Fifteen studies were reviewed by Bornschier and Chase-Dunn (1985), of which only one (Weede and Tiefenbach, 1981) reported that FDI did not lead to an increase in inequality. More recently, using the proxy of FDI inflows/GDP and the Gini coefficient, Tsai (1995) argued unambiguously that FDI inflows are very likely to lead to a worsening of developing countries' income distributions. The question of FDI and inequality can also be addressed by micro-studies comparing wages paid by FDI to local companies and to skilled and unskilled workers. Unfortunately, not all studies differentiate between skilled and unskilled workers, and research focuses on FDI in manufacturing. In general, the empirical evidence suggests that FDI wages are higher than local wages and differentials between skilled and unskilled workers are significant (for a summary of studies see Morrissey and te Velde, 2002:3). In terms of the impact of FDI on total investment, the results are also mixed (see Table 6.3). Borenzstein *et al.* (1998) report crowding-in overall, and Bosworth and Collins (1999) found a one-for-one relationship between FDI and domestic investment – $1 of FDI raised domestic investment by $1. However, de Mello (1999) argues that impacts are dependent on the complementarity of FDI and domestic investment. Kumar and Pradhan (2002) found mixed results, with crowding-out effects dominating. The same was true for Agosin and Mayer (2000) and UNCTAD (1999b). Both of these studies argue that crowding-in is prevalent in less liberal FDI policy regimes, and underdeveloped economic sectors, such as Asia (especially before liberalisation, between 1976 and 1985), and crowding-out is the norm in more liberal FDI policy regimes, and if domestic firms are already in existence, such as Latin America and Africa. Additionally, the World Bank (2004:63) has noted that the elasticity of FDI to domestic investment had significantly weakened – more than halving – in the more liberal 1990s compared with the 1970–1989 period. Cross-country findings on whether FDI uses local suppliers are also mixed, with certain studies positive (e.g. UNCTAD, 2001:134–5) and others negative (e.g. Moran, 1998).

There have been numerous country studies, focused primarily on manufacturing, covering spillover effects such as local firms' productivity gains, local sourcing, and propensity to export. A number of studies have identified positive impacts of local sourcing – largely in Asia (e.g. Sjoholm, 1999; Xia and Yuebing, 2001) and weak, neutral, or negative spillovers – largely in Latin America (e.g. Carrillo, 2001; Haddad and Harrison, 1993), or spillovers to export firms only (Aitken *et al.*, 1997) or smaller firms only (Aitken and Harrison, 1999) or the benefits dependent on human capital (Mody and Wang, 1997). Overall, local sourcing varies by industry and region. For example, local sourcing has been very low in Mexico but very high in Thailand and Malaysia (Brimble, 2001; Carrillo, 2001).

To summarise, we think that:

* FDI leads to aggregate economic growth *but only if* prerequisites are in place (such as human capital) and thus probably increases in GDP per capita.
* The benefits of FDI seem to be more prominent in those times/ regions of less liberal FDI policy regimes.

What about globalisation, the MDGs and poverty reduction? Cross-country research on trade and poverty is disputed between proponents, who largely rely on trade volumes as a proxy (Dollar and Kraay, 2004; 2002; Santarelli and Figini, 2003) and sceptics, who measure reductions in trade barriers (Agénor, 2002; Hertel *et al.*, 2003; Lundberg and Squire, 2000). Many studies on FDI (measured as the US$ volume of foreign direct investment and poverty) argue that there is no link (Agénor, 2002; Carkovic and Levine, 2002; Milanovic, 2002; Santarelli and Figini, 2003). Others argue there is a positive link for poverty reduction (Dollar and Kraay, 2004; Soto, 2000). The literature on capital account integration (measured as the US$ volume of non-FDI capital flows and poverty) is very thin and polarised between globalisation proponents (Eichengreen, 2001) and sceptics (Agénor and Aizenman, 1999). Taking the more expansive literature on globalisation–growth, more is agreed. Studies based on globalisation as a policy outcome (internationalism), measured by trade or capital volumes, tend to find globalisation is good for growth (see for example, Alfaro *et al.*, 2000; Dollar and Kraay, 2004; Frankel and Roemer, 1999; Irwin and Tervio, 2002; Lensink and Morrissey, 2001). In contrast, studies that measure globalisation as an input/policy (liberalisation), measured by changes in trade or capital barriers, tend to be more sceptical (see for example, Arteta *et al.*, 2001; Hertel *et al.*, 2003; Greenaway *et al.*, 1997; Klein, 2003; Rodrik, 1997; 1998). Not surprisingly, a limited number of notable exceptions exist (such as Dollar and Kraay, 2004; Edwards, 1998). In sum, the 'conventional wisdom' that globalisation is good for the poor, is accepted or disputed depending on what we take 'openness' to mean.

Public capital-led globalisation

What about public capital-led globalisation? A new direction on the macroeconomic effectiveness of development aid was initiated with the World Bank's (1998) *Assessing Aid* report. The report emphasised the role of governance, strong institutional environment and good policies in aid effectiveness. It concluded that the policy environment of the recipient countries should be an important criterion for aid allo-cation. A number of background studies contributed to the discussions and the conclusions of *Assessing Aid*. The best-known (and most con-tentious) studies are those that formed the basis of the *Assessing Aid* report – those of Burnside and Dollar (2000) and Collier and Dollar (2002). Burnside and Dollar show the positive impact of aid on real GDP when interacted with a policy index variable. When the recipient country puts in place 'good' fiscal, monetary and trade policies, aid will lead to growth. The study deployed a cross-country regression analysis for 40 low-income countries and 16 middle-income countries over the 1970–93 period. Collier and Dollar's study further reinforced these arguments. They show that poor countries with 'good' policy regimes would reduce the number of poor by an additional 18 million per year if aid were reallocated to these countries. The conclusions of both studies have been supported and contested. The strongest support for the role of economic environment on aid effectiveness is found in Collier and Dehn (2001) and Collier and Hoeffler (2002).

Studies that strongly contest the results are Easterly *et al.* (2004) and Roodman (2004). Both papers (using the same data set) found the rela-tionship between policy environment and aid effectiveness to be rather weak. Both papers question Burnside and Dollar's deletion of some observations that prove to be deterministic. The positive aid–policy link has been further criticised for the policy index used in the model. The use of variables such as budget surplus, inflation rate, trade open-ness and the absence of measures on privatisation, financial market liberalisation, educational policies and tax reforms remains arbitrary and unexplained.

Assessing Aid and the responses it generated created intense debate. Alternative stances on the aid–policy relationship cover a wide spec-trum including the decreasing returns of aid, influences of external shocks and climatic conditions on aid, influences of political con-ditions and the impact of institutions on aid (see for further discussion McGillivray *et al.*, 2006). Unfortunately, there have been few studies on aid and poverty that seek to provide a macro-view. Levine *et al.* (2004) on health outcomes is one exception. Its findings were positive on a range of aid in the health sector. Modalities of aid are likely to be increasingly important as we move from project aid to direct budget support. Nevertheless, much aid of course is channelled through NGOs. Again there are relatively few studies that provide a macro-view. The World Bank (1999) found that NGOs were more effective than states but still do not reach the poorest. This reflected a range of other studies (see for discussion Chapter 3 in Feeny and Clarke, 2009 for review of NGOs' contributions to the MDGs).

Such research on aid is intertwined with public expenditure research. The 'conventional wisdom' is that 'infrastructure for productive sectors, water, health and education are priorities for public expenditure' *but* one might tentatively note the importance of social protection including food insecurity and malnutrition (Maxwell, 2005:2, 4). This is a point accepted by *The Millennium Project Report to the United Nations Secretary-General*. However, the DAC Guidelines, recent *Human Development Reports*, the 2000/1 *World Development Report*, and the more recent 2004 *World Development Report* (on services and poverty) emphasise the need for public expenditure while, in places, they focus on the failings of public expenditure in poverty reduction, and to some extent promote the case for 'fostering' and 'balancing' private interventions in infrastructure for health, education and water (OECD, 2001:78, 82; UNDP, 2003:85–122; UNMP, 2005:49–50, 66–94, 140–2; World Bank, 2000:1; World Bank, 2004b:66–91). End of story? Not quite. Whether or not public expenditure is good for the poor depends on whether the expenditures reach the poor or benefit the non-poor. A number of cross-country studies have shown that government spending on public goods in health and education makes an overall positive contribution to multi-dimensional poverty reduction and to the income poor; however there is a wide variation in country experience (for a range, see Anand and Ravallion, 1993; Barro, 1991; Bidani and Ravallion, 1997; Hojman, 1996; Gundlach *et al.*, 2001; Tanzi and Chu, 1998; Van de Walle, 1996). Nevertheless, many studies have questioned to what extent the income poor do benefit from public expenditure (Demery and Walton, 1998; Dollar and Kraay, 2002; Filmer *et al.*, 1998; Filmer and Pritchett, 1997; Flug *et al.*, 1998; Gupta *et al.*, 2002; Landau, 1986; Noss, 1991; Mingat and Tan, 1998; Ravallion *et al.*, 1993). Additionally, a number of studies have argued public expenditure is good for growth (see for example, Kneller *et al.*, 1999; Ramirez and Nazmi, 2003) but that the composition may be crucial to the benefits of growth (Mourmouras and Lee, 1999; Tanzi and Zee, 1997) and who benefits (Mosley *et al.*, 2004). In sum, the 'conventional wisdom' is that public expenditure is good for the poor, but many researchers would not agree.

4.   The future of globalisation

So, in light of the above what do Collier, Sachs, Easterly, Rodrik, Chang and Stiglitz say about policy and trade, investment and aid? Given

Table 6.4   Selected Studies on Aid Effectiveness

Authors	Findings
Earlier studies	
Rahman (1968)	Foreign capital flows have a negative impact on growth
Griffin (1970)	Foreign capital flows have a negative impact on domestic savings
Gupta (1970)	Foreign capital has no impact on domestic savings
Weisskopf (1972)	Foreign aid has a negative impact on domestic savings
Papanek (1973)	Aid has a positive impact on growth
Mosley (1980)	Aid has no impact on growth
Dowling and Hiemenz (1982)	Aid has a positive impact on growth
Voivodas (1973)	Aid has no impact on growth
Gupta and Islam (1983)	Aid has a positive impact on growth
Mosley (1987)	Aid has no impact on growth
Boone (1996)	Aid has no impact on growth
Later studies	
Burnside and Dollar (1997, 2000)	Aid effectiveness depends on the policy environment
Durbarry *et al.* (1998)	Aid has diminishing returns
Collier and Dehn (2001)	Aid effectiveness depends on the policy environment
Dalgaard and Hansen (2001)	Aid is effective with diminishing returns and is independent from the policy environment
Guillaumont and Chauvet (2001)	Aid effectiveness does not depend on the policy environment, but on climatic conditions
Hansen and Tarp (2001)	Aid is effective with diminishing returns and is independent of the policy environment
Hudson and Mosley (2001)	Aid is effective with diminishing returns and is independent of the policy environment
Lensink and White (2001)	Aid is effective with diminishing returns and is independent of the policy environment
Lu and Ram (2001)	Aid is effective with diminishing returns and is independent of the policy environment
Chauvet and Guillaumont (2002)	Aid effectiveness depends on political stability

Table 6.4   **Selected Studies on Aid Effectiveness** – *continued*

Authors	Findings
Collier and Dollar (2002)	Aid effectiveness depends on the policy environment
Islam (2002)	Aid effectiveness does not depend on the policy environment, but on political stability
Gomanee *et al.* 2003)	Aid is effective after a threshold value of growth has been reached
Jensen and Paldam (2003)	Aid is not effective in stimulating growth
Kosack (2003)	Aid is effective in improving quality of life in democratic countries
Dalgaard *et al.* (2004)	Aid is effective with diminishing returns, is less effective in tropical regions and is independent of the policy environment
Burnside and Dollar (2004)	Aid effectiveness depends on institutional quality
Easterly *et al.* (2004)	Aid effectiveness does not depend on the policy environment

Source: Adapted from McGillivray *et al.* (2006:1045–6).

that we discussed Collier, Sachs, and Easterly in Chapter 1 we recap and then focus the discussion here on Chang, Rodrik and Stiglitz (see Table 6.5).

For Collier, aid has been little more than a 'holding operation', and left to itself, globalisation is not going to solve development problems – the bottom-billion countries need to diversify into manufacturing trade. This will not happen by removing OECD trade barriers, or through fair trade. The key is temporary protection from successful exporters in Asia in certain sectors such as textiles.

For Easterly, aid has been a failure because big institutions do not motivate people to implement policy and are lacking in accountability. Aid should be implemented with local contexts in mind and at grassroots level with accountability, evaluation and reward mechanisms. What matters are incentives, markets and 'searchers'. Planners apply a 'global blueprint' to foreign aid plans without checking grassroots realities. Further, planners take no responsibility for not delivering the plans and meeting the set objectives. Searchers on the other hand find an opportunity, deliver and seek reward. They are far better connected

Table 6.5 Collier *et al.* on Trade and Aid

	The problem		The solution	
	Aid	Trade	Aid	Trade
Collier	Aid has been a 'holding operation'.			Diversification into manufacturing trade via temporary protection from successful exporters in Asia in certain sectors such as textiles.
Easterly	Big plans through 'global blueprints' and big institutions that do not motivate people to implement policy and also are lacking in accountability.		Understanding of local contexts and grassroots level implementation of foreign aid. Inclusion of accountability, feedback, evaluation and reward systems.	
Sachs	Small unpredictable flows and governments' capacity to deal with aid.	Trade barriers in the rich countries.	Harmonise aid through a UN system towards poverty reduction within the MDG agenda.	Pro-poor trade liberalisation accompanied by public investment.

Table 6.5 Collier *et al.* on Trade and Aid – *continued*

	The problem		The solution	
	Aid	Trade	Aid	Trade
Rodrik		Rapid and unstructured trade liberalisation without consideration of the domestic market configurations.		Restrictions and regulations to trade openness as a precursor to the establishment of a strong institutional and domestic entrepreneurial culture. Restrictions should then be eased to engage with international trade. Trade is a means and not an end.
Chang	Neo-liberal thinking that foreign aid does not work.	Free trade restricts choices for the poor countries. Trade liberalisation has led to reduction in government revenues.	Emphasis on aid not motivated by geo-politics.	Restrict free trade in the short term, regulate financial markets and foreign investment and invest in capacity-building.
Stiglitz		Rapid trade liberalisation, poor infrastructure, high cost of capital, skills scarcity and low productivity in developing countries.	Aid and trade as complements: both needed for successful development.	

with the grassroots, aspire to find answers to individual problems through experimentation and bear responsibility for their actions. They rely heavily on understanding local contexts and knowledge to find solutions. Easterly points to feedback and accountability as two key elements that the searchers take seriously and achieve their targets while the planners tend to ignore and continue to fail. The way forward in making aid work for the poor, according to Easterly, is to introduce accountability into the actions of aid agents via feedback, evaluation, rewards and penalties. Further, the donors should insist that the agents carry out an exhaustive search into what works and what doesn't and experiment on the basis of these outcomes. Easterly urges the aid regime be managed by the searchers to enable the aid money to reach the poor.

Sachs's (2005) *The End of Poverty* draws mostly on Sachs's own field experiences and research in Bolivia, Poland, Russia, China, India and Kenya. The premise of the book is Sachs's belief that extreme poverty can be ended by 2025 largely via aid and trade. The book emphasises the creation of the preconditions for market to become the driver of development, focusing strongly on Keynesian mechanisms to achieve this. Sachs's critique of the International Financial Institutions – in particular IMF's restrictive 'one treatment for all symptoms' – is sharp. Aid occupies a central role in Sachs's proposed framework for an end to global poverty. He argues against the 'trade not aid' lobby in favour of the 'trade plus aid' model. However, the book points to mixed outcomes of trade liberalisation in agriculture for the poor. Large net food exporters stand to benefit while net importers – most developing countries – will pay higher prices. Without strong infrastructure and capacity-building, most developing countries will be negatively affected by trade reforms.

Ha-Joon Chang's *Bad Samaritans* (2007), which builds upon the earlier *Kicking Away the Ladder* (2002), tells the story that rich countries, want poor countries to do what they say they should do, and not what they themselves did. Rich countries protected their economies to industrialise but now deny poor countries the chance to do so with WTO rules and thus are 'bad Samaritans' who are 'kicking away the ladder'. Chang argues for selective strategic integration with the world economy via trade with trade protection. Chang reviews the industrialisation of Great Britain, Japan and South Korea and notes infant industry protectionism and government subsidies that were crucial contributors. Chang sets out to challenge the foundations of any success stories of globalisation. Chang points out that almost all of the current developed countries embarked upon clearly defined state-led development. The book provides numerous examples of market leaders of today – such as Nokia and Samsung – arriving at their global positions through adopting a 'defying the market' stance (via infant industry protection).

In *One Economics, Many Recipes* Dani Rodrik rejects over-simplification arguing neither the globalisers nor the anti-globalisers have got it right. He notes orthodox outcomes may result from unorthodox policies and vice versa. Economic globalisation can reduce poverty but success depends on policies that promote local development. Poor countries that have developed have not done so by copying a Washington-led universal model but by carefully crafting their own unique strategies. Industrial policy, institutions and governance matter. Rodrik's approach is not to push his own prescriptions but to propose a practical approach to policy formation based on 'growth diagnostics'. He argues that by trying to assess what hinders growth first (i.e. weak infrastructure or low levels of education or the investment climate) governments can design policies accordingly. Rodrik's faith in role of the state in economic development is visible throughout as is his support for the context-specific growth policies, rejecting the 'one shoe fits all' stance. The book draws out successful countries as those where policy formulation is grounded in domestic limitations and opportunities. Rodrik highlights the distinction between attaining economic growth and sustaining it – the latter being the more challenging task, requiring long-term institutional support and infrastructure. A forceful argument is made for open, participatory political systems that foster democratic institutions for sustained economic growth. Despite the sharp progress of most of the East Asian economies under authoritarian models, such regimes need not be emulated as the only path to prosperity. Rodrik points to the many success stories under democratic regimes during the same period. The book revisits the debate on protectionism, trade openness and growth. It highlights the fact that nearly all of today's developed countries adopted protectionism and tariff barriers to achieve growth. While no country has prospered by insulating itself from international trade, it is also true that no country can develop by embarking on purely a liberalisation of its economy to trade and foreign investment. Rodrik points to 'gradualism' as the proven route to engaging with international trade but one that is not necessarily professed by the globalisers of today. Amongst the 21st-century successful countries, China in particular completely violated globalisation rules while India even today continues to practise many regulatory mechanisms. The earlier successes of South

Korea and Taiwan have well documented for such practices of protectionism and tariff use in their early development.

Finally, the work of Stiglitz and the related post-Washington Consensus is discussed in Chapter 1. Stiglitz's *Making Globalisation Work* (2007) and Stiglitz and Charlton's *Fair Trade for All* (2007) add to these discussions. He argues we need fairer trade and better governance of international finance, arms trade and narcotics. We also need leadership on climate change from the rich countries and support to civil society to make globalisation more inclusive.

5. What next?

In sum, there have been different findings on both private capital/ trade-led globalisation and public-led globalisation in the form of aid because different research has assessed different things. It is surprisingly difficult to conclude on public capital-led globalisation but we can be more conclusive on private-capital or trade-led globalisation. The available empirical evidence is fairly conclusive that trade and private-capital volumes and growth are associated (although the direction of causality may be disputed). However, on the question of the association between reductions in trade and private capital barriers/ controls and growth there is no unambiguous conclusion. In short, private capital/trade-led globalisation as internationalism is linked to growth, but we do not know for sure whether liberalisation is. It is something of an understatement to say this is an unfortunate conclusion for policy-makers, given that the former (volumes) are not under the direct control of governments and the latter (barriers) are.

However, this is not the end of the story. The literature is beginning to evolve into 'new' issues that could be summed up as an interest in the heterogeneity of experience. Indeed, more generally, there is an increased interest in the quality of private capital/trade-led globalisation growth (and in particular the growth–inequality impact of globalisation), the direction of causation, non-linearity and thresholds. Examples include Greenaway *et al.* (2002), who took both input and output trade measures and found negative short-run growth effects, but positive long-run effects. On the direction of causality, both Basu *et al.* (2003) and Chowdhury and Mavrotas (2003) found evidence of causality in both directions between growth and foreign direct investment. On non-linearity, growth-inequality and disaggregation, both Milanovic (2002) and Agénor (2002) have argued that only after reaching a certain threshold is the growth from 'openness' broad-based. The evolution of globalisation research into these 'new' issues seems likely to stimulate a new round of heterogeneity-led work. This may have the effect of somewhat blurring the 'proponent' versus 'sceptic' separation because there are winners and losers from globalisation across various disaggregations. The ambiguity over the effect of liberalisation might be addressed through some attention to the heterogeneity of experience that is already emerging in the literature, especially with regard to time horizons, disaggregation, thresholds and non-linearity between and within countries.

Notes

1   This chapter draws upon and builds on Rugraff *et al.* (2008), Sumner (2004; 2007) and Sumner and Tiwari (2005). Not only must policies (such as tariffs and non-tariffs) be aggregated, there are also further issues of the credibility and enforcement of any regime itself that further complicates quantification matters (Winters *et al.*, 2002:8). For greater discussion of trade measures see Pritchett (1996).
2   Although the IMF has guidelines on capital flow accounting, data is of questionable consistency for international comparison. For example, statistics may include double counting, and/or omissions of reinvested earnings; or intra-company loans, overseas commercial borrowings (trade credits, financial leasing) and portfolio holdings over 10% held by institutional investors may not be fully included (see for more detail UNCTAD, 2000:113; 2003:231–48; World Bank, 2003:88–93). Gross and net flows further complicate matters.
3   For greater discussion of measuring globalisation of the capital account see Edison *et al.* (2002).

References

Agénor, P. and Aizenman, J. (1999) Volatility and the welfare cost of financial market integration, in Agénor, P., Miller, M., Vines, D., Weber, A. (eds) *The Asian Financial Crisis: Causes, Contagion and Consequences*. Cambridge: Cambridge University Press.

Agénor, P. (2002) Does Globalisation Hurt the Poor? Mimeograph. Washington DC: World Bank.

Agosin, M. and Mayer, R. (2000) Foreign Direct Investment in Developing Countries. UNCTAD Discussion Paper No. 146. Geneva: UNCTAD.

Aitken, B., G.H., Hanson, and Harrison, A.E. (1997) 'Spillovers, Foreign Investment and Export Behaviour', *Journal of International Economics*, 43(1):103–32.

Aitken, B. and Harrison A.E. (1999) 'Do Domestic firms Benefit from Foreign Direct Investment? Evidence from Venezuela', *American Economic Review*, 89(3):605–18.

Alfaro, L., Chanda, A., Kalemli-Ozcan, S. and Sayek, S. (2000) FDI and Economic Growth: the Role of Financial Markets. Working Paper 01-083. Boston, MA: Harvard Business School.

Amsden, A. (1989) *Asia's Next Giant: South Korea and Late Industrialisation*. New York: Oxford University Press.

Anand, S. and Ravallion, M. (1993) 'Human Development in Poor Countries: On the Role of Private Incomes and Public Services', *Journal of Economic Perspectives*, 7:133–50.

Arteta, C., Eichengreen, B. and Wyplosz, C. (2001) On the Growth Effects of Capital Account Liberalisation. Mimeo. Berkeley, California: University of California.

Bacha, E.L. (1990) 'A Three-Gap Model of Foreign Transfers and the GDP Growth Rate in Developing Countries', *Journal of Development Economics*, 32(2):279–96.

Balasubramanyam, V.N., Salisu, M. and Sapsford, D. (1996) 'Foreign Direct Investment and Growth in EP and IS Countries', *The Economic Journal*, 106(434):92–105.

Barro, R. (1991) 'Economic Growth in a Cross-Section of Countries', *Quarterly Journal of Economics*, 106:407–44.

Basu, P., Reagle, D. and Chakraborty, C. (2003) Empirical Dynamics of FDI and Growth in Developing Countries: Does Liberalisation Matter? Paper presented at Global Business and Economic Development. School of Management, Asian Institute of Technology, Bangkok, Thailand. January.

Bhattacharya, A. and Pangestu, M. (1993) Indonesia: Development Transformation Since 1965 And The Role Of Public Policy, World Bank Country Study. Washington DC: World Bank.

Bidani, B. and Ravallion, M. (1997) 'Decomposing Social Indicators Using Distributional Data', *Journal of Econometrics*, 77:125–39.

Blomstrom, M. and Kokko, A. (1994) 'Multinational Corporations and Spillovers', *Journal of Economic Surveys*, 12(3):247–77.

Boone, P. (1996) 'Politics and the Effectiveness of Aid', *European Economic Review*, 40(2):289–329.

Borenzstein, E., De Gregorio, J. and Lee, J. (1998) 'How Does Foreign Direct Investment Affect Growth?', *Journal of International Economics*, 45:115–35.

Bornschier, V. and Chase-Dunn, C. (1985) *Transnational Corporations and Underdevelopment*. New York, NY: Praeger Press.

Bosworth, B. and Collins, S. (1999) Capital Flows to Developing Economies: Implications for Saving and Investment. Brookings Papers on Economic Activity: Spring.

Brimble, P. (2001) The Thai Hard Disk Drive Industry, mimeograph. Geneva: UNCTAD.

Burnside, C. and Dollar, D. (1997) Aid, Policies and Growth. World Bank Policy Research Working Paper No. 1777. Washington, DC: The World Bank.

Burnside, C. and Dollar, D. (2000) 'Aid, Policies and Growth', *American Economic Review*, 90(4):847–68.

Burnside, C. and Dollar, D. (2004a) A Reply to 'New Data, New Doubts: A Comment on Burnside and Dollar's Aid, Policies and Growth', *American Economic Review*, 94(3):774–80.

Burnside, C. and Dollar, D. (2004b) Aid, Policies and Growth: Revisiting the Evidence. World Bank Policy Research Working Paper No.3251. Washington DC: World Bank.

Carkovic, M. and Levine, R. (2002) Does Foreign Direct Investment Accelerate Growth? Mimeo. University of Minnesota.

Carrillo, J. (2001) Foreign Direct Investment and Local Linkages: Experiences and the Role of Policies. The Case of the Mexican Television Industry in Tijuana, mimeograph. Geneva: UNCTAD.

Cassen, R. and Associates (1994) *Does Aid Work?* New York: Oxford University Press.

Chang, H-J. (1994) *The Political Economy of Industrial Policy*. London: Anthem Press.

Chang, H-J. (2002) *Kicking Away the Ladder: Development*. Strategy in Historical Perspective. London: Anthem Press.

Chang, H-J. (2007) *Bad Samaritans*. London: Random House.

Chauvet, L. and Guillaumont, P. (2002) Aid and Growth Revisited: Policy, Economic Vulnerability and Political Instability. Paper presented at the Annual Bank Conference of Development Economics, Oslo.

Chenery, H. and Bruno, M. (1962) 'Development Alternatives in an Open Economy: The Case of Israel', *Economic Journal*, 77(285):79–103.

Chenery, H. and Strout, S. (1966) 'Foreign Assistance and Economic Development', *American Economic Review*, 66(4 Part 1):679–753.

Chowdhury, A. and Mavrotas, G. (2003) FDI and Growth: What Causes What? Paper prepared for Paper prepared for United Nation University, World Institute for Development Economics Research (WIDER) conference, 'Sharing global Prosperity, Helsinki, September 6–7.

Collier, P. and Dehn, J. (2001) Aid, Shocks and Growth. Policy Research Working Paper No.2688. Washington DC: World Bank.

Collier, P. and Dollar, D. (2002) 'Aid Allocation and Poverty Reduction', *European Economic Review*, 46(8):1475–500.

Collier, P. and Hoeffler, A. (2002) Aid, Policy, and Growth in Post-Conflict Societies. Policy Research Working Paper No. 2902. Washington: World Bank.

Dalgaard, C.J. and Hansen, H. (2001) 'On Aid, Growth and Good Policies', *Journal of Development Studies*, 37(6):17–41.

Dalgaard, C.J., Hansen, H. and Tarp, F. (2004) 'On the Empirics of Foreign Aid and Growth', *Economic Journal*, 114(496):F191–F216.

De Mello, L. (1997) 'Foreign Direct Investment in Developing Countries and Growth: A Selective Survey', *The Journal of Development Studies*, 34(1):1–24.

De Mello, L. (1999) 'Foreign Direct Investment-Led Growth: Evidence from Time Series and Panel Data', *Oxford Economic Papers*, 51(1):133–51.

Demery, L. and Walton, M. (1998) Are Poverty Reduction and the Other 21st Century Social Goals Attainable? Washington, DC: World Bank.

Dollar, D. and Kraay, A. (2001) 'Trade, Growth and Poverty', *Economic Journal*, 114(493): 22–49.

Dollar, D. and Kraay, A. (2002) 'Growth is Good for the Poor', *Journal of Economic Growth*, 7:195–225.

Dollar, D. and Kraay, A. (2003) 'Institutions, Trade and Growth', *Journal of Monetary Economics*, 50(1):133–62.

Dollar, D. and Kraay, A. (2004) 'Trade, Growth and Poverty', *Economic Journal*, 114(493):22–49.

Dowling, M. and Hiemenz, U. (1982) Aid, Savings and Growth in the Asian Region. Economic Office Report Series 3, Manila: Asian Development Bank.

Durbarry, R., Gemmell, N. and Greenaway, D. (1998) New Evidence on the Impact of Foreign Aid on Economic Growth. CREDIT Research Paper No. 98/9. Nottingham: University of Nottingham.

Easterly, W., Levine, R. and Roodman, D. (2004) 'New Data, New Doubts: A Comment on Burnside and Dollar's "Aid, Policies and Growth (2000)"', *American Economic Review*, 94(3):781–4.

Edison, H., Klein, M., Ricci, L. and Sløk, T. (2002) Capital Account Liberalisation and Performance: Survey and Synthesis. IMF Working Paper, Number 120. Washington, DC: IMF.

Edwards, S. (1998) 'Openness, Productivity and Growth: What Do We Really Know?', *Economic Journal*, 108:383–98.

Eichengreen, B. (2001) Capital Account Liberalisation: What Do the Cross-Country Studies Tell Us? Mimeo. University of California at Berkeley.

Feeny, S. and Clarke, M. (2009) *The Millennium Development Goals and Beyond: International Assistance to the Asia-Pacific*. London: Palgrave.

Filmer, D. and Pritchett, L. (1997) Child Mortality and Public Spending on Health: How Much Does Money Matter? Policy Research Working Paper, No. 1864. Washington, DC: World Bank.

Filmer, D., Hammer, J. and Pritchett, L. (1998) Health Policy in Poor Countries: Weak Links in the Chain. World Bank Working Paper, No. 1874. Washington, DC: World Bank.

Flug, K., Spilimbergo, A. and Wachtenheim, E. (1998) 'Investment in Education: Do Economic Volatility and Credit Constraints Matter?', *Journal of Development Economics*, 55:465–81.

Frankel, J. and Roemer, D. (1999) 'Does Trade Cause Growth?', *American Economic Review*, 89:379–99.

George, S. (2001) Corporate Globalisation, in Bircham, E. and Charlton, J. (eds) *Anti-capitalism: A Guide to the Movement*. London: Bookmarks.

Gomanee, K., Girma, S. and Morrissey, O. (2003) Searching for Aid Threshold Effects. School of Economics. University of Nottingham: CREDIT Research Paper 03/15.

Greenaway, D., Morgan, W. and Wright, P. (1997) 'Trade Liberalisation and Growth in Developing Countries: Some new evidence', *World Development*, 25(11):1885–92.

Greenaway, D., Morgan, W. and Wright, P. (2002) 'Trade Liberalisation and Growth in Developing Countries', *Journal of Development Economics*, 67:229–44.

Griffin, K. (1970) 'Foreign Capital, Domestic Savings and Economic Development', *Bulletin of the Oxford University Institute of Economics and Statistics*, 32(2):99–112.

Griffin, K. and Enos, J. (1970) 'Foreign Assistance: Objectives and Consequences', *Economic Development and Cultural Change*, 18(3):313–27.

Guillaumont, P. and Chauvet, L. (2001) 'Aid and Performance: A Reassessment', *Journal of Development Studies*, 37(6):66–87.

Gundlach, E., de Pablo, J. and Weisert, N. (2001) Education is Good for the Poor. Paper presented at World Institute for Development Economics Research (WIDER) conference on economic growth and poverty reduction, WIDER, Helsinki, May 25–26.

Gupta, S., Verhoeven, M. and Tiongson, E. (2002) 'The Effectiveness of Government Spending on Education and Health Care in Developing and Transition Economies', *European Journal of Political Economy*, 18:717–37.

Gupta, K.L. (1970) 'Foreign Capital and Domestic Savings: A Test of Haavelmo's Hypothesis with Cross-Country Data: A Comment', *Review of Economics and Statistics*, 52(2):214–16.

Gupta, K.L. and Islam, M.A. (1983) *Foreign Capital, Savings and Growth – An International Cross-Section Study*. Dordrecht: Reidal Publishing Company.

Haddad, M. and Harrison, A. (1993) 'Are There Positive Spillovers from Direct Foreign Investment? Evidence from Panel Data for Morocco', *Journal of Development Economics*, 42:51–74.

Hansen, H. and Tarp, F. (2001) 'Aid and Growth Regressions', *Journal of Development Economics*, 64(2):547–70.

Hansen, H. and Rand, J. (2006) 'On the Causal Links between FDI and Growth in Developing Countries', *World Economy*, 29(1):21–41.

Hertel, T., Ivanic, M., Preckel, P. and Cranfield, J. (2003) Trade Liberalisation and the Structure of Poverty in Developing Countries. Paper prepared for 'Globalisation, agricultural development and rural livelihoods'. Ithaca, NY: Cornell University. April 11–12.

Herzer, D., Klasen, S. and Nowak-Lehmann, F. (2006) In Search of FDI-Led Growth in Developing Countries. Ibero America Institute for Economic Research Discussion Paper Number 150. Göttingen, Germany: Ibero-America Institute for Economic Research.

Hill, H. (1996) *The Indonesia Economy Since 1966*. Cambridge: Cambridge University Press.

Hojman, D. (1996) 'Economic and Other Determinants of Infant and Child Mortality in Small Developing Countries: The Case of Central America and the Caribbean', *Applied Economics*, 28:281–90.

Hudson, J. and Mosley, P. (2001) 'Aid, Policies and Growth: In Search of the Holy Grail?', *Journal of International Development*, 13(7):1023–38.

Irwin, D. and Tervio, M. (2002) 'Does Trade Raise Income: Evidence from the Twentieth Century', *Journal International Economics*, 58:1–18.

Islam, N. (2002) Regime Changes, Economic Policies and the Effects of Aid on Growth. Paper presented at the conference 'Exchange Rates, Economic Integration and the International Economy', May 17–19, Ryerson University, Canada.

Jensen, P.S. and Paldam, M. (2003) Can the New Aid-Growth Models Be Replicated? Working Paper No. 2003–17. Aarhus: Institute for Economics.

Johnstone, R., Darbar, S. and Echeverria, C. (1997) Sequencing Capital Account Liberalisation: Lessons from Experience in Chile, Indonesia, Korea and Thailand. IMF Working Paper. Washington DC: IMF.

Jomo, K. (1998) (ed.). *Tigers in Trouble: Financial Governance, Liberalisation and Crises in East Asia*. London: Zed Books.

Kanbur, R. (2001) Growth and Trade: The Last Redoubt? Mimeo. Ithaca, NY: Cornell University.

Khor, M. (2001) *Rethinking Globalisation: Critical Issues and Policy Choices*. London: Zed Books.

Klein, M. (2003) Capital Account Openness and the Varieties of Growth Experience. National Bureau of Economic Research (NBER) Working Paper, Number 9500. Cambridge, MA: NBER.

Kneller, R., Bleaney, M.F. and Gemmell, N. (1999) 'Fiscal Policy and Growth: evidence from OECD Countries', *Journal of Public Economics*, 74(2):171–90.

Kosack, S. (2003) 'Effective Aid: How Democracy Allows Development Aid to Improve the Quality of Life', *World Development*, 31(1):1–22.

Kumar, N. and Pradhan, J. (2002) Foreign Direct Investment, Externalities and Economic Growth in Developing Countries. Research and Information System for the non-aligned and other developing countries: RIS Discussion Paper 27. New Delhi: RIS.

Landau, D. (1986) 'Government and Economic Growth in the Less Developed Countries: An Empirical Study for 1960–80', *Economic Development and Cultural Change*, 35:35–75.

Lensink, R. and Morrissey, O. (2001) Foreign Direct Investment: Flows, Volatility and Growth. Paper prepared for Development Economics Study Group conference. University of Nottingham. April 5–7.

Lensink, R. and White, H. (2001) 'Are There Negative Returns to Aid?', *Journal of Development Studies*, 37(6):42–65.

Lewis, W.A. (1954) Economic Development with Unlimited Supplies of Labour. The Manchester School, 22(2):139–91.

Lu, S. and Ram, R. (2001) 'Foreign Aid, Government Policies and Economic Growth: Further Evidence from Cross-Country Panel Data for 1970 to 1993', *Economia Internazionale*, 54(1):14–29.

Lundberg, M. and Squire, L. (2000) The Simultaneous Evolution of Growth and Inequality. Mimeograph. Washington DC: World Bank.

Maxwell, S. (2005) The Washington Consensus is Dead! Long Live the Mera-narrative. ODI Working Paper. London: ODI.

Mbabazi, J., Morrissey, O. and Millner, C. (2002) The Fragility of the Evidence on Inequality, Trade Liberalisation, Growth and Poverty. CREDIT Working Paper. CREDIT: Nottingham University, UK.

McGillivray, M., Feeny, S., Hermes, N. and Lensink, R. (2006) 'Controversies Over the Impact of Development Aid: It Works; It Doesn't; It Can, But That Depends ....', *Journal of International Development*, 18(6):1031–50.

Milanovic, B. (2002) Can We Discern The Effect of Globalisation on Income Distribution? World Bank Policy Research Working Paper. Washington, DC: World Bank.

Mingat, A. and Tan, J. (1998) The Mechanics of Progress in Education: Evidence from Cross-Country Data. Working Paper, No 2015. Washington, DC: World Bank.

Mody, A. and Wang F.-Y. (1997) 'Determinants of Industrial Growth in Coastal China 1986–89', *World Bank Economic Review*, 11(2):293–325.

Moran, T. (1998) *FDI and Development: The New Policy Agenda for Developing Countries and Economies in Transition*. Washington, DC: Institute for International Economics.

Morrissey, O. and te Velde, D. (2002) 'Foreign Direct Investment: Who Gains?', ODI Briefing Paper (April), London: ODI.

Mosley, P. (1980) 'Aids, Savings and Growth Revisited', *Oxford Bulletin of Economics and Statistics*, 42(2):79–95.

Mosley, P. (1987) *Overseas Development Aid: Its Defence and Reform*. Brighton: Wheatsheaf.

Mosley, P., Hudson, J. and Verschoor, A. (2004) 'Aid, Poverty Reduction and the New Conditionality', *Economic Journal*, 114:214–43.

Mourmouras, I. and Lee, J. (1999) 'Government Spending on Infrastructure in an Endogenous Growth Model with Finite Horizons', *Journal of Economics and Business*, 51(5):395–407.

Nair-Reichert, U. and Weinhold, D. (2001) 'Causality Tests for Cross-Country Panels: New Look at Foreign Direct Investment and Economic Growth in Developing Countries', *Oxford Bulletin of Economics and Statistics*, 2:153–72.

Noss, A. (1991) Education and Adjustment: A Review of the Literature. Working Paper No. 701. Washington DC: World Bank.

Nurkse, R. (1953) *Problems of Capital Formation in Underdeveloped Countries*. New York: Oxford University Press.

OECD (Organization of Economic Co-operation and Development) (2001) *Development Assistance Committee Poverty Guidelines*. Paris: OECD.

Oxfam (2002) *Rigged Rules and Double Standards: Trade, Globalisation and The Fight Against Poverty*. Oxford: Oxfam Publishing.

Papanek, G.F. (1973) 'Aid, Foreign Private Investment, Savings and Growth in Less Developed Countries', *Journal of Political Economy*, 81(1):120–30.

Pritchett, L. (1996) 'Measuring Outward Orientation: Can It Be Done?', *Journal of Development Economics*, 49:307–35.

Quinn, D. (1997) 'The Correlates of Change in International financial Regulation', *American Political Science Review*, 91(3):531–51.

Rahman, M.A. (1968) 'Foreign Capital and Domestic Savings: A Test of Haavelmo's Hypothesis with Cross-Country Data', *Review of Economics and Statistics*, 50(1): 137–8.

Ramirez, M. and Nazmi, N. (2003) 'Public Investment and Economic Growth in Latin America: An Empirical Test', *Review of Development Economics*, 7(1): 115–26.

Ravallion, M., Datt, G. and Chaudhuri, S. (1993) 'Does Maharashtra's Employment Guarantee Scheme Guarantee Employment?', *Economic Development and Cultural Change*, 41(2):251–75.

Reisen, H. and Soto, M. (2001) 'Which Types of Capital Inflow Foster Developing Country Growth?', *International Finance*, 4(1):1–14.

Rodrik, D. (1997) Trade Policy and Performance in Sub-Saharan Africa, Mimeo. Cambridge, MA: Harvard University.

Rodrik, D. (1998) Who Needs Capital-Account Convertibility?, in Fischer, S. *et al. Should the IMF Pursue Capital Account Convertibility?* Essays in International Finance, No. 207, International Finance Section, Department of Economics, (May) Princeton, N.J.: Princeton University.

Rodrik, D. (2000) Comments on 'Trade, Growth and Poverty', by D. Dollar and A. Kraay. Dani Rodrik. Harvard University. October. Available at ksghome. harvard.edu/~drodrik/rodrik%20on%20dollar-kraay.pdf

Rodrik, D. (2008) *One Economic, Many Recipes: Globalisation, Institutions and Economic Growth*. Princeton, NJ: Princeton University Press.

Rugraff, E., Sanchez, E. and Sumner, A. (2008) *Transnational Corporations and Development Policy*. Basingstoke: Palgrave Macmillan.

Sachs, J. (2005) *The End of Poverty*. London: Penguin.

Sakong, I. (1993) *Korea in the World Economy*. Washington DC: Institute for International Economics.

Salleh, I., Yeah, K. and Meyanathan, S. (1993) 'Growth, Equity and Structural Transformation in Malaysia: The Role of the Public Sector. Lessons in East Asia'. World Bank Country Study. Washington DC: World Bank.

Santarelli, E. and Figini, P. (2003) Does Globalisation Reduce Poverty? Some Empirical Evidence for Developing Countries. Paper prepared for WIDER Conference, 'Inequality, Poverty and Human Well-being', Helsinki, May 30–31.

Sjoholm, F. (1999) 'Productivity Growth in Indonesia: The Role of Regional Characteristics and Direct Foreign Investment', *Economic Development and Cultural Change*, 47(3):559–84.

Soto, M. (2000) Capital Flows and Growth in Developing Countries: Recent Empirical Evidence. Organisation of Cooperation and Development (OECD) Development Centre Technical Paper No. 160. Paris: OECD.

Stern, N. (2001) Proceedings of press conference for launch of *Globalisation, Growth and Poverty: Building an Inclusive World Economy*, Washington DC: World Bank, 5 December.

Stiglitz, J. (2007) *Making Globalisation Work*. New York: WW Norton.

Stiglitz, J. and Charlton, A. (2008) *Fair Trade for All*. New York: Oxford University Press.

Sumner, A. (2004) 'Why Are There Still Arguing about Globalisation?', *Journal of International Development*, 16(7):1015–22.

Sumner, A. (2007) 'Foreign Direct Investment in Developing Countries: Have We Reached a Policy "Tipping Point"?', *Third World Quarterly*, 29(2):239–53.

Sumner, A. and Tiwari, M. (2005) 'Poverty and Economic Policy: What Happens When Researchers Disagree?', *Journal of International Development*, 17(6): 781–801.

Tanzi, V. and Chu, K. (1998) *Income Distribution and High Quality Growth*. Cambridge, MA: MIT Press.

Tanzi, V. and Zee, H. (1997) 'Fiscal Policy and Long-run Growth', *International Monetary Fund Staff Papers*, 44:179–209.

Taylor, L. (1990) Foreign Resource Flows and Developing Country Growth: A Three-Gap Model. In Problems of Developing Countries in 1990s. World Bank Discussion Paper 97, Washington DC: World Bank.

Tsai, Pan-Long (1995) 'Foreign Direct Investment and Income Inequality: Further Evidence', *World Development*, 23(3):469–83.

UNCTAD (United Nations Conference on Trade and Development) (1999a) *Transfer Pricing. UNCTAD Series on Issues in International Investment Agreements*. Geneva: UNCTAD.

UNCTAD (1999b) *World Investment Report: FDI and the Challenge of Development*. Geneva: UNCTAD.

UNCTAD (2000) *World Investment Report: Cross-border Mergers and Acquisitions and Development*. Geneva: UNCTAD.

UNCTAD (2001) *World Investment Report: Promoting Linkages*. Geneva: UNCTAD.

UNCTAD (2003) *Foreign Direct Investment Policies for Development: National and International Perspectives*. Geneva: UNCTAD.

UNDP (2003) *Human Development Report (2003) Millennium Development Goals: A Compact Among Nations to End Human Poverty*. Oxford: Oxford University Press.

UNMP (United Nations Millennium Project) (2005) *Investing in Development: A Practical Plan to Achieve the Millennium Development Goals*. London: Earthscan.

Van de Walle, J. (1996) Assessing the Welfare Impacts of Public Spending. Working Paper No. 1670. Washington, DC: World Bank.

Voivodas, C.S. (1973) 'Exports, Foreign Capital Inflow and Economic Growth', *Journal of International Economies*, 3(4):337–49.

Wade, R. (1990) *Governing the Market: Economic Theory and The Role of Government in East Asian Industrialisation*. Princeton: Princeton University Press.

WDM (World Development Movement) (2003) *States of Unrest III: Resistance to IMF and World Bank Polices in Poor Countries*. London: WDM.

Weede, E. and Tiefenbach, H. (1981) 'Some Recent Explanations of Income Inequality: An Evaluation and Critique', *International Studies Quarterly*, 25:255–82.

Weisskopf, T. (1972) 'The Impact of Foreign Capital Flows on Domestic Savings in Undeveloped Countries', *Journal of International Economics*, 2(1):25–38.

White, H. (1992) 'The Macroeconomic Impact of Development Aid: A Critical Survey', *Journal of Development Studies*, 28(2):163–240.

White, H. and Anderson, E. (2001) 'Growth versus Distribution: Does the Pattern of Growth Matter?', *Development Policy Review*, 19(3):267–89.

Winters, A., McCulloch, N. and McKay, A. (2002) *Trade Liberalisation and Poverty: The Empirical Evidence*. CREDIT Working Paper. CREDIT: University of Nottingham, UK.

World Bank (1993) *East Asia Miracle: Economic Growth And Public Policy*. Oxford: Oxford University Press.

World Bank (1998) *East Asia: The Road to Recovery*. Washington, DC: World Bank.

World Bank (2000) *World Development Report 2000/1*. Washington, DC: World Bank.

World Bank (2002) *Globalisation, Growth and Poverty: Building an Inclusive World Economy*. Washington DC: World Bank.

World Bank (2003) *Global Development Finance*. Washington, DC: World Bank.

World Bank (2004) *Global Development Finance*. Washington, DC: World Bank.

World Bank (2004) *World Development Indicators*. Washington, DC: World Bank.

World Bank (2004a) *Progress in Reaching the Millennium Development Goals*. Washington, DC: World Bank. Downloaded on 1 November 2004 from http:www.developmentgoals.org/

World Bank (2004b) *World Development Report: Making Services Work for Poor People*. Washington, DC: World Bank.

Xia, Y. and Lu, Y. (2001) FDI and Host Country Linkages: Assessing the Effectiveness and Development Impact of the Policy Measures: The Case of the Automobile Industry in China, mimeograph. Geneva: UNCTAD.

7
Conclusions

> Today's world is experiencing social, technological and environmental change at an unprecedented pace, across a variety of scales... processes are not only dynamic in themselves, but also interact in complex ways. The result is a variety of possible patterns – or pathways – of change (Leach *et al.*, 2007:1).

1. Introduction

The world in 2015 and beyond is difficult to predict. Thinking back, who would have imagined the spread of the Internet, the collapse of the Soviet bloc or the post-9/11 world? What can we say at this stage? International development post-2015 is likely to be more global, more complex and about more than material well-being. This would suggest new policy roles, goals and means for state and non-state actors alike. Development problems are no longer the preserve of the South with answers in the North. Parts of Glasgow have lower life expectancy than Sub-Saharan Africa. Four of the world's richest billionaires are Indian. Indeed, many policy issues are common to countries at different levels of economic or social development. This increased global interconnectedness is expressing itself in a growing variety of ways. Take, for example:

- volatility in global markets (i.e. food, fuel and credit);
- climate change and natural resources;
- technology (notably ICTs and industrial biofuels);
- terrorism and security.

The net outcome of all the above is a lot of change – of lifestyles and livelihoods. Larger migratory movements nationally as well as

197

internationally are likely as is an increased potential for conflict over resources as a result of people on the move. One might then be forgiven for feeling overwhelmed when thinking about policy planning amid so many changes. Even development policy itself is reconfiguring. We have:

- new actors – China and other new donors, and the new large private foundations such as the Gates Foundation;
- new contexts and institutions – a new aid architecture, decentralisation – terrorism legislation;
- newly emerging policy narratives – the resurgence of economic growth as crucial to development, and the more nuanced agendas of citizenship, participation.

Such changes may reshape policy processes in favour or not of the poor and marginalised. So, how can we promote pro-poor policy after the MDGs and amid all these complex changes, some of which mediate in favour of the poor, many do not?

2.   Policy, complexity and the 3Gs

We chose to focus discussions in our book on the 3Gs – governance, growth and globalisation. This was because they provided a 'centre of gravity', by which we mean there is consensus, we argue, that the 3Gs matter. However, the apparent common themes hide much in terms of nuance. The discussion on complexity science in Chapter 1 suggested looking out for several things. First, focus on the processes of change rather than solely on outcomes. Second, focus on interrelationships and juxtapositions producing co-evolving processes and outcomes. Third, don't forget diversity of pathways and contexts – any claims to universality need to be balanced with commentary on the outliers. Whilst at first glance it may appear the search has been for the universal and the linear in all three areas – governance, growth and globalisation – a search now being shaped by thresholds or tipping points, heterogeneity of contexts, attention to timelines, juxtapositions and non-linearity is evident. For example, in growth research there is a new interest in heterogeneity of country experience and 'going beyond averages'. In governance there is increased interest in actor and context-specificity. Finally, in globalisation there is increased attention to the quality of globalisation-led growth, the direction of causation, non-linearity and thresholds. For example, only after reaching a certain threshold in economic development is the growth from 'openness' broad based.

3.   Three key take-away messages

If you are looking for the 'take-away' or key messages of the book, here are three:

i.   The MDGs have been important in focusing public policy (though they are limiting).
ii.   Post-2015 development is likely to be more global, more complex and about more that just material deprivation or consumption.
iii.   So, we need something different to promote pro-poor policy after the MDGs. Three options are (we favour the third option in the list):

   • We could carry forward the same MDGs without a timeline.
   • We could take the same MDG targets but with a new timeline.
   • We could have new or different kinds of targets with/without a timeline (e.g. process rather than outcome targets such as genuinely nationally 'owned' development strategies and targets and/or new or different kinds of targets that go beyond the 'traditional' lens of material consumption/deprivation.

In terms of something new, a 'well-being approach' is emerging as a complement – and even perhaps an alternative – to the more traditional ways of thinking about and measuring poverty and deprivation. It extends attention from what people can do and be to how people feel about what they can do and be. Well-being thus goes beyond the material to consider relationships and values, beliefs and behaviour. Breaking the inter-generational transmission of poverty requires not only disrupting the transmission of material deprivation via public policy such as nutrition or education programmes and projects but also the creation of progressive norms and values in terms of relationships and behaviour via public policy campaigns that seek to influence how people think. This suggests public policy would move beyond material provision (public expenditure, growth, etc.) into areas in which policy intervention is considered at best highly controversial – values, relationships, norms and behaviour. Yet, it is this line of thinking that underpins the recent popularity in behavioural economics books such as Dan Ariely's *Predictably Irrational* and Thaler and Sunstein's *Nudge*.

   In short, international development policy post-2015 is certain to be more global as we all become more connected by global markets, climate change, migration and information technology. International development policy post-2015 is also likely to be more complex and less predictable because of all these global changes – and the speed at which they are happening. Much greater national as well as international migration and conflict over resources is a very real possibility. In response development policy is likely to evolve. Further support for society-owned strategies and goals for adaptation to changing circumstances are needed. Reflecting on the patterns of these global flows and adaptations and how they reproduce or disrupt the inter-generational transmission of poverty in both North and South will provide opportunities for public policy to think beyond material deprivation, taking into account values, norms and behaviour. A sobering outlook and call to action awaits President Clooney and Vice President Jolie when they enter office.

In a rapidly changing world the poor in particular need voice and visibility in policy processes either directly via participatory institutions for adaptation (i.e. voice) or in pro-poor indicators (i.e. visibility) used by policy-makers. The various 'crises' we face cannot be solved without those involved in them.

Reference

Leach, M., Bloom, G., Ely, A., Nightingale, P., Scoones, I., Shah, E. and Smith, A. (2007) *Understanding Governance: Pathways to Sustainability*. STEPS Working Paper 2, STEPS Centre. Brighton, UK: IDS.

Epilogue
The Global Financial Crisis, the MDGs and Global Poverty Reduction

1. Whose panic?

As this book goes to production the global financial crisis is unfolding. We've heard a lot on the global financial crisis of panic in terms of banks and bankers. We've heard a lot about panic among policy-makers and the media. Look further and a silent panic may be evolving – a pro-poor panic – that we haven't heard much about yet.

Who really suffers during a crisis – the person or family whose income falls most or the person or family whose income falls when they already live near the minimum? Policy-makers beware. Urban populations are likely to lose most in the current turbulence and the round of food riots from Latin America and Asia in 2008 in response to the food price spike may rock urban politics again.

2. Who's vulnerable?

Quite a few developing countries are vulnerable in one way or another. The World Bank President has said 30 countries will need emergency loans. Actually, around 80 countries are probably at risk (in the sense of having large trade deficits). There are broadly speaking two groups. First, there are those developing countries that are at risk because they are primarily linked financially to the global economy by hot money (e.g. Nigeria, Brazil) and international banks (e.g. Ukraine, Pakistan). Second, there are those developing countries at risk because they are primarily linked by their real economy to the global economy via non-oil exports, particularly so as commodities fall in price (e.g. Zambia is one example – *The Economist* commodity prices index fell 40% in the last six months of 2008 alone) but also manufactures exported to western markets with falling demand, or countries linked by remittances from workers (e.g. India, Mexico), or countries linked by aid flows which are aid dependent and which will suffer if aid falls (e.g. Uganda and Tanzania). Some countries fall into more than one category and thus potentially face multishocks. One visible dimension of the crisis is what happens to currencies. Exchange rates in many developing countries are falling rapidly (relative to the dollar). At the time of writing (January 2009), there is a 40% fall in South Africa, 30% in South Korea, 25% in Pakistan, Zambia, Brazil, Chile and Mexico, 20% in India and 10–15% in Indonesia, Russia and Ukraine according to *The Economist*'s Slumpometer. But what does this actually mean at street level outside the panic in the dealing rooms?

3.   How are traders in New York and London linked to farmers and labourers in Pakistan or Nigeria?

Small losses of income make big differences when you live on around a dollar-a-day. Small changes can push people below the minimum. A financial crisis is transmitted to street level as follows: stock markets and exchange rates fall; capital flows out; rates of interest may rise to arrest outflows (for example rates of interest are very low in the US but 12% in Hungary, South Africa, Russia, and Indonesia, 15% in Brazil and Pakistan, 21% in Argentina). Import inflation can result from the exchange rate fall as imported goods become more expensive. Inflation may also occur from scarcity of certain goods and increases in the money supply as central banks provide emergency credit to prevent the credit crunch (for example, inflation in Kenya is running at 15%, 12–15% in South Africa, Russia, and Indonesia, 24% in Pakistan). These inflation spikes may though be short-lived in the current climate. However, at the same time as exchange rates fall there is a rush for dollars as companies try to service foreign debts and in the process trigger further currency falls. As debts rise and credit and demand contracts, investment and thus output slows or even falls as companies become insolvent or bankrupt. Central banks may try again to provide emergency liquidity to banks to ease the credit crunch. If output does slow or fall, redundancies follow and household income falls, leading to changes in consumption. People may replace meat with carbohydrates, for example. Health and children's education costs may be cut. Depending on severity there is migration back to rural areas and real rural incomes fall as a result. For example, when the crisis hit Indonesia in 1998 it was thought to be an urban phenomenon but there was a hidden rural dimension. Retrenched urban workers returned to their villages, depressing rural wages.

4. What will be the impact of the crisis on the MDGs and poverty reduction?

Prior to the crisis, the Millennium Development Goals were on-track in some countries but off-track in many (in Sub-Saharan Africa in particular). MDG 1 on income and food poverty (those living on under a dollar-a-day and with under-nutrition respectively) is linked to growth and to food prices to some considerable extent. It was looking hopeful globally but slowing growth, and in particular slowing growth in China and India, is now worrying. For the many African countries that were off-track anyway the picture simply gets worse. With regard to the other MDGs – health and education for example – these are linked to public expenditures and aid flows. Things were more mixed pre-crisis but the risks are that any crisis-induced squeezing of public expenditure in developing countries as tax revenues fall and/or any shrinking of the aid budget may hit these other MDGs hard. Further, there is the cost of bail-outs in terms of higher taxes and lower public expenditures at some point in the future and these are big loans so far – US$12bn to Pakistan, US$16bn to Ukraine, US$25bn to Hungary.

What to do about all of this? We can't stop the crisis but we can mitigate its impacts. Here are a few ideas. We need an evidence base – what's going on at street level? We need global civil society at the table in terms of Bretton Woods II negotiations. For countries linked to the crisis primarily via finance, temporary capital controls and medium-term banking reform (reserve ratio requirements for example) are important. For countries connected not primarily via finance but via the real economy – via remittances, exports, and threats to the aid budget – we need some ring-fencing of social expenditures as a minimum and more on social protection and social safety nets. For both groups of countries, low-interest loans from the World Bank and IMF credit are important, though with process (i.e. civil society oversight) rather than macro-economic policy conditionality.

5. What will be the Black Swans?

Tangible beneficiaries have been Japanese firms, which have made US$71bn of acquisitions so far. One less tangible beneficiary from the crisis may be the MDG that seems to get most forgotten – MDG 8 on global partnerships. The crisis is likely to lead to greater emphasis on multilateralism (and the end of the G8), on new alliances and changes in the balance of global power (such as the G20 and the role of the

BRICs – Brazil, Russia, India and China), and to create new policy space (the resurgence of Keynesianism and the space to think the unthinkable on part-state ownership of banks and the regulation of markets and financial risk?).

Much depends on the larger developing countries' power in the G20. Seven of the G8 countries are in recession. China too has seen industrial production fall from 18% expansion a year ago to 8% now. China may gain depending on how it exploits the situation – when Pakistan needed a loan it turned to China before the IMF and the idea of an Asian Monetary Fund – a challenge to the IMF's monopoly – has re-emerged. However, China has its own problems – mass redundancies at 3–4 million or more and the other BRICs are suffering too – Brazil, Russia and India to a greater or lesser extent. One thing remains, however. A recession in the US will only bring closer the date when China will overtake the US as the world's largest economy and the political power that comes with this.

6.   What does the crisis mean for post-2015 development policy?

i.   Post-2015 development policy as global

The global financial crisis has demonstrated the extent of North–South, East–West global inter-connectedness. Development policy needs to catch up. As noted in earlier chapters, the MDGs ghettoise 'development' as something that happens in the South, i.e to the 'poor'. What about 'development' beyond developing countries – i.e. in the North and/or the inter-connectedness of poverty and wealth, vulnerability and risk in North and South? All countries are developing in some sense. There is wealth and poverty in both North and South. Many development problems, notably the current crisis, are neither the preserve of the North or the South. Further, given international migration, well-being in North and South is increasingly connected via transnational identities and well-being and remittances. Finally, given that many of the EPICs including volatile markets previously outlined are North and South problems alike (climate change and terrorism for example) addressing them also requires North–South collaboration.

ii.   Post-2015 development policy as (complex) change

The global financial crisis has demonstrated the increasing complexity of that global inter-connectedness. Again, development policy needs to catch up. As noted in earlier chapters, a body of ideas that has emerged in development research could be loosely called Complexity Science or Complex Adaptive Thinking. This focuses on *inter-relationships* rather than linear cause and impact and pays attention to *processes of change* rather than snapshots. The point of departure is that systems are made of multiple elements and processes which are not only connected but interdependent. Development includes processes and outcomes which are the product of a juxtaposition of often non-linear factors. Thus changes are often highly uncertain and cause is the product of a juxtaposition of factors (one could argue a demarcation of dependent and independent variable is thus problematic). What are the things one might look out for? First, focus on the processes of change rather than focus solely on outcomes – what led to the current crisis. Second, a focus on inter-relationships and juxtapositions producing co-evolving processes and outcomes of the current crisis for example. Third, don't forget diversity of pathways and contexts – any claims to universality need to be balanced with commentary on the outliers.

iii. Post-2015 development policy as material plus

The global financial crisis has demonstrated the increasingly evident relationship between material well-being and ill-being and non-material factors – for example, (in)security, vulnerability, risk, and psychological wellbeing – and the importance of relational wellbeing in times of crisis. Again, development policy needs to catch up. As noted in earlier chapters, the MDGs emphasise development as poverty reduction in largely material terms. This is important. However, as the wellbeing discussion noted, development is beyond the material to include relational and subjective aspects of human life. This raises issues of governments' involvement in matters not traditionally their realm – in relationships, in subjectivities (values, norms, etc.) and in behaviour. Wellbeing thus goes beyond the material to consider relationships and values, beliefs and behaviour. Breaking the inter-generational transmission of poverty requires not only disrupting the transmission of material deprivation via public policy such as nutrition or education programmes and projects but also the creation of progressive norms and values in terms of relationships and behaviour via public policy campaigns that seek to influence how people think. This suggests public policy would move beyond material provision (public expenditure, growth, etc.) into areas in which policy intervention is considered at best highly controversial – values, relationships, norms and behaviour. Yet, it is this line of thinking that underpins the recent popularity in behavioural economics books such as Dan Ariely's *Predictably Irrational* and Thaler and Sunstein's *Nudge*.

iv.   Post-2015 development policy as politics

The global financial crisis has demonstrated the increasing importance of politics and governance – political and of markets. Once again, development policy needs to catch up. As noted in earlier chapters, there is a revived interest in self- or endogenously defined development evident in wellbeing and, derived from that, a revival of interest in politics and governance, and in the concept of 'voice' in decision-making that relates to people's lives. This resurgence of interest in politics raises the issues of the inter-connectedness of the 'poor' or those with ill-being and the 'rich' or those with wellbeing and the inter-connection of the South and the North. Research focused on explanation of individual deprivation does not study the politics i.e. the social relations and inequality in power, voice, governance and ultimately wealth. In short, studying poverty is not the same as studying the poor and the processes of development are inherently social and political processes.

In sum, international development policy post-2015 is certain to be more global as we all become more connected by global markets, climate change, migration and information technology. International development policy post-2015 is also likely to be more complex and less predictable because of all these global changes – and the speed at which they are happening. Much greater national as well as inter-national migration and conflict over resources is a very real possibility. In response development policy needs to evolve towards genuinely society-owned strategies and goals for adaptation to changing circum-stances and public policy that thinks beyond material deprivation, taking into account non-material wellbeing and values, norms and behaviour.

The MDGs have provided a rallying call. We should be bolder about heralding a new development agenda which has a wider scope, but which anchors around the MDGs. It would be aimed at encouraging policy makers in all countries to give greater weight to tackling sys-temic inter-related global issues of which poverty is one in itself and strongly influenced by others such as the global economic crisis and climate change.

Andy Sumner and Meera Tiwari, January 2009
a.sumner@ids.ac.uk
m.tiwari@uel.ac.uk

Index